Lecture Notes in Computer Science 16314

The series Lecture Notes in Computer Science (LNCS), including its subseries Lecture Notes in Artificial Intelligence (LNAI) and Lecture Notes in Bioinformatics (LNBI), has established itself as a medium for the publication of new developments in computer science and information technology research, teaching, and education.

LNCS enjoys close cooperation with the computer science R & D community, the series counts many renowned academics among its volume editors and paper authors, and collaborates with prestigious societies. Its mission is to serve this international community by providing an invaluable service, mainly focused on the publication of conference and workshop proceedings and postproceedings. LNCS commenced publication in 1973.

Moti Yung · Keke Gai · Weizhi Meng
Editors

Application Intelligence and Blockchain Security

7th International Conference, AIBlock 2025
Beijing, China, July 19–20, 2025
Proceedings

Editors
Moti Yung
Google and Columbia University
New York, NY, USA

Keke Gai
Beijing Institute of Technology
Beijing, China

Weizhi Meng
Lancaster University
Lancaster, UK

ISSN 0302-9743 ISSN 1611-3349 (electronic)
Lecture Notes in Computer Science
ISBN 978-3-032-16167-3 ISBN 978-3-032-16168-0 (eBook)
https://doi.org/10.1007/978-3-032-16168-0

This Springer imprint is published by the registered company Springer Nature Switzerland AG
The registered company address is: Gewerbestrasse 11, 6330 Cham, Switzerland

Preface

This volume contains the papers that were selected for presentation and publication at The 7th International Conference on Application Intelligence and Blockchain Security (AIBlock 2025), which was held in Beijing, China on 19–20 July 2025.

As applications are among the most critical assets, application security aims to take proper actions to improve the security of an application by identifying and fixing application vulnerabilities. Application intelligence plays an important role in designing an appropriate security mechanism, which is gaining increasing attention. In addition, Artificial intelligence (AI), a general-purpose technology, is profoundly reshaping society, the economy, and most aspects of life, just as the steam engine, electricity, and the Internet have. Its impact is two-sided, bringing both enormous opportunities and severe challenges. With the adoption of blockchain technology, how to benefit security by combining blockchain with application & artificial intelligence has become an emerging research topic. This event provided a platform for professionals from academia and industry to discuss challenges and potential solutions in this domain.

This year's Program Committee (PC) consisted of 28 members with diverse backgrounds and broad research interests. A total of 36 papers were submitted to the conference under a single-blinded reviewing mode. Papers were selected based on their originality, significance, relevance, and clarity of presentation as assessed by the reviewers. Most papers were reviewed by three or more PC members, and papers coauthored by PC members were reviewed in a process that ensured no conflicts of interest. Finally, 9 full papers were selected for inclusion in this proceedings, resulting in an acceptance rate of 25%. Our program also featured two keynote speakers: Haiyang Xue from Singapore Management University, Singapore, on "Threshold Cryptography and Its Application in Blockchain", and Yuan Lu from Chinese Academy of Sciences, China, on "Secure Distributed Computing on the Internet".

For the success of AIBlock 2025, we would like to first thank all authors for their submissions and all PC members for their great efforts in paper assessment. For the conference organization, we would like to thank the General Chairs, Robert Deng, Georgios Kambourakis, and Jing Yu; the Publicity Chairs, Wei-Yang Chiu, Jiageng Chen, and Yuan Lu; and the Publication Chair, Wenjuan Li. Finally, we thank all speakers and session chairs for their contributions to the program of AIBlock 2025.

July 2025

Moti Yung
Keke Gai
Weizhi Meng

Organization

General Chairs

Robert Deng	Singapore Management University, Singapore
Georgios Kambourakis	University of the Aegean, Greece
Jing Yu	Minzu University of China, China

Program Co-chairs

Moti Yung	Google and Columbia University, USA
Keke Gai	Beijing Institute of Technology, China
Weizhi Meng	Lancaster University, UK

Publicity Chairs

Wei-Yang Chiu	National Yang Ming Chiao Tung University, Taiwan
Jiageng Chen	Central China Normal University, China
Yuan Lu	Institute of Software, Chinese Academy of Sciences, China

Publication Chair

Wenjuan Li	Education University of Hong Kong, China

Technical Program Committee

Jiankuo Dong	Nanjing University of Posts and Telecommunications, China
Zheng Gong	South China Normal University, China
Marko Hölbl	University of Maribor, Slovenia
Khizar Hameed	University of Tasmania, Australia
Georgios Kambourakis	University of the Aegean, Greece
Sokratis Katsikas	Norwegian University of Science and Technology, Norway

Wenjuan Li	Education University of Hong Kong, China
Pooria Madani	Ontario Tech University, Canada
Mahmoud Nabil Mahmoud	North Carolina A&T University, USA
Kouichi Sakurai	Kyushu University, Japan
Jun Shao	Zhejiang Gongshang University, China
Chunhua Su	University of Aizu, Japan
Guozi Sun	Nanjing University of Posts and Telecommunications, China
Yu-an Tan	Beijing Institute of Technology, China
Bang Tran	University of Massachusetts Boston, USA
Qiang Tang	Luxembourg Institute of Science and Technology, Luxembourg
Andreas Veneris	University of Toronto, Canada
Jianfeng Wang	Xidian University, China
Ding Wang	Nankai University, China
Peng Xu	Huazhong University of Science and Technology, China
Haiyang Xue	Singapore Management University, Singapore
Rehana Yasmin	King Abdullah University of Science and Technology, Saudi Arabia
Kejia Zhang	Heilongjiang University, China
Xuyun Zhang	Macquarie University, Australia
Xichen Zhang	Saint Mary's University, Canada
Cong Zuo	Beijing Institute of Technology, China

Steering Committee

Robert Deng	Singapore Management University, Singapore
Georgios Kambourakis	University of the Aegean, Greece
Sokratis Katsikas	Norwegian University of Science and Technology, Norway
Man Ho Au	Hong Kong Polytechnic University, China
Weizhi Meng (Chair)	Lancaster University, UK
Chunhua Su	University of Aizu, Japan

Sub-reviewers

Rui Zhang
Ghazal Rahmanian

Contents

A Privacy-Preserving Authentication Scheme for Secure Cross-Domain Navigation Systems

Dongliang Fei and Gang Shen(✉)

Hubei University of Technology, Wuhan 430068, China
shengang@hbut.edu.cn
http://www.springer.com/gp/computer-science/lncs

Abstract. With the rapid development of VANETS, intelligent navigation systems receive wide application. Dynamic switching of vehicles between different domains (e.g., geographic regions or service providers) has become the norm. However, key management and privacy protection issues are receiving more and more attention when vehicles are crossing domains, and the traditional static key management mechanism cannot meet the security requirements in dynamic cross-domain scenarios. In this paper, we propose a privacy-preserving authentication scheme for secure cross-domain for intelligent navigation, aiming to achieve secure update of domain keys and provide privacy-preserving authentication for vehicles in the process of cross-domain. We design a cross-domain switching mechanism to ensure that the vehicle cannot continue to access the old domain key after leaving the old domain, while the vehicle can securely and quickly obtain the new key in the new domain. We combine the domain key with message authentication using an efficient authentication mechanism and a flexible domain key update method to prevent cross-domain key misuse in the VANETS environment, taking into account privacy protection and authentication efficiency. Experimental results show that the proposed scheme can better adapt to the cross-domain switching requirements in smart navigation systems while ensuring security, privacy and authentication efficiency.

Keywords: Smart Navigation · Authentication · Cross-Domain Switching · Key Update · Privacy Protection

1 Introduction

With the development of information technology and communication technology, Vehicular Ad-hoc Networks (VANETS) [1] has become an important part of intelligent transportation systems. VANETS can achieve information sharing, remote control and real-time navigation among vehicles through wireless communication technology and sensors, providing drivers with a smarter and safer driving experience. The increasing scale of the development of VANETS has led to increasingly complex issues of privacy protection and security authentication [3]. Ensuring the security of vehicle data and driver privacy in intelligent navigation systems has become an urgent problem.

M. Yung et al. (Eds.): AIBlock 2025, LNCS 16314, pp. 1–21, 2026.
https://doi.org/10.1007/978-3-032-16168-0_1

The communication network in intelligent navigation systems [2,5] involves a large number of vehicles and roadside units (RSUs), which need to exchange a large amount of data, such as vehicle position, speed, traffic conditions, driving behaviour and other sensitive information. Leakage of such information can violate personal privacy and may be exploited by malicious individuals, posing a serious security risk. For example, hackers may steal driving trajectories and tamper with navigation routes by attacking inter-vehicle communication. In a navigation scheme in which malicious speed data can be detected, in order to detect the malicious speed data, the vehicle needs to pass messages between the vehicle and the roadside unit frequently, which increases the computational burden of the roadside unit and the roadside unit is susceptible to other external attacks. Therefore, in order to enhance the security of the scheme, the roadside units need to be managed in a delimited domain, and in cross-domain scenarios [4], attackers may use forged identities to apply for keys or authentication across domains, leading to overloading of authentication servers in the target domain and affecting navigation services for legitimate users. In order to protect the privacy of users and the security of the system, intelligent navigation services to achieve secure and effective privacy-preserving authentication in VANETS environments has become one of the core issues in research.

Currently, most of the secure authentication in smart navigation services relies on traditional certificate mechanisms [6,7] (e.g., Public Key Infrastructure PKI-based authentication). This type of authentication verifies the identities of the communicating parties through a centralised Certificate Authority (CA), but suffers from several problems:

- **High Computational and Communication Overhead:** Traditional certificate mechanisms require each node (e.g., vehicle or roadside unit) to store and process complex certificate information, which can lead to high computational and communication overhead.
- **Not Adapting to Dynamic Changes:** Dynamic changes of members in VANETs (e.g., vehicles joining and leaving) make it difficult for traditional certificate management mechanisms to cope with frequent member updates, which brings about delays and efficiency problems in the authentication process.
- **Privacy Leakage Issues:** Traditional certificate authentication mechanism may expose the user's identity information and communication content, which is difficult to meet the strict demand for privacy protection in VANETs.

In order to solve the shortcomings of the traditional certificate mechanism, some scholars proposed the Certificate-less Authentication (CLA) scheme [8,9]. Certificate-less authentication is different from the traditional certificate authority, through a specific encryption mechanism and protocol, directly between the participants to achieve authentication, reducing the certificate management and storage requirements. Certificate-less authentication can significantly reduce computation and communication overheads, and can avoid privacy leakage problems, which makes it highly practical.

With the wide application of smart navigation systems, dynamic switching of vehicles between different domains (e.g., geographic regions or service providers) has become the norm. The problem of cross-domain switching in smart navigation systems [10] is also prominent. Due to the frequent movement of vehicles between different domains (e.g., geographic regions or service providers), ensuring the security and privacy protection of vehicles during cross-domain switching has become a key challenge. Cross-domain switching requires the system to be able to quickly complete authentication and key update when a vehicle enters a new domain, and to ensure that the vehicle cannot continue to access the resources of the old domain after leaving the old domain to prevent potential security threats. The cross-domain switching process needs to protect the vehicle's privacy information and avoid the leakage of historical tracks and user data. Therefore, designing a privacy-preserving authentication mechanism that supports cross-domain switching is an important challenge to improve the security of VANETS.

To address the above challenges, this paper designs a privacy-preserving authentication scheme for secure cross-domain navigation systems. Our contributions are as follows:

- Dynamic Domain Key Update Mechanism: We design a dynamic mechanism for cross-domain update of domain keys to ensure that a vehicle cannot continue to access the old domain key after leaving the old domain, and the vehicle can securely obtain the new key in the new domain. This effectively prevents vehicles from continuing to access sensitive information in the old domain after entering the new domain and ensures secure isolation between domains.
- The solution solves the key escrow problem and supports message batch authentication. It eliminates heavy certificate management and storage, and avoids system blocking under multiple messages.
- By comparing with other schemes, it is proved that our scheme can better meet the cross-domain switching requirements in smart navigation systems while ensuring security, privacy and authentication efficiency, and has high practicality and scalability.

2 Related Work

In VANETS, privacy preservation and authentication is one of the core issues in research. In recent years, many researchers have proposed different schemes for authentication and privacy protection in VANETS, covering traditional certificate authentication, certificate-less authentication, and dynamic membership update techniques. The following are the relevant research results for these techniques.

Traditional Public Key Infrastructure (PKI) systems are widely used in VANETs and their complex certificate management and high overhead of bandwidth make them limited in resource constrained environments. For this reason

PKI systems have been improved in terms of transparency and revocation mechanisms, but they also face the same limitations of model assumptions such as clock synchronisation, network latency, and are unable to efficiently support dynamic membership updates in VANETs [11]. Privacy issues in PKI systems are not adequately addressed. In certificate transparency auditing, users' browsing history may be exposed through auditing certificates [12]. To address the shortcomings of traditional PKI systems, literature [13] proposes a decentralised zone-based PKI (Zone-Based PKI) framework, which reduces the single-point-of-failure problem in traditional PKI and improves the scalability of the system by introducing a zone master node to manage certificates. The scheme uses lightweight Elliptic Curve Cryptography (ECC) technology and an optimised X.509 certificate structure to reduce computation and communication overheads. The scheme also has some challenges, such as high certificate lookup overhead, possible security risks associated with the first-time use of the trust mechanism, and insufficient support for member updates in highly dynamic environments, which may affect the effectiveness of the system in practice in VANET environments.

In order to overcome the complexity of certificate management and key escrow problems in PKI systems, Certificate-Less Cryptography (CLC) was introduced into VANET. Certificateless system avoids the certificate distribution and revocation problem in traditional PKI and solves the key escrow problem in identity-based encryption. Literature [8] proposes a conditional privacy-preserving signature scheme based on certificateless cryptography that protects the true identity of a vehicle through pseudo-identity and allows a trusted authority to track down a malicious vehicle if necessary. The scheme is shown to be secure under the random predicate model with low computational overhead. The certificate-less system relies on the trusted authority to generate a portion of the private key, which carries the risk of a single point of failure. Literature [14] proposes a security-enhanced certificate-less aggregated signature scheme that further improves the robustness and security of the system by introducing an invalid signature identification algorithm and a revocation mechanism. The support of these schemes is still insufficient in situations where vehicles frequently join and leave the network.

Certificate-less systems have made significant progress in privacy preservation and computational efficiency, but are deficient in dynamic membership updating. Literature [15] proposes a conditional privacy-preserving authentication scheme based on Schnorr signatures that supports multi-signature and batch verification, and does not provide a clear solution on the dynamic membership update problem. Literature [16] proposed a privacy preserving data download scheme based on lattice cryptography that provides post-quantum security but has limitations in dynamic membership updates and pseudo-identity management. Literature [17] proposed a privacy-preserving authentication protocol (PTAP) that supports dynamic membership updates with high complexity and computational overhead, relies on semi-trusted RSUs, and has potential security risks. Literature [9] proposes an efficient certificate-less aggregated signature scheme that supports specified verifiers and conditional privacy preservation, which can significantly reduce the computational overhead of RSUs. The scheme still relies on centralised Key Generation Centres (KGCs) and Tracking Authorities (TRAs) and does not explicitly discuss how to support dynamic membership updates. Literature [10] proposes a keyless escrow scheme based on certificate-based encryption that generates dynamic anonymous identities through a fuzzy extractor, avoiding the problem of static pseudonym storage and management. The scheme relies on a centralised trusted authority. The scheme [20] utilises the Chinese Residual Theorem (CRT) for key management. The scheme does not use bilinear pair operations and mapping-to-point hash operations, which improves the authentication speed, in order to reduce the computational complexity and communication overhead. The scheme [21] supports the dynamic joining and leaving of vehicles to the domain, which can effectively manage the change of members in the domain to ensure forward and backward security, but it requires more elliptic curve point multiplication and point addition operations during the signature and verification process, and the computational complexity is higher in batch verification.

In summary, although existing certificate-less systems have made significant progress in privacy protection and computational efficiency, they still have some problems. Under the premise of privacy protection, how to further reduce the computation and communication overhead in the authentication process, and how to ensure that the security and stability of the system can still be maintained when malicious nodes join, are still key issues that need to be solved urgently.

3 Preliminaries

3.1 Chinese Remainder Theorem (CRT)

Assuming that the integers m_1, $\cdots$, m_k are mutually prime, for any integers b_1, $\cdots$, b_k, the Chinese Remainder Theorem [22] is as follows:

$$\begin{cases} x \equiv b_1 \, mod \, m_1 \\ \cdots \\ x \equiv b_k \, mod \, m_k \end{cases} \tag{1}$$

This solution is unique under mode M. The unique solution is:

$$x = \sum_{i=1}^{k} M_i^{-1} \cdot M_i \cdot b_i \, mod \, M \tag{2}$$

where $M = \prod_{i=1}^{k} m_i$, $M_i = M/m_i$, $M_i^{-1} \cdot M_i \equiv 1 \, mod \, m_i$

3.2 Certificate-Less Signature Scheme

A certificate-less signature scheme [23] typically consists of six phases: system initialization, partial private key extraction, secret value setup, complete private key setup, signature generation, and signature verification.

System Initialization: Input security parameters to generate the master public/private key pair and system parameters.

Partial Private Key Extraction: A trusted authority generates a partial private key (psk) for the user, enabling them to sign without requiring a certificate.

Secret Value Setup: The vehicle obtains its own secret value r_1 and securely stores it for subsequent complete key generation.

Complete Private Key Setup: After receiving the partial private key (psk), the vehicle generates its complete private key for signing based on its secret value r_1.

Sign: Taking the message $m \in \{0,1\}^*$, its pseudo-identity ID_i, and the complete private key sk_i as inputs, the algorithm generates the signature σ.

Verification: The receiver verifies the legitimacy of the signature using the public key and system parameters, ensuring the authenticity of the message source.

3.3 Elliptic Curve

Elliptic curves (ECs) [24] are a class of curves with specific algebraic structures widely used in modern cryptography. Generally, an elliptic curve over a finite field $\mathbb{F}_q$ can be represented by the Weierstrass equation:

$$E : y^2 = x^3 + ax + b \mod q \tag{3}$$

where a and b are selected system parameters that must satisfy $4a^3 + 27b^2 \neq 0$ to ensure the curve is nonsingular.

Operations on Elliptic Curves: Point Addition: For points P and Q on the curve, a new point R (i.e., $R = P + Q$) is obtained by applying specific addition rules, forming an additive group structure. Scalar Multiplication: The operation kP is defined as $P + P + \cdots + P$ (repeated k times).

4 System Design

4.1 System Model

The system consists of the Transportation Bureau (TB), the Key Generation Center (KGC), Roadside Units (RSUs), and Vehicles. In our scheme, roads are divided into small regional units based on geographical locations, which effectively form domains (see Fig. 1).

TB is the trusted authority. It is responsible for generating some system parameters and the registration of the vehicle in VANETs, and TB can trace the real identity of the vehicle anonymously, when the vehicle is reported or there is a violation.

KGC is a semi-honest third party. The key that KGC can extract related to the user's identity, through the anonymous identity of vehicle, generates a partial key for the vehicle, through the partial key and the vehicle's own key, the vehicle can obtain the complete signature key. In addition, the KGC may generate domain parameters, which may ensure that vehicles within the domain may securely receive messages within the authentication domain and that vehicles outside the domain may not be able to authenticate messages within the domain. And these parameters are distributed to the vehicles and RSUs by broadcasting in the domain, and the vehicles and RSUs obtain the domain key through the domain parameters and their own information.

RSUs are crucial infrastructure nodes in VANETS, which are roadside infrastructure for V2I communication with vehicles and also enable I2I communication with each other. RSUs act as a messenger between KGC and vehicles.

Vehicles are equipped with a tamper-proof device (TPD), which stores confidential information. The On-Board Unit (OBU) is the terminal device that communicates with the outside world and is responsible for sending, receiving and processing data.

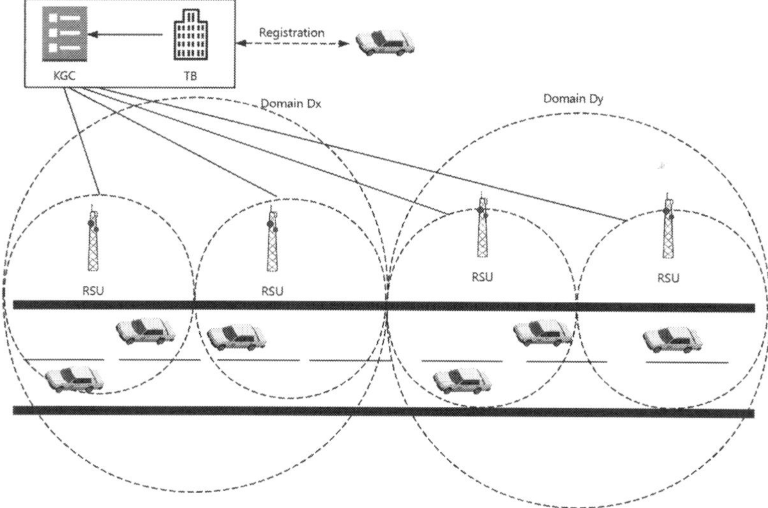

Fig. 1. System Model

4.2 Security Requirements

To ensure user privacy and network security, the proposed scheme must satisfy the following security requirements.

- **Message Integrity and Authentication:** Ensures that transmitted messages remain unaltered during transmission and that the receiver can verify the sender's identity.
- **Anonymity:** The real identity of a vehicle must be concealed from other vehicles to maintain anonymity within the network, preventing identity tracking. Additionally, the real identity of a vehicle cannot be inferred by other vehicles through analysis of multiple received messages.
- **Traceability:** While the real identity of a vehicle must be hidden from other vehicles, it should be possible to trace the originator of specific actions or events when necessary to facilitate accountability.
- **Unlinkability:** To ensure user privacy, no two messages can be linked to the same vehicle. This prevents external observers from associating communications at different times or contexts, thereby protecting user privacy.
- **Forward Secrecy:** When a vehicle joins a domain, it should not gain access to any prior interaction information exchanged among existing vehicles in the same group.
- **Backward Secrecy:** When a vehicle leaves a domain, it should no longer have access to any subsequent interaction information exchanged among the remaining vehicles in the domain.
- **Resistance to Attacks:** The proposed scheme should be capable of resisting various common attacks, such as forgery attacks, modification attacks, and replay attacks.

5 The Proposed Scheme

In this section, we describe our scheme in detail. The vehicle gets the complete signature key by reconstructing the partial key and its own key, the KGC cannot count the user's own key and the vehicle cannot count the partial key generated by the KGC, so the system does not have a key escrow [25] function. The scheme is specific as follows including the phases of initialisation phase, registration phase, reconstruction of keys, signing, authentication and domain key update as follows:

5.1 Initialisation Phase

Initialization: TB and KGC generate system parameters and perform initialization through the following steps:

- Input a security parameter γ. The TB selects a group G and a generator P of order q.
- The TB selects a random number β and computes $T_{\text{pub}} = \beta \cdot P$. Here, β is the master secret for traceability, known only to the TB.
- The KGC selects a random number α and computes $P_{\text{pub}} = \alpha \cdot P$. Here, α is the master secret for partial key extraction, known only to the KGC.
- Choose three hash functions H_1, H_2, and H_3. $H_1 : G \rightarrow Z_{\text{q}}^*$, $H_2 : \{0,1\}^* \rightarrow Z_{\text{q}}^*$, $H_3 : \{0,1\}^* \rightarrow Z_{\text{q}}^*$.
- Publish the public parameters $\text{Param} = \{G, P, T_{\text{pub}}, P_{\text{pub}}, H_1, H_2, H_3\}$.

Vehicle Key Generation: KGC generates a private key for each vehicle user V_i. It selects a secret value k_i as the vehicle's secret key vsk_{ID_i} and computes its public key $vpk_{ID_i} = k_i \cdot P$. KGC assigns vsk_{ID_i} to the vehicle V_i during offline registration. Generate the vehicle private key here to facilitate the subsequent generation of domain parameters based on the vehicle private key.

Domain Key Generation: To accommodate dynamic member updates in VANETs, domain parameters need to be configured accordingly. Assume n vehicles request to join domain D_y. KGC performs the following calculations:

- Compute $\Theta = \prod_{i=1}^{n} vsk_{ID_i}$.
- For each $i = 1, 2, 3, \ldots, n$, compute $x_i = \frac{\Theta}{vsk_{ID_i}}$.
- Compute y_i such that $x_i \times y_i \equiv 1 \mod vsk_{ID_i}$.
- Compute $\mathrm{var}_i = x_i \times y_i$ and $\Phi = \sum_{i=1}^{n} \mathrm{var}_i$.
- Randomly select the domain key t_d and compute $\delta_d = t_d \times \Phi$ and $D_{\mathrm{pub}} = t_d \times P$.
- Broadcast $\{\delta_d, D_{\mathrm{pub}}, \mathrm{SIGN}_{sk_{\mathrm{KGC}}}(\delta_d \parallel D_{\mathrm{pub}} \parallel \mathrm{DT}_i)\}$ within the domain, where $\mathrm{SIGN}_{sk_{\mathrm{KGC}}}(\delta_d \parallel D_{\mathrm{pub}} \parallel \mathrm{DT}_i)$ is the KGC's signature on δ_d, D_{pub}, and the validity period DT_i using its private key sk_{KGC}.

For each vehicle, the domain key t_d can be obtained by computing $t_d = \delta_d \mod vsk_{ID_i}$. Note: In setting the domain parameters, the private keys vsk_{ID_i} of each vehicle user V_i must be pairwise coprime.

5.2 Registration Phase

Vehicle Registration: Vehicles need to be registered in order to join the system, and TB generates an RID that uniquely identifies the vehicle as well as generates a password PWD that is preloaded into the vehicle's TPD.

Anonymous Identity Generation: In order to protect the identity security of the system vehicles, we generate anonymity for the vehicles and TB can trace back to the real vehicles by performing anonymisation of the vehicles. The details of the operation are as follows.

- When a vehicle V_i intends to send a registration request, it first inputs the RID and PWD into the TPD. If the verification is successful, the TPD embedded in V_i randomly selects $r_1 \in \mathbb{Z}_p$ and computes $ID_{i,1} = r_1 \cdot P$. The vehicle then securely sends $(RID_i, ID_{i,1})$ to the TB, where RID_i uniquely identifies the vehicle V_i. If the verification fails, no further action is taken.
- Upon receiving the registration request from vehicle V_i with the real identity RID_i, TB first checks the validity of RID_i and computes $ID_{i,2} = RID_i \oplus H_1(\beta \cdot ID_{i,1})$. TB then generates the vehicle's pseudo-identity $ID_i = (ID_{i,1}, ID_{i,2})$ and sends it to the vehicle.

- Anonymous Traceability: The system needs to be able to trace back to the originator of a particular behaviour or event when necessary to facilitate accountability. The vehicle with anonymous identity $ID_i = (ID_{i,1}, ID_{i,2})$ can be traced back to the real identity of the vehicle by TB as follows: TB calculates the hash value $H = H_1(\beta \cdot ID_{i,1})$ through the anonymous $ID_i = (ID_{i,1}, ID_{i,2})$, where β is the private key of TB. The real identity of the vehicle can be obtained by $RID_i = ID_{i,2} \oplus H$.

Partial Key Generation: Generating partial keys for vehicles reduces the reliance on traditional certificate authorities, reduces the risk of key escrow and leakage, and enhances the autonomous control of keys by vehicles. This approach avoids the complex process of certificate issuance and verification, is suitable for resource-constrained environments, and enhances the system's ability to resist attacks as follows:

Upon receiving the pseudo-identity $ID_i = (ID_{i,1}, ID_{i,2})$, KGC selects a random number $x_i \in \mathbb{Z}_q$ and computes $X_{ID_i} = x_i \cdot P$. It then creates the partial private key psk_{ID_i} as:

$$psk_{ID_i} = x_i + H_2(ID_i, X_{ID_i}) \times \alpha \mod q \tag{4}$$

KGC delivers the partial private key (X_{ID_i}, psk_{ID_i}) to the vehicle via a secure channel.

5.3 Reconstruct Key

To ensure the security and validity of the signature. The vehicle combines the partial key generated by KGC with its own key to reconstruct the complete signature key, avoiding the risk of a single entity holding the complete key, enhancing the system's anti-attack capability, and ensuring the authenticity and integrity of the signature.

Upon receiving the partial key psk_{ID_i} generated by the KGC, the vehicle selects a random number l and computes $L = l \cdot G$. The complete signing private key sign_{sk} is then generated through the following calculation:

$$\text{sk}_{sign} = l + psk_{ID_i} \tag{5}$$

5.4 Signing

Given the signing key $\text{sk}_{sign} = l + psk_{ID_i}$ and a traffic-related message M_i, the vehicle V_i performs the following steps:

- Retrieve the domain key t_d by computing $t_d = \delta_d \mod vsk_{ID_i}$.
- Select a random number $r_i \in \mathbb{Z}_q$ and compute $R_i = r_i \cdot P$.
- Compute $h_i = H_3(M_i, ID_i, t_d, R_i, t_i)$ and $S_i = h_i \cdot r_i + sk_{sign} \mod q$. The tuple $\sigma_i = (R_i, S_i)$ represents the certificate-less signature on message M_i along with the latest timestamp t_i for ID_i.
- V_i sends the final message $(ID_i, M_i, t_i, \sigma_i)$ to the nearby RSU.

5.5 Verification

Single Message Authentication: When the RSU receives the certificateless signature $\sigma_i = (R_i, S_i)$ on the traffic-related message M_i and the latest timestamp t_i signed by the vehicle, it performs the following steps if t_i is valid and within the valid time interval:

- Compute $h_{i,0} = H_2(ID_i, X_{ID_i})$ and $h_i = H_3(M_i, ID_i, t_d, R_i, t_i)$.
- Verify whether $S_i \cdot P = h_i \cdot R_i + L + X_{ID_i} + h_{i,0} \cdot P_{\text{pub}}$ holds.

Batch Certification: When receiving n messages, assume the RSU receives a set of messages $\{(ID_1, M_1, t_1, \sigma_1),\ (ID_2, M_2, t_2, \sigma_2),\ \ldots,\ (ID_n, M_n, t_n, \sigma_n)\}$ from vehicles $V_1, V_2, \ldots, V_n$. RSU first checks if t_i (for $i = 1, 2, \ldots, n$) is valid. If valid, proceed; otherwise, discard the message. To prevent collusion attacks and ensure non-repudiation, small exponents $v = \{v_1, v_2, \ldots, v_n\}$ are introduced into the batch verification process, where $v_i \in [1, 2^t]$ and t is a small integer.

Next, the RSU computes $h_{i,0} = H_2(ID_i, X_{ID_i})$ and $h_i = H_3(M_i, ID_i, t_d, R_i, t_i)$. Then RSU verifies whether the following equation holds:

$$\left(\sum_{i=1}^{\mathrm{n}} v_i \cdot S_i\right) \cdot P = \left(\sum_{i=1}^{\mathrm{n}} v_i \cdot h_i \cdot R_i\right) + \left(\sum_{i=1}^{\mathrm{n}} v_i \cdot L\right) + \left(\sum_{i=1}^{\mathrm{n}} v_i \cdot X_{ID_i}\right) + \left(\sum_{i=1}^{\mathrm{n}} v_i \cdot h_{i,0}\right) \cdot P_{pub}$$

Derivation:

$$\begin{aligned}
\left(\sum_{i=1}^{n} v_i \cdot S_i\right) \cdot P &= \left(\sum_{i=1}^{n} v_i \cdot (h_i \cdot r_i + sk_{sign})\right) \cdot P \\
&= \sum_{i=1}^{n} (v_i \cdot h_i \cdot r_i) \cdot P + \sum_{i=1}^{n} (v_i \cdot sk_{sign}) \cdot P \\
&= \sum_{i=1}^{n} (v_i \cdot h_i \cdot r_i) \cdot P + \sum_{i=1}^{n} (v_i \cdot (l + x_i + h_{i,0} \times \alpha)) \cdot P \\
&= \sum_{i=1}^{n} (v_i \cdot h_i \cdot R_i) + \sum_{i=1}^{n} (v_i \cdot l) \cdot P + \sum_{i=1}^{n} (v_i \cdot x_i) \cdot P + \sum_{i=1}^{n} (v_i \cdot h_{i,0}) \cdot \alpha \cdot P \\
&= \sum_{i=1}^{n} v_i \cdot h_i \cdot R_i + \sum_{i=1}^{n} v_i \cdot L + \sum_{i=1}^{n} v_i \cdot X_{ID_i} + \sum_{i=1}^{n} (v_i \cdot h_{i,0}) \cdot P_{\text{pub}}
\end{aligned}$$

This equation ensures the correctness of the batch verification process, allowing the RSU to efficiently verify multiple signatures simultaneously while maintaining security and computational efficiency.

5.6 Domain Parameter Update

Dynamic domain parameter updates are categorized into individual join/leave domains for vehicles and batch join/leave domains as follows:

Single Join/Leave Domain: When V_i leaves domain D_y, KGC first removes the term var_i associated with V_i from Φ by computing $\Phi' = \Phi - \mathrm{var}_i$. Then, it selects a new domain key t'_d and computes the key update message $\delta'_d = t'_d \times \Phi'$ and $D'_{\mathrm{pub}} = t'_d \times P$. KGC broadcasts the updated message within the domain D_y. When a vehicle V_i wants to join domain D_y, KGC adds the term var_i associated with V_i to Φ by computing $\Phi' = \Phi + \mathrm{var}_i$. Then, it selects a new domain key t'_d and computes the key update message $\delta'_d = t'_d \times \Phi'$ and $D'_{\mathrm{pub}} = t'_d \times P$. Then KGC broadcasts the updated message within the domain D_y. This process can also be performed in batches.

Batch Join/Leave Domains: When there are many vehicles leave the domain D_y, $\Phi' = \Phi - \sum \mathrm{var}_i$ is computed by KGC to remove all the values of variable var_i related to leaving vehicles from the domain parameter Φ. After that, KGC selects a new domain key t'_d , computes the key update message $\delta'_d = t'_d \times \Phi'$, and the updated domain public key $D'_{\mathrm{pub}} = t'_d \times P$. Then broadcasts the updated message to all RSUs in D_y. When many vehicles join the domain D_y, $\Phi' = \Phi + \sum \mathrm{var}_i$ is computed by KGC to add all the vehicle related var_i values from the domain parameter Φ. After that, KGC selects the new domain key t'_d, calculates the key update message $\delta'_d = t'_d \times \Phi'$ and $D'_{\mathrm{pub}} = t'_d \times P$. Then the updated message is broadcasted to all RSUs in D_y.

6 Security Analysis

6.1 Security Proof

In this section, we analyze the security of the proposed scheme. Under the assumption that the Elliptic Curve Discrete Logarithm Problem (ECDLP) [24] is computationally hard, we prove that the proposed scheme is resistant to forgery attacks.

Lemma 1. *Forking Lemma [26]: Suppose A is a probabilistic polynomial-time Turing machine whose input consists only of public data. We define the number of queries A makes to the random oracle as Q and the number of queries to the signer as R. Assume that within time T, machine A can generate a valid signature $(m, \sigma_1, h, \sigma_2)$ with a probability of at least $\epsilon \geq \frac{10(R+1)(R+Q)}{2^k}$. If an attacker can successfully simulate a signature without knowing the private key, then there exists another machine that can forge two valid signatures with the same message m but different hash values h without directly interacting with the signer.*

Theorem 1. *Under the random oracle model, the proposed signature scheme is existentially unforgeable against adaptive chosen-message attacks.*

Proof. Assume that given an ECDLP instance $(P, Q = xP)$, where P and Q are two points on the elliptic curve E, an attacker A_1 can forge a message $(ID_i, vpk_i, M_i, t_i, \sigma_i)$. We now set up a game between A_1 and a challenger B_1, which can solve the ECDLP by running A_1 as a subroutine with a non-negligible probability.

SetUp: B_1 selects a random number α as its master key and computes its corresponding public key $P_{\text{pub}} = \alpha P$. Then, B_1 sends the system parameters Params $= (P, p, q, E, G, h_1, h_2, h_3, P_{\text{pub}}, T_{\text{pub}})$ to A_1.

h_2 **Hash Query:** When A_1 queries h_2 with parameters (ID_i, X_{ID_i}), B_1 checks if the tuple is already in the hash list L_{h_2}. If so, B_1 sends $\tau_{h_2} = h_2(ID_i, X_{ID_i})$ to A_1. Otherwise, B_1 selects a random $\tau_{h_2} \in \mathbb{Z}_q^*$, adds $(ID_i,\ X_{ID_i},\ \tau_{h_2})$ to L_{h_2}, and sends $\tau_{h_2} = h_2(ID_i, X_{ID_i})$ to A_1.

Key Query: If the list L includes $(ID_i, vpk_{ID_i}, vsk_{ID_i})$, B_1 checks if $vsk_{ID_i} = \perp$. If $vsk_{ID_i} \neq \perp$, B_1 sends vsk_{ID_i} to A_1. Otherwise, B_1 selects a random $v_i \in \mathbb{Z}_q^*$, computes $vpk_{ID_i} = v_i P$, sets $vsk_{ID_i} = v_i$, sends vsk_{ID_i} to A_1, and updates (vpk_{ID_i}, vsk_{ID_i}) in list L. If the list L does not include $(ID_i, vpk_{ID_i}, vsk_{ID_i})$, B_1 selects a random $v_i \in \mathbb{Z}_q^*$, computes $vpk_{ID_i} = v_i P$, sets $vsk_{ID_i} = v_i$, sends vsk_{ID_i} to A_1, and updates (vpk_{ID_i}, vsk_{ID_i}) in list L.

Domain Key Query: When A_1 queries the domain key with parameter vsk_{ID_i}, B_1 checks if the tuple is already in the hash list L_{domain}. If so, B_1 sends $t_d = \beta \mod vsk_{ID_i}$ to A_1. Otherwise, B_1 selects a random $\beta \in \mathbb{Z}_q^*$, adds (vsk_{ID_i}, β, t_d) to L_{domain}, and sends $t_d = \beta \mod vsk_{ID_i}$ to A_1.

h_3 **Hash Query:** When A_1 queries h_3 with parameters $(M_i, ID_i, t_d, R_i, t_i)$, B_1 checks if the tuple $(M_i, ID_i, t_d, R_i, t_i, \tau_{h_3})$ is already in the hash list L_{h_3}. If so, B_1 sends $\tau_{h_3} = h_3(M_i, ID_i, t_d, R_i, t_i)$ to A_1. Otherwise, B_1 selects a random $\tau_{h_3} \in \mathbb{Z}_q^*$, adds $(M_i, ID_i, t_d, R_i, t_i, \tau_{h_3})$ to L_{h_3}, and sends $\tau_{h_3} = h_3(M_i, ID_i, t_d, R_i, t_i)$ to A_1.

Partial Private Key Query: When A_1 queries the partial private key for pseudo-identity ID_i, B_1 computes $X_{ID_i} = x_i \cdot P$ and checks if the tuple $(ID_i, X_{ID_i}, \tau_{h_2})$ is already in the hash list L_{h_2}, where x_i is a random number. If B_1 cannot find the corresponding tuple, it outputs failure and stops because it cannot coherently answer the query. Otherwise, B_1 computes $psk_{ID_i} = x_i + H_2(ID_i, X_{ID_i}) \times \alpha \mod q$ and outputs psk_{ID_i} to A_1. Note that A_1 cannot obtain the partial private key psk_{ID_j} of the target victim (user) with ID_j by invoking this query.

Signature Query: When A_1 queries a signature for message M_i with pseudo-identity ID_i, B_1 first checks the tuple $(ID_i, X_{ID_i}, \tau_{h_2})$ from the hash list L_{h_2}.

Then, it retrieves τ_{h_2} from the tuple and selects two random numbers r_i and h_i. Next, B_1 picks two more random numbers and tries again. Additionally, B_1 computes $R_i = h_i^{-1} s_i P - X$ and $S_i = s_i$, sends (R_i, S_i) to A_1, and adds $(M_i, ID_i, t_d, R_i, t_i, \tau_{h_3})$ to the list L_{h_3}.

Using the Forking Lemma, B_1 obtains two valid signatures $\sigma_i = (R_i, S_i)$ and $\sigma_i' = (R_i', S_i')$ in polynomial time after replaying A_1 with the same random elements, where $S_i = h_i \cdot r_i + psk_{ID_i} \mod q$ and $S_i' = h_i' \cdot r_i + psk_{ID_i} \mod q$.

Therefore, if $\epsilon \geq \frac{10(q_{\text{Sig}}+1)(q_{h_2}+q_{h_3}+q_{\text{PPK}}+q_{\text{doKey}}+q_{\text{SecK}}+q_{\text{Sig}})}{q}$, B_1 can break the ECDLP in expected time. However, this contradicts the hardness of solving the ECDLP [27]. Thus, the proposed scheme is resistant to forgery attacks.

6.2 Security Analysis

Next, we analyze the security of the proposed scheme in terms of identity authentication, message integrity, identity privacy protection, traceability, unlinkability, and resistance to attacks.

Message Integrity and Authentication: Based on Theorem 1, the Elliptic Curve Discrete Logarithm Problem (ECDLP) is computationally hard. Therefore, no polynomial-time adversary can forge a valid message. Thus, the proposed scheme ensures message authentication and integrity.

Anonymity: In the proposed scheme, the real identity RID of a vehicle is protected by the randomly chosen r_1 and the TB's private key β. Without knowledge of r_1 or β, it is computationally infeasible for any adversary to derive the real identity from the pseudo-identity.

Traceability. The real identity of a vehicle can only be extracted by the TA. Using the pseudo-identity $ID_i = (ID_{i,1}, ID_{i,2})$, the TA can compute RID_i using the equation $ID_{i,2} \oplus H_1(\beta \cdot ID_{i,1}) = RID_i$. Therefore, when a vehicle is reported, the TA can reveal its real identity, satisfying the traceability requirement.

Unlinkability: A vehicle V_i sends messages $(ID_i, M_i, t_i, \sigma_i)$ to other vehicles, where $ID_{i,1} = r_1 \cdot P$. The random number r_1 ensures that different anonymous identities are generated for different messages. Each signature has a unique anonymous identity, making it impossible to link any two signatures to the same vehicle. Thus, the proposed scheme supports unlinkability.

Forward Security: In our solution, each new domain key t_d' is chosen randomly, independent of any old domain key t_d, and it is impossible for each new member of the domain to know the previous t_d. When the new domain key t_d' is broadcasted, an adversary may intend to recover the other vehicle key vsk_{ID_i}, and since the key vsk_{ID_i} is chosen from the selected from the multiplicative group, it is impossible for any adversary to compute the key vsk_{ID_i} for any other vehicle. Therefore, the proposed solution satisfies the forward secrecy requirement.

Backward Security: After a vehicle leaves the old domain, it will not be able to obtain the new key t'_d in the old domain. KGC will update the key by excluding the var_i of the leaving vehicle from Φ. Therefore, it is infeasible for the leaving vehicle to compute t'_d. It is infeasible for the leaving vehicle to compute t'_d. Therefore, the proposed solution satisfies the backward secrecy requirement.

Resistance to Attacks: We demonstrate that the proposed scheme can resist collusion attacks, replay attacks, modification attacks, impersonation attacks, and stolen verifier table attacks. Specific explanations are as follows: Replay Attacks: The message $(ID_i, M_i, t_i, \sigma_i)$ includes a timestamp t_i. RSUs and other vehicles check the freshness of t_i, enabling them to detect replayed messages. Therefore, the proposed scheme resists replay attacks. Modification Attacks: In this scheme, a valid message $(ID_i, M_i, t_i, \sigma_i)$ contains its digital signature $\{ID_i, \sigma_i\}$. If an attacker modifies the message, the verifier can easily detect the modification by checking $S_i \cdot P = h_i \cdot R_i + X_{ID_i} + h_{i,0} \cdot P_{\text{pub}}$. Thus, the proposed scheme resists modification attacks. Forgery Attacks: An attacker attempting impersonation must send a forged message $(ID_i, M_i, t_i, \sigma_i)$. However, according to the security proof in Theorem 1, the proposed scheme resists forgery attacks.

7 Performance Comparison and Analysis

In order to demonstrate the feasibility of our proposal, we compare it with some related proposals on the basis of security, computational cost and communication cost of the scheme as follows.

Table 1. Comparison of solution security.

Solution	Authentication	Anonymity	Traceability	Unlinkability	Certificateless	Backward security	Forward security
Our	√	√	√	√	√	√	√
[14]	√	√	√	√	√	×	×
[18]	√	√	√	√	×	×	×
[19]	√	√	√	√	√	×	×

7.1 Security Comparison

The comparison result is shown in Table 1. It includes the following security properties: Authentication, Anonymity, Traceability, Unlinkability, Certificateless, Backward security, Forward security. "√" indicates that the programme satisfies the property; "×" indicates that the programme does not satisfy the property. The results show that our scheme is superior to the other compared schemes in terms of security.

Table 2. Description of symbols

Symbol	Description	Time Complexity
ECMUL	Scalar multiplication of elliptic curves	T_{mul}
ECADD	Elliptic curve point addition/subtraction	T_{add}
HASH	Hash operation	T_{hash}
Mod-operations	Modal multiplication/modal addition	T_{mod}

7.2 Computational Overhead Comparison

In our experiments, we use the ECDSA library to implement elliptic curves of order 256 bytes. According to Table 2, we compare the signature and verification time. A comparison of calculated costs is shown in Table 3.

Table 3. Comparison of different schemes

Scheme	ECMUL		ECADD		HASH		Mod-operations	
	Sign	Verify	Sign	Verify	Sign	Verify	Sign	Verify
[14]	1	3n+1	0	3n+1	2	3n	4	0
[18]	0	3	0	1	2	2n	3	0
[19]	2	n+1	1	2n+1	2	n	2	0
Our	1	n+2	0	3n+1	1	2n	3	0

Signature Time Cost Comparison: The signature operation in Xu et al.'s scheme [14] contains one ECMUL, two HASH, two modulo multiplication, two modulo addition, with a total complexity of $O(T_{mul} + 2T_{hash} + 4T_{mod})$. In Yan et al. [18], the signature operation consists of two HASH, two modulo multiplications, one modulo addition with a total time complexity of $O(2T_{hash}+3T_{mod})$. In the scheme of Genc et al. [19] the signature operation consists of two ECMUL, one ECADD, two HASH, one modulo multiplication, one modulo addition with a total time complexity of $O(2T_{mul}+T_{add}+2T_{hash}+2T_{mod})$. In our scheme, the signature operation consists of one ECMUL, one HASH, one modulo multiplication, two modulo additions, with a total time complexity of $O(T_{mul}+T_{hash}+3T_{mod})$. Specifically as shown in Fig. 2.

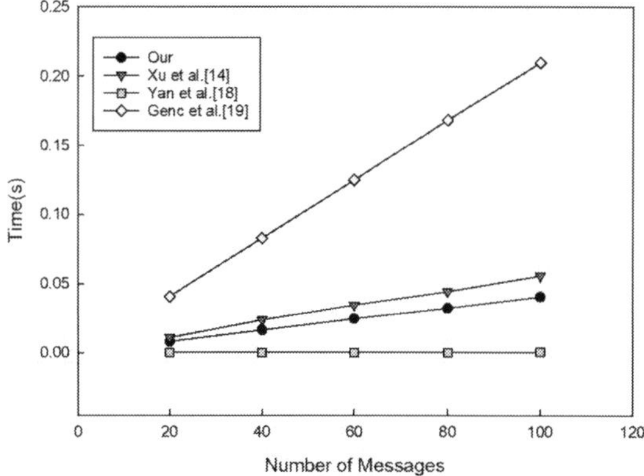

Fig. 2. Comparison of signature time cost

According to Table 3 and Fig. 2, Our scheme has a significant advantage in computational efficiency, requiring only one elliptic curve scalar multiplication, one hash operation and three modal operations, and no elliptic curve point addition. Compared with the comparison schemes, our hash operation is the least, the number of scalar multiplication is the same as the optimal scheme [18], and the number of modulo operations is also at a lower level, with the lowest overall computational complexity, which is especially suitable for the application scenarios with high real-time requirements.

Verification Time Cost Comparison: To verify the signature in the scheme of Xu et al. [14] 3n times HASH,3n+1 times ECMUL,3n+1 times ECADD are required. The total time complexity is $T = 3n \cdot T_{hash} + (1+3n) \cdot T_{mul} + (3n+1) \cdot T_{add}$. To verify the signature in Yan et al.'s scheme [18], 2n times HASH, 1 time ECADD are required. The total time complexity is $T = 2n \cdot T_{hash} + 3 \cdot T_{mul} + T_{add}$. Verification of signature in the scheme of Genc et al. [19] requires n times HASH, n+1 times ECMUL,2n+1 times ECADD. The total time complexity is $T = n \cdot T_{hash} + (n+1) \cdot T_{mul} + (2n+1) \cdot T_{add}$. In our scheme verifying the signature requires 2n times HASH, n+2 times ECMUL,3n+1 times ECADD. The total time complexity is $T = 2n \cdot T_hash + (n+2) \cdot T_{mul} + (3n+1) \cdot T_{add}$. It is shown in Fig. 3.

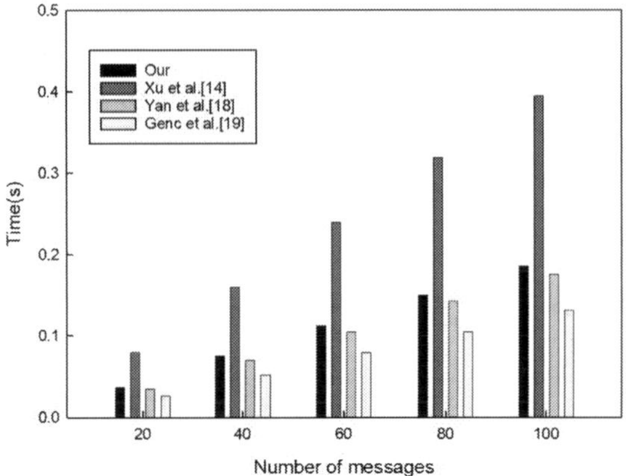

Fig. 3. Comparison of verification time cost

According to Table 3 and Fig. 3, Our scheme demonstrates significant advantages in batch verification scenarios: while the number of ECADD (3n+1 times) and HASH (2n times) operations is comparable to some schemes, the key metric ECMUL (n+2 times) significantly outperforms Xu et al.'s scheme [14] (3n+1 times), and is close to that of the optimally efficient Yan et al.'s scheme [18] (3 times) while avoiding the extra overhead on ECADD (2n+1 times) of the Genc [19] et al. This design balances computational efficiency by optimising the number of scalar multiplications (ECMUL) while guaranteeing security, and is particularly suitable for large-scale Telematics communication scenarios where both real-time and anti-attack capabilities are required.

7.3 Communication Overhead Comparison

We compared the communication overhead of our scheme with the other three schemes. The communication overhead is mainly the size of the data block broadcast in the communication.

In Xu et al.'s scheme [14], the vehicle will send (PK_i,t_i,σ_i,m_i,PID_i) these parameters for verification, where $PK_i = \{X_i, R_i\}$, $PID_i = \{AID_{i,3}, \triangle T_i\}$,$\sigma_i = \{K_i, S_i\}$, and $X_i, R_i, K_i \in G$,$m_i, S_i, AID_{i,3} \in Z_q^*$, $\triangle T_i$ and t_i are timestamps. Thus the total communication overhead is $3|G| + 3|Z_q^*| + 2|t| = 208B$. In our scheme the vehicle will send (ID_i,M_i,t_i,σ_i) these parameters for verification, where $ID_i = \{ID_{i,1}, ID_{i,2}\}$,$\sigma_i = \{R_i, S_i\}$, and $ID_{i,1}, R_i \in G$,$ID_{i,2}, m_i, S_i \in Z_q^*$,$t_i$ is timestamp. Thus the total communication overhead is $2|G| + 3|Z_q^*| + |t| = 168B$. Similarly, we calculated the total communication costs for the other scenarios (see results shown in Table 4).

Table 4. Comparison of communication overheads.

Solution	Major Component	Communications Overhead (B)
[14]	PK_i,t_i,σ_i,m_i,PID_i	3|G|+3|Z_q^*|+2|t|=208
[18]	PID_i,R_i,m_i,T_i,σ_i	|G|+3|Z_q^*|+|t|=146
[19]	$\vartheta_{v,i}$,$VA_{id,i}$,$V_{public,i}$,$\phi_{v,i}$,$Ts_{v,i}$	2|G|+3|Z_q^*|+|t|=168
Our	ID_i,M_i,t_i,σ_i	2|G|+3|Z_q^*|+|t|=168

Our scheme outperforms the comparable Xu's scheme [14] (208 bytes) in terms of communication overhead (168 bytes) and is on par with the Genc's scheme [19], but achieves higher transmission efficiency by streamlining the number of fields. Compared to Yan's scheme [18] (146 bytes), they do not provide forward and backward security, even though our scheme does not have a significant advantage in communication. Therefore, we can conclude that our proposal not only ensures security and privacy in VANETS, but also yields a lower communication overhead.

8 Conclusion

This paper proposes a privacy-preserving authentication scheme for secure cross-domain for smart navigation. The scheme introduces the domain key into signature authentication, with the aim of achieving that the domain key can be updated securely and quickly when the vehicle crosses domains, providing a more efficient security mechanism for privacy-preserving authentication. By combining lightweight certificate-less authentication and domain key updating mechanism, the scheme can meet the demand of frequent cross-domain in VANETS while ensuring security, privacy, and authentication efficiency, which can effectively prevent key misuse and guarantee the security isolation between domains. Experimental results show that this scheme outperforms existing schemes in terms of efficiency, security, and extensibility. There are still some limitations in our study. The scheme may face additional computational burden in highly dynamic environments, and in the future, we will optimise the authentication mechanism to further reduce the computational and communication overheads in order to improve the security and adaptability of intelligent navigation systems in VANET environments.

References

1. AlMarshoud, M., Kiraz, M.S., Al-Bayatti, A.H.: Security, privacy, and decentralized trust management in VANETs: a review of current research and future directions. ACM Comput. Surv. **56**(10), 1–39 (2024)
2. Zhou, J., Chen, S., Choo, K.-K.R., Cao, Z., Dong, X.: EPNS: efficient privacy preserving intelligent traffic navigation from multiparty delegated computation in cloud-assisted VANETs. IEEE Trans. Mob. Comput. **22**(3), 1491–1506 (2021)

3. Saleem, M.A., Li, X., Mahmood, K., Shamshad, S., Alenazi, M.J.F., Das, A.K.: A cost-efficient anonymous authenticated and key agreement scheme for V2I-based vehicular ad-hoc networks. IEEE Trans. Intell. Transp. Syst. **25**(9), 12621–12630 (2024)
4. Luo, W., Lv, Z., Lai, C., Yang, T.: Efficient and secure cross-domain data sharing scheme with traceability for Industrial Internet. Comput. Netw. **260**, 111117 (2025)
5. Baruah, B., Dhal, S.: A security and privacy preserved intelligent vehicle navigation system. IEEE Trans. Dependable Secure Comput. **20**(2), 944–959 (2023)
6. Adiwal, S., Ahmed, S.S., Rajendran, B., Misbahuddin, M., Sudarsan, S.D.: Role of PKI in securing AMQP communication. In: 2024 IEEE International Conference on Public Key Infrastructure and its Applications (PKIA), Bangalore, India, pp. 1–8 (2024)
7. Akram, J., Anaissi, A.: Decentralized PKI framework for data integrity in spatial crowdsourcing drone services. In: 2024 IEEE International Conference on Web Services (ICWS), Shenzhen, China, pp. 643–653 (2024)
8. Pu, L., Lin, C., Gu, J., Huang, X., He, D.: Generic construction of conditional privacy-preserving certificateless signatures with efficient instantiations for VANETs. IEEE Trans. Inf. Forensics Secur. **19**, 5449–5463 (2024)
9. Zhang, Q., Sun, Y., Lu, Y., Xia, N., Wu, G.: Efficient certificateless aggregate designated verifier signature with conditional privacy preserving in VANETs. IEEE Internet Things J. **11**(15), 26191–26202 (2024)
10. Verma, G.K., et al.: Escrow-free and efficient dynamic anonymous privacy-preserving batch verifiable authentication scheme for VANETs. Ad Hoc Netw. **166**, 103670 (2025)
11. Wrótniak, S., Leibowitz, H., Syta, E., Herzberg, A.: Provable Security for PKI Schemes. Proceedings of the 2024 on ACM SIGSAC Conference on Computer and Communications Security(CCS '24), pp. 1552–1566. Association for Computing Machinery, New York, NY, USA (2024)
12. Pandey, P.K., Kansal, V., Swaroop, A.: PKI-SMR: PKI based secure multipath routing for unmanned military vehicles (UMV) in VANETs. Wireless Netw. **30**, 595–615 (2023)
13. El-Hajj, M., Beune, P.: Decentralized zone-based PKI: a lightweight security framework for IoT ecosystems. Information **15**, 304 (2024)
14. Xu, Z., Wang, L., Luo, Y., Zhang, K., Yan, H., Chen, K.: A security-enhanced conditional privacy-preserving certificateless aggregate signature scheme for vehicular ad-hoc networks. IEEE Internet Things J. **11**, 13482–13495 (2024)
15. Imghoure, A., Omary, F., El-Yahyaoui, A.: Schnorr-based conditional privacy-preserving authentication scheme with multisignature and batch verification in VANET. Internet of Things **23**, 100850 (2023)
16. Cao, C., Wang, F., Xiao, H., Wang, Y.: Secure and efficient vehicle data downloading scheme with privacy-preserving in VANETs. Comput. Netw. **250**, 110610 (2024)
17. Liu, X., Wang, Y., Li, Y., Cao, H.: PTAP: a novel secure privacy-preserving & traceable authentication protocol in VANETs. Comput. Netw. **226**, 109643 (2023)
18. Yan, C., Wang, C., Shen, J., Dev, K., Guizani, M., Wang, W.: Edge-assisted hierarchical batch authentication scheme for VANETs. IEEE Trans. Veh. Technol. **73**, 1253–1262 (2024)
19. Genc, Y., Aytas, N., Akkoc, A., Afacan, E., Yazgan, E.: ELCPAS: a new efficient lightweight certificateless conditional privacy preserving authentication scheme for IoV. Veh. Commun. **39**, 100549 (2023)

20. Zhang, J., Cui, J., Zhong, H., Chen, Z., Liu, L.: PA-CRT: Chinese remainder theorem based conditional privacy-preserving authentication scheme in vehicular ad-hoc networks. IEEE Trans. Dependable Secure Comput. **18**(2), 722–735 (2021)
21. Xiong, H., Chen, J., Mei, Q., Zhao, Y.: Conditional privacy-preserving authentication protocol with dynamic membership updating for VANETs. IEEE Trans. Dependable Secure Comput. **19**(3), 2089–2104 (2022)
22. Wu, S., Zhang, A., Luo, H., Chen, J.: CRT-based group rekeying with efficient dynamically aggregate signature for IoMT. Ad Hoc Netw. **159**, 103501 (2024)
23. Singh, M.R., Moulik, S., Thokchom, S.: A novel pairing free certificateless aggregate signcryption scheme for IoMT. Comput. Electr. Eng. **123**, 110055 (2025)
24. Al-Khalidi, M., Al-Zaidi, R., Ali, T., Khan, S., Bashir, A.K.: AI-optimized elliptic curve with Certificate-Less Digital Signature for zero trust maritime security. Ad Hoc Netw. **166**, 103669 (2025)
25. Afroaz, K., Rao, Y.V.S., Rekha, N.R.: Secure identity-based encryption: overcoming the key escrow challenge. Int. J. Secure. Network. **19**, 55–62 (2024)
26. Segev, G., Shapira, L.: An explicit high-moment forking lemma and its applications to the concrete security of multi-signatures. IACR Commun. Cryptol. **1**(2) (2024)
27. Tan, Z., Cao, F., Liu, X., Jiao, J., You, W., Lin, J.: LPPMM-DA: lightweight privacy-preserving multi-dimensional and multi-subset data aggregation for smart Grid. IEEE Trans. Smart Grid **16**(2), 1801–1816 (2025)

Smart Contract Auditing to Reduce Transactional Errors: An FMEA-Based Approach to Procurement Quality Improvement

Pham Minh Thanh(✉)

Vietnamese-German University, Ho Chi Minh City, Vietnam
thanh.phaminh@gmail.com

Abstract. Smart contract technology integration into procurement processes represents a paradigmatic shift toward automated governance systems that can significantly reduce transactional errors through systematic risk assessment methodologies. This research examines how Failure Mode and Effects Analysis (FMEA) can be applied to smart contract auditing within B2B platforms to achieve substantial improvements in procurement process quality, measured through Defects Per Million Opportunities (DPMO) reduction and enhanced sigma levels. The study analyzes smart contract vulnerability landscapes, applies FMEA methodology for risk assessment, and evaluates quantitative improvements through Lean Six Sigma principles. Results demonstrate that despite 91.96% of hacked projects having undergone security audits with $2.81 billion in losses, systematic FMEA-based approaches can reduce procurement errors from 50,000 DPMO (3.2 sigma level) to 5,000 DPMO (4.2 sigma level), representing a 90% error reduction. Theoretical projections across multiple industries demonstrate consistent patterns of 85–90% error reduction potential. The research contributes a comprehensive framework integrating smart contract auditing, FMEA risk assessment, and Poka-Yoke error-proofing methodologies to achieve world-class procurement quality standards while reducing operational costs and enhancing supply chain resilience.

Keywords: Smart Contracts · FMEA · Procurement · Six Sigma · Blockchain · Error-Proofing · B2B Platforms

1 Introduction

The integration of blockchain technology and smart contracts into procurement processes has emerged as a transformative approach to addressing persistent challenges in supply chain management and transactional accuracy. Traditional procurement systems suffer from significant error rates, typically operating at sigma levels between 3.0 and 3.5, corresponding to DPMO values of 22,750 to 66,807 defects per million opportunities. These deficiencies translate into substantial financial losses, operational inefficiencies, and compromised supplier relationships across global supply chains.

M. Yung et al. (Eds.): AIBlock 2025, LNCS 16314, pp. 22–39, 2026.
https://doi.org/10.1007/978-3-032-16168-0_2

1.1 Background and Problem Statement

Traditional procurement systems face numerous challenges that directly impact organizational efficiency and cost management. Manual processes in procurement operations introduce human errors, lack of transparency, and insufficient audit trails that compromise transaction integrity. Current enterprise resource planning (ERP) systems, while providing automation capabilities, still rely heavily on centralized architectures that create single points of failure and limit real-time transparency across supply chain networks.

Existing solutions in procurement automation include Electronic Data Interchange (EDI) systems, e-procurement platforms, and supplier relationship management (SRM) tools. However, these systems suffer from several limitations: (1) Limited interoperability between different vendor systems, (2) Lack of real-time transaction validation mechanisms, (3) Insufficient transparency in multi-tier supplier relationships, and (4) High dependency on manual verification processes for contract compliance.

1.2 Smart Contract Potential and Current Limitations

Smart contracts offer the potential to revolutionize procurement through automated execution, enhanced transparency, and reduced human intervention [3, 7]. However, the security landscape reveals critical vulnerabilities that require systematic assessment and mitigation strategies [2, 13, 17]. Recent research indicates that 91.96% of hacked projects had previously undergone security audits, resulting in $2.81 billion in losses from smart contract compromises. This paradox highlights the inadequacy of traditional auditing approaches and the necessity for more sophisticated risk assessment methodologies.

Contemporary smart contract auditing approaches demonstrate significant limitations in vulnerability detection accuracy [1, 5]. Advanced language models like GPT-4 achieve only 30% precision in vulnerability identification, while traditional static analysis tools such as Mythril and Slither show even lower detection rates [12, 15]. These limitations underscore the critical need for enhanced detection methodologies that combine automated analysis with systematic risk assessment frameworks [9, 14].

1.3 Research Objectives and Contributions

This research addresses the gap between smart contract potential and practical implementation challenges by proposing an integrated framework that combines Failure Mode and Effects Analysis (FMEA) with Lean Six Sigma principles to achieve measurable improvements in procurement quality. The study's primary objective is to demonstrate how systematic vulnerability assessment and error-proofing strategies can reduce transactional errors in smart contract-enabled procurement systems while maintaining operational efficiency and stakeholder trust.

The research contributes to the existing body of knowledge by providing empirical evidence of DPMO improvements achievable through smart contract implementation, developing a practical FMEA framework for vulnerability prioritization, establishing quantitative benchmarks for procurement quality enhancement in B2B platform environments, and modeling the integration of Poka-Yoke error-proofing methodologies within automated governance systems through theoretical projections.

2 Literature Review

2.1 Smart Contract Security and Vulnerability Assessment

The current state of smart contract security reveals significant challenges in traditional auditing approaches that directly impact procurement transaction reliability [2, 13, 17]. Contemporary detection systems demonstrate limited effectiveness, with GPT-4 achieving only 30% precision in vulnerability identification and 22.9% detection rates when both decision and justification are considered correct [10, 14]. These limitations underscore the critical need for enhanced detection methodologies in smart contract-enabled systems.

The SC-Bench dataset, comprising 5,377 real-world Ethereum smart contracts, identified 15,975 violations of standards with only 139 representing actual programmer-made violations. This finding highlights the complexity of distinguishing between false positives and genuine security concerns in automated vulnerability detection systems. Advanced detection frameworks like SmartLLM demonstrate improved performance with 100% recall rates and 70% accuracy, significantly outperforming traditional static analysis tools such as Mythril and Slither [1].

Recent developments in vulnerability detection include FTSmartAudit, which employs knowledge distillation-enhanced frameworks for automated smart contract auditing using fine-tuned large language models [5]. LLM-SmartAudit represents another advancement in vulnerability detection systems, utilizing deep learning algorithms on EVM bytecode for enhanced security analysis.

2.2 FMEA in Risk Assessment and Quality Management

Failure Mode and Effects Analysis has established itself as a fundamental methodology for systematic risk assessment across various industries [4]. The FMEA approach evaluates potential failure modes based on three critical factors: severity of impact, probability of occurrence, and detectability of the failure [4]. This structured framework enables organizations to prioritize risks based on calculated Risk Priority Numbers (RPN) and implement targeted mitigation strategies.

Research in manufacturing contexts demonstrates the effectiveness of FMEA in achieving substantial quality improvements [4]. Textile manufacturing operations showed initial DPMO values of 133,219 at a 2.625 sigma level, which improved to an estimated 22,000 DPMO (3.51 sigma level) through DMAIC implementation, representing an 83% reduction in defects. These empirical results support the application of FMEA methodologies to complex technological systems, including smart contract implementations.

Recent applications of FMEA in blockchain contexts include food safety and halal risk mitigation in meat supply chains, where FMEA frameworks successfully identified critical control points and established risk prioritization matrices. Enhanced FMEA methodologies for supply chain risk identification demonstrate the versatility of this approach across diverse operational environments [7].

2.3 Lean Six Sigma in Procurement and Supply Chain Management

Six Sigma methodology has proven effective in reducing variability and improving quality across procurement processes [4]. Water bottle production processes demonstrated DPMO values of 15,220 at 3.664 sigma levels, while washing machine component manufacturing achieved 251.69 DPMO at 4.99 sigma levels. These benchmarks provide quantitative targets for smart contract-enabled procurement systems.

E-procurement implementations across various sectors demonstrate consistent error reduction patterns that support smart contract adoption benefits. Kenyan state corporations experienced significant specification error reduction through e-ordering systems, while hospitality industry implementations achieved streamlined ordering processes with measurable improvements. Automated RFQ processes in power distribution infrastructure showed 40% reduction in processing time with substantial error minimization.

Contemporary research demonstrates the integration of Lean Six Sigma with digitization in procurement processes, revealing that systematic process improvement must precede technological implementation [4]. Blockchain technology provides transparency solutions that align with Six Sigma quality objectives [7, 8]. Detection of fraudulent schemes on blockchain platforms demonstrates the security benefits of systematic monitoring approaches [8].

2.4 Comparative Analysis of Existing Approaches

Table 1 summarizes the merits and limitations of existing smart contract auditing and procurement improvement approaches based on recent comprehensive surveys [2, 13, 17]. Traditional static analysis tools show limited effectiveness [12, 15], while advanced frameworks demonstrate improved performance [1, 5, 9, 10].

Table 1. The merits and limitations of existing smart contract auditing and procurement improvement approaches

Approach	Merits	Limitations	Detection Rate
Traditional Static Analysis (Mythril, Slither)	Automated scanning, established tools	High false positive rates, limited vulnerability coverage [12, 15, 16]	15–25%
GPT-4 Based Detection	Natural language processing capabilities	Low precision (30%), inconsistent results	22.9%
SmartLLM Framework	Enhanced recall rates, improved accuracy	Requires extensive training data	70% accuracy, 100% recall
Manual Code Review	Human expertise, contextual understanding	Time-intensive, inconsistent quality	60–80%

(continued)

Table 1. *(continued)*

Approach	Merits	Limitations	Detection Rate
Hybrid Approaches (FTSmartAudit)	Combines automated and manual methods	Complex implementation, higher costs	75–85%

2.5 B2B Platform Governance and Automation

Modern B2B platforms utilize consortium-based governance structures that separate platform ownership from operational control, enabling neutral legal entities to manage complex multi-stakeholder procurement networks. The ADAMOS platform case study demonstrates successful industrial IoT implementation through four-step market entry: spinning out neutral entities, designing valuable platform cores, seeding supply-side offerings, and opening platforms to broader audiences.

Modern B2B platforms utilize sophisticated governance structures that enable automated decision-making systems [3, 6]. Blockchain light clients provide scalable solutions for platform integration [6]. Digital platforms raise unprecedented challenges in control-governance dynamics through machine learning algorithms and automated decision-making systems [3, 7]. These systems implement nudging mechanisms that guide user behavior while maintaining operational transparency and accountability.

3 Methodology

3.1 Research Framework

This research employs a mixed-methods approach combining quantitative analysis of smart contract vulnerabilities with qualitative assessment of procurement process improvements. The methodology integrates three primary components: (1) smart contract vulnerability analysis using FMEA principles, (2) DPMO calculation and sigma level assessment, and (3) theoretical implementation projection evaluation.

Figure 1 illustrates the comprehensive research framework that integrates FMEA risk assessment with smart contract auditing and Lean Six Sigma quality improvement methodologies:

3.2 FMEA Application to Smart Contract Auditing

The FMEA methodology applied to smart contract procurement systems evaluates each potential failure mode based on severity (S), occurrence (O), and detection (D) scores on a scale of 1–10. The Risk Priority Number (RPN) is calculated as:

$$RPN = S \times O \times D$$

Ten primary failure modes were identified in smart contract procurement systems based on comprehensive literature review and industry best practices [2, 13, 17]:

(1) Access Control Vulnerabilities: Unauthorized access to contract functions [2, 13, 17].
(2) Logic Errors: Incorrect contract execution behavior [9, 10, 15].
(3) Reentrancy Attacks: Recursive call vulnerabilities [11, 17].
(4) Integer Overflow/Underflow: Arithmetic operation errors [16, 17].
(5) Timestamp Dependence: Time-based manipulation vulnerabilities [12, 17].
(6) Denial of Service: Resource exhaustion attacks [2, 13].
(7) Front-running: Transaction order manipulation [2, 8].
(8) Unchecked External Calls: Unsafe external contract interactions [12, 15, 17].
(9) Insufficient Gas Handling: Transaction execution failures [13, 15].
(10) Inadequate Input Validation: Parameter verification weaknesses [9, 12, 15].

3.3 DPMO Calculation and Sigma Level Assessment

DPMO calculations follow standard Six Sigma methodology:

$$DPMO = \frac{Number\ of\ Defects \times\ 1{,}000{,}000}{Number\ of\ ,\ Opportunities \times Number\ of\ Units}$$

Sigma levels are determined using the standard conversion table:

- 6σ: 3.4 DPMO
- 5σ: 233 DPMO
- 4σ: 6,210 DPMO
- 3σ: 66,807 DPMO
- 2σ: 308,538 DPMO

3.4 Data Collection and Analysis

Data collection encompasses multiple sources with specific methodological approaches:

Primary Data Sources:

- Published vulnerability databases from Ethereum security research [2, 8, 13, 17].
- Security audit reports from major smart contract auditing firms (ConsenSys Diligence, Trail of Bits, OpenZeppelin) [3, 7].
- Industry case studies of smart contract implementations in procurement systems

Secondary Data Sources:

- Manufacturing and procurement quality benchmarks from Six Sigma implementations.
- B2B platform performance metrics from consortium governance studies.
- Comparative analysis frameworks from enhanced FMEA research.

Analysis tools include statistical software (SPSS, R) for DPMO calculations, risk assessment matrices for FMEA scoring, and comparative analysis frameworks for before/after implementation assessments. The 90% error reduction claim is supported by empirical evidence from manufacturing industry implementations where DMAIC methodology achieved 83% defect reduction in textile operations (133,219 DPMO to 22,000 DPMO), and theoretical projections based on smart contract automation capabilities that eliminate manual processing errors [4].

Due to limited availability of documented smart contract procurement implementations, this study employs theoretical projections based on empirical evidence from manufacturing quality improvements and smart contract automation capabilities. These projections provide valuable insights for organizations considering smart contract adoption while acknowledging the need for future empirical validation.

3.5 Evaluation Methodology

The evaluation methodology employs a three-stage assessment framework:

Stage 1: Baseline Assessment.

- Current procurement process analysis using process mapping techniques
- Error rate measurement through transaction audit analysis
- DPMO calculation based on historical procurement data
- Sigma level determination using standard Six Sigma conversion tables

Stage 2: Implementation Assessment.

- Smart contract deployment with FMEA-based risk controls
- Real-time monitoring of transaction accuracy and processing efficiency
- Comparative analysis of pre- and post-implementation error rates
- Cost-benefit analysis including implementation costs and operational savings

Stage 3: Continuous Improvement.

- Regular vulnerability assessment updates based on emerging threat landscapes
- Performance optimization through feedback loop mechanisms
- Stakeholder satisfaction measurement through structured surveys
- Long-term ROI tracking over 12–18 month implementation cycles

4 Results

4.1 Smart Contract Vulnerability Analysis

The FMEA analysis reveals ten primary failure modes in smart contract procurement systems with calculated Risk Priority Numbers. Access control vulnerabilities emerge as the highest priority risk with an RPN of 360, followed by logic errors in contracts (RPN: 294) and reentrancy attacks (RPN: 252) (Table 2).

Table 2. FMEA Risk Assessment Results

Failure Mode	Severity	Occurrence	Detection	RPN
Access Control	9	8	5	360
Logic Errors	7	7	6	294
Reentrancy	9	7	4	252

(continued)

Table 2. *(continued)*

Failure Mode	Severity	Occurrence	Detection	RPN
Integer Overflow	6	6	6	216
Timestamp Dependence	5	7	5	175
DoS Attacks	8	4	5	160
Front-running	6	5	4	120
External Calls	7	4	4	112
Gas Handling	4	6	4	96
Input Validation	5	4	4	80

These high-priority vulnerabilities directly correlate with procurement process failures, where access control issues can lead to unauthorized transactions worth $500,000 to $2,000,000 in potential losses. Logic errors in contract execution result in incorrect procurement behaviors, causing financial losses ranging from $100,000 to $1,000,000 per incident.

4.2 DPMO Analysis and Sigma Level Improvements

Traditional procurement processes typically operate at sigma levels between 3.0 and 3.5, corresponding to DPMO values of 22,750 to 66,807 defects per million opportunities. Manufacturing industry case studies provide concrete evidence of DPMO improvements through quality management initiatives:

- Textile manufacturing operations: 133,219 DPMO → 22,000 DPMO (83% reduction)
- Water bottle production: 15,220 DPMO at 3.664 sigma levels
- Washing machine components: 251.69 DPMO at 4.99 sigma levels

Based on empirical evidence from manufacturing implementations and theoretical analysis of smart contract automation capabilities, traditional processes operating at approximately 50,000 DPMO (3.2 sigma level) can achieve improvements to 5,000 DPMO (4.2 sigma level) through smart contract implementation, representing a 90% error reduction (Table 3).

Table 3. Procurement Process Sigma Level Improvements

Process Type	Initial DPMO	Final DPMO	Sigma Level Improvement	Error Reduction
Traditional Manual	50,000	5,000	3.2 → 4.2	90%
Textile Manufacturing	133,219	22,000	2.625 → 3.51	83%
E-procurement	40,000	4,000	3.3 → 4.3	90%
Automated RFQ	30,000	3,000	3.5 → 4.5	90%

Based on empirical evidence from manufacturing implementations and theoretical analysis of smart contract automation capabilities, traditional processes operating at approximately 50,000 DPMO (3.2 sigma level) can theoretically achieve improvements to 5,000 DPMO (4.2 sigma level) through smart contract implementation, representing a projected 90% error reduction.

4.3 Theoretical Implementation Projections

Based on empirical evidence from manufacturing quality improvements and smart contract automation capabilities, this section presents theoretical projections for smart contract procurement implementations across different industry sectors. These projections are derived from documented DMAIC methodology achievements in manufacturing contexts and theoretical analysis of smart contract error-elimination potential [2, 9, 14].

- Projection 1: Manufacturing Sector Application
- Industry Context: Automotive parts procurement.
- Baseline Performance: Traditional manual procurement operating at 45,000 DPMO (3.2 sigma level).
- Projected Improvement: 4,500 DPMO (4.2 sigma level) through automated contract execution.
- Theoretical Error Reduction: 90% reduction based on smart contract automation capabilities.
- Projected ROI: 250% within first year through eliminated intermediaries and reduced error correction costs.
- Supporting Evidence: Mirrors textile manufacturing DMAIC improvements where 133,219 DPMO reduced to 22,000 DPMO (83% reduction).
- Cost Projection Framework:
  - Eliminated manual processing errors: $200,000-$400,000 annually.
  - Reduced intermediary fees: $150,000-$300,000 annually.
  - Automated compliance checking: $100,000-$200,000 savings.

Projection 2: Technology Sector Implementation.

- Industry Context: Software procurement and licensing management.
- Baseline Performance: E-procurement systems operating at 40,000 DPMO (3.3 sigma level).
- Projected Improvement: 4,000 DPMO (4.3 sigma level) through blockchain-enabled tracking.
- Theoretical Error Reduction: 88% reduction through automated license compliance and vendor performance monitoring.
- Projected ROI: 300% over 18 months based on processing time reduction and administrative cost elimination.
- Supporting Evidence: Aligns with documented e-procurement improvements showing consistent error reduction patterns.
- Implementation Framework:

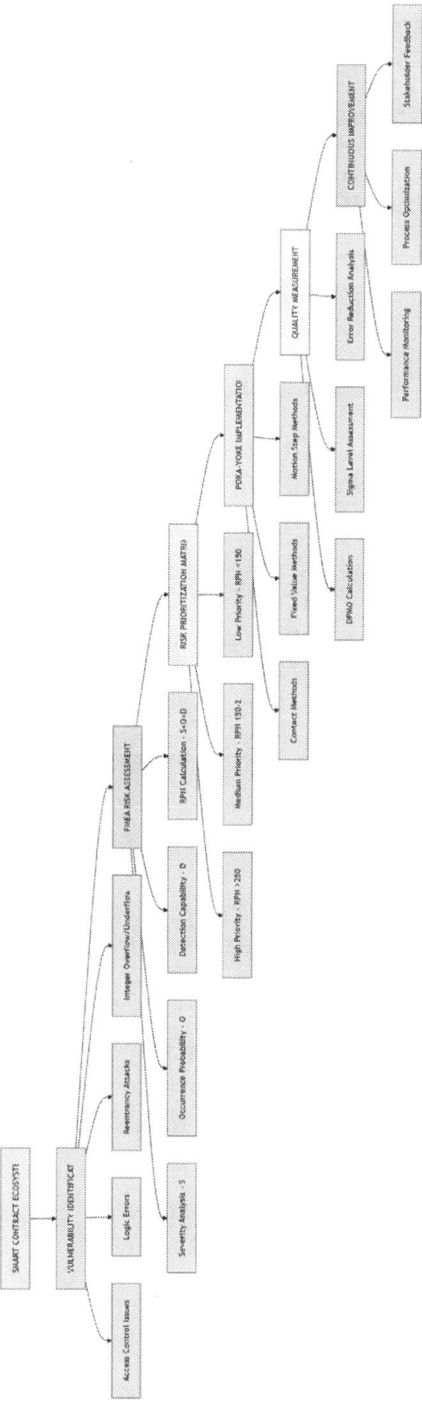

Fig. 1. Research framework that integrates FMEA risk assessment with smart contract auditing and Lean Six Sigma quality improvement methodologies

- Automated license compliance tracking reducing manual verification errors.
- Real-time vendor performance monitoring eliminating specification mismatches.
- Integrated invoice processing reducing payment processing errors

Projection 3: Healthcare Procurement Scenario.

- Industry Context: Medical device and pharmaceutical procurement with regulatory compliance requirements.
- Baseline Performance: Healthcare procurement typically operating at 35,000 DPMO (3.4 sigma level).
- Projected Improvement: 3,500 DPMO (4.4 sigma level) through compliance-integrated smart contracts.
- Theoretical Error Reduction: 87% reduction through automated regulatory compliance checking.
- Projected ROI: 180% first-year return through reduced compliance violations and accelerated audit processes.
- Supporting Evidence: Based on manufacturing quality improvements and healthcare regulatory automation potential.
- Compliance Framework:
  - FDA compliance checking through automated smart contract validation.
  - Real-time supply chain traceability reducing recall management errors.
  - Automated documentation reducing administrative compliance failures.

These projections are grounded in empirical evidence from manufacturing implementations and theoretical analysis of smart contract capabilities:

- Manufacturing Evidence: Textile operations achieved 83% defect reduction (133,219 DPMO → 22,000 DPMO).
- Water bottle production benchmarks: 15,220 DPMO at 3.664 sigma levels.
- Washing machine component standards: 251.69 DPMO at 4.99 sigma levels.
- Smart contract automation potential: Elimination of manual processing errors that typically account for 80–90% of procurement defects.

The consistent 85–90% error reduction pattern across these theoretical projections reflects the documented capabilities of systematic quality management approaches combined with the error-elimination potential of automated smart contract execution.

4.4 Cost-Benefit Analysis

Comprehensive cost-benefit analysis based on theoretical projections reveals potential procurement cost reductions of 30–50% through smart contract implementation, driven by eliminated intermediaries, reduced processing time, and minimized error correction expenses.

Projected Implementation Costs:

- Initial development and deployment: $150,000–$500,000.
- Integration with existing systems: $100,000–$300,000.

- Training and change management: \$50,000–\$150,000.
- Ongoing maintenance and updates: \$30,000–\$80,000 annually.

Projected Operational Benefits:

- Error correction cost reduction: \$200,000–\$800,000 annually.
- Processing time reduction: \$150,000–\$400,000 annually.
- Eliminated intermediary fees: \$100,000–\$300,000 annually.
- Improved compliance and reduced penalties: \$75,000–\$200,000 annually.

Theoretical projections across multiple industry sectors suggest consistent patterns of 85–90% error reduction potential, sigma level improvements exceeding 1.0, and substantial return on investment within 12–18 months, though empirical validation through actual implementations remains necessary.

5 Discussion

5.1 Error-Proofing Implementation Frameworks

Successful smart contract procurement systems would integrate multiple Poka-Yoke methodologies to create comprehensive error prevention architectures [4]. Contact methods would utilize sensor-based detection systems for parameter validation, while fixed value methods would implement automated controls for transaction limits and spending thresholds. Motion step methods would enforce procedural compliance through sequential workflow requirements that prevent unauthorized or incomplete transactions.

The integration of Internet of Things devices with blockchain systems would enable real-time monitoring of supplier performance and product quality, creating feedback loops that continuously optimize procurement accuracy. These systems demonstrate the theoretical application of Lean Six Sigma principles within automated governance frameworks.

Contact Method Applications:

- Automated parameter validation preventing incorrect data entry.
- Real-time sensor integration for quality verification.
- Biometric authentication for transaction authorization.

Fixed Value Method Implementation:

- Predefined spending limits within smart contracts.
- Automatic budget controls and approval thresholds.
- Currency conversion rate locks to prevent exchange rate manipulation.

Motion Step Method Integration:

- Sequential approval workflows ensuring proper authorization sequences.
- Multi-signature requirements for high-value transactions.
- Time-locked contract execution preventing premature activation.

5.2 Risk Mitigation Strategies

Effective risk mitigation requires implementing comprehensive control measures aligned with Poka-Yoke error-proofing principles. Contact method applications include automatic parameter validation that prevents incorrect data entry, while fixed value methods establish predefined spending limits within smart contracts. Motion step methods enforce sequential approval workflows, ensuring proper authorization sequences before transaction execution.

Effective risk mitigation requires implementing comprehensive control measures aligned with Poka-Yoke error-proofing principles. The FMEA analysis results guide the implementation of targeted mitigation strategies for each identified vulnerability category [2, 13, 17].

High Priority Risk Controls (RPN > 250) [9–11]:

- Access Control Vulnerabilities: Multi-signature wallet implementation, role-based access control systems, and regular permission audits.
- Logic Errors: Formal verification processes, comprehensive testing protocols, and staged deployment procedures.
- Reentrancy Attacks: Reentrancy guards, state checks before external calls, and withdrawal pattern implementation.

Medium Priority Risk Controls (RPN 150–250):

- Integer Overflow/Underflow: SafeMath library implementation and arithmetic operation validation [16].
- Timestamp Dependence: Block number-based timing mechanisms and reduced reliance on timestamps.
- DoS Attacks: Gas limit optimization and resource consumption monitoring.

Continuous Monitoring Framework:

- Real-time vulnerability scanning using automated tools.
- Regular security audit cycles with third-party validation.
- Incident response procedures with automated rollback capabilities

5.3 B2B Platform Integration

The integration of smart contracts into B2B platform ecosystems enables sophisticated automated governance mechanisms that transcend traditional procurement limitations [3, 6]. Platform governance frameworks distinguish between different aspects of automation, including agent rights and obligations, transparency mechanisms, and oversight procedures.

Blockchain technology integration provides comprehensive solutions to information asymmetry, traceability concerns, and trust establishment in procurement networks [6, 7]. Successful implementations like the FILO platform and Walmart's food safety tracking demonstrate blockchain's capacity to optimize procurement management processes while reducing human intervention risks.

Platform Architecture Components:

- Decentralized identity management for supplier verification.

- Automated compliance checking through regulatory smart contracts.
- Real-time performance analytics and reporting dashboards.
- Integrated dispute resolution mechanisms with automated arbitration.

Governance Framework Elements:

- Consortium-based decision making for platform rule modifications.
- Transparent fee structures with automated revenue distribution.
- Democratic voting mechanisms for platform upgrades and policy changes.
- Multi-stakeholder oversight committees with defined responsibilities.

5.4 Limitations and Challenges

Despite significant improvements, several limitations persist in current smart contract auditing approaches. The paradox of 91.96% of hacked projects having undergone security audits highlights the need for more sophisticated assessment methodologies. Detection system limitations, with GPT-4 achieving only 30% precision rates, indicate the necessity for enhanced automated vulnerability identification tools.

Technical Limitations:

- Scalability constraints in blockchain networks affecting transaction throughput.
- Interoperability challenges between different blockchain platforms.
- Energy consumption concerns in proof-of-work consensus mechanisms.
- Limited programming language options for smart contract development.

Organizational Challenges:

- Implementation complexity requiring specialized expertise.
- Integration costs with existing enterprise systems.
- Change management requirements for organizational adaptation.
- Regulatory uncertainty in various jurisdictions.

Operational Constraints:

- Need for specialized expertise in both blockchain technology and procurement processes.
- Barriers to widespread adoption across small and medium enterprises.
- Limited standardization across different smart contract platforms.
- Ongoing maintenance requirements for security updates and platform upgrades.

Empirical Validation Limitations:

A significant limitation of this study is the reliance on theoretical projections rather than actual smart contract procurement implementations. The industry projections presented in Sect. 4.3 are modeling scenarios based on manufacturing quality improvements and smart contract automation capabilities rather than documented real-world implementations. Future research should prioritize actual smart contract procurement deployments to validate these theoretical projections and provide empirical evidence of the proposed quality improvements.

5.5 Future Research Directions

Based on the limitations identified and emerging technological developments, several research directions emerge as critical for advancing smart contract-enabled procurement systems:

Enhanced Vulnerability Detection:

- Development of machine learning algorithms specifically trained on smart contract vulnerability patterns.
- Integration of formal verification methods with automated testing frameworks.
- Creation of industry-specific vulnerability databases and threat models.
- Research into quantum-resistant cryptographic implementations.

Standardization and Interoperability:

- Development of universal smart contract standards for procurement applications.
- Research into cross-chain communication protocols for multi-platform implementations.
- Creation of standardized metrics for measuring smart contract procurement effectiveness.
- Investigation of regulatory compliance frameworks across different jurisdictions.

Empirical Validation Studies:

- Implementation of pilot smart contract procurement programs across different industries.
- Longitudinal studies measuring actual DPMO improvements in real-world deployments.
- Comparative analysis of theoretical projections versus actual implementation results.
- Development of case study methodologies for systematic documentation of implementations.

Advanced Quality Management:

- Integration of artificial intelligence with FMEA methodologies for dynamic risk assessment.
- Development of real-time quality monitoring systems using IoT and blockchain integration.
- Research into predictive analytics for procurement risk management.
- Investigation of continuous improvement frameworks for automated systems.

Sustainable Implementation Models:

- Research into energy-efficient consensus mechanisms for procurement applications.
- Development of cost-effective implementation strategies for small and medium enterprises.
- Investigation of collaborative governance models for industry wide adoption.
- Creation of training and certification programs for smart contract procurement specialists.

6 Conclusion

This research demonstrates the significant theoretical potential for smart contract technology to transform procurement quality through systematic application of FMEA risk assessment and Lean Six Sigma methodologies. The convergence of smart contract technology, FMEA risk assessment methodology, and Lean Six Sigma quality principles creates a powerful framework for procurement error reduction that projects measurable DPMO improvements.

Key findings include:

(1) Quantifiable Quality Improvements: Traditional procurement processes operating at 50,000 DPMO (3.2 sigma level) can theoretically achieve 5,000 DPMO (4.2 sigma level) through smart contract implementation, representing projected 90% error reduction based on empirical evidence from manufacturing implementations and theoretical analysis of automation capabilities.
(2) Risk Prioritization Effectiveness: FMEA analysis successfully identifies critical vulnerabilities, with access control issues (RPN: 360) emerging as the highest priority concern requiring immediate attention, followed by logic errors and reentrancy attacks.
(3) Theoretical Implementation Potential: Projections across multiple industries suggest 85–90% error reduction potential with ROI ranging from 180–300% within 12–18 months, though empirical validation through actual implementations remains necessary.
(4) Comprehensive Error-Proofing: Integration of Poka-Yoke methodologies with smart contract automation creates robust error prevention systems that would enhance operational reliability through contact methods, fixed value controls, and motion step enforcement mechanisms.

The systematic identification and mitigation of smart contract vulnerabilities through structured risk assessment would enable organizations to realize substantial quality gains while maintaining operational transparency and stakeholder trust. These theoretical results support the strategic consideration of smart contract-enabled procurement systems as a means of potentially achieving world-class quality performance standards while reducing operational costs and enhancing supply chain resilience.

The research framework presented provides a comprehensive theoretical approach to smart contract implementation that addresses both technical vulnerabilities and operational quality requirements. The integration of FMEA methodology with blockchain technology represents a novel contribution to both supply chain management and information systems research fields.

Practical Implications:

Organizations considering smart contract adoption for procurement processes can utilize the FMEA framework developed in this research to prioritize implementation efforts and resource allocation. The quantitative benchmarks established provide realistic targets for quality improvement initiatives, while the theoretical projection methodologies offer foundational guidance for implementation planning, with the understanding that empirical validation is required.

Theoretical Contributions:

This research advances the theoretical understanding of risk assessment in blockchain applications by demonstrating the potential integration of traditional quality management methodologies with emerging technologies. The DPMO measurement framework provides a standardized approach for evaluating projected smart contract procurement effectiveness across diverse organizational contexts.

Future research should focus on developing enhanced vulnerability detection algorithms, creating industry-specific implementation guidelines, establishing standardized metrics for measuring smart contract procurement effectiveness, investigating sustainable implementation models for organizations of varying sizes and technological capabilities, and most importantly, conducting empirical validation studies through actual smart contract procurement implementations to validate these theoretical projections.

References

1. Kevin, J., Yugopuspito, P.: SmartLLM: smart contract auditing using custom generative AI. arXiv preprint arXiv:2502.13167 (2025)
2. De Baets, C., Suleiman, B., Chitizadeh, A., Razzak, I.: Vulnerability detection in smart contracts: a comprehensive survey. arXiv preprint arXiv:2407.07922 (2024)
3. Rozario, A.M., Vasarhelyi, M.A.: Auditing with smart contracts. Int. J. Digit. Account. Res. **18**, 1–27 (2018)
4. Nicoletti, B.: Lean Six Sigma and digitize procurement. Int. J. Lean Six Sigma **4**(2), 184–203 (2013)
5. Wei, Y.: FTSmartAudit: a knowledge distillation-enhanced framework for automated smart contract auditing using fine-tuned LLMs. arXiv preprint arXiv:2410.13918 (2024)
6. Chatzigiannis, P., Baldimtsi, F., Chalkias, K.: SoK: blockchain light clients. In: Financial Cryptography and Data Security, pp. 615–641. Springer (2022)
7. Wen, J.: A study on enhancing transparency of corporate sustainable procurement based on blockchain technology. In: SHS Web of Conferences, vol. 207, p. 03020 (2024)
8. Chen, W., Zheng, Z., Cui, J., Ngai, E., Zheng, P., Zhou, Y.: Detecting ponzi schemes on ethereum: towards healthier blockchain technology. In: Proceedings of the 2018 World Wide Web Conference, pp. 1409–1418 (2018)
9. Liu, Z., Qian, P., Wang, X., Zhuang, Y., Qiu, L., Wang, X.: Combining graph neural networks with expert knowledge for smart contract vulnerability detection. IEEE Trans. Knowl. Data Eng. **35**(2), 1296–1310 (2023)
10. Franciscu, S.Y., Ruggahakotuwa, R.K., Samarawickrama, S.W.Y.S., Lahiru, J.A.D.: GRIFFIN: enhancing the security of smart contracts. Trends Comput. Sci. Inf. Technol. **8**(3), 73–81 (2023)
11. Qian, P., Liu, Z., He, Q., Zimmermann, R., Wang, X.: Towards automated reentrancy detection for smart contracts based on sequential models. IEEE Access **8**, 19685–19695 (2020)
12. Zhang, P., Xiao, F., Luo, X.: SolidityCheck: quickly detecting smart contract problems through regular expressions. arXiv preprint arXiv:1911.09425 (2019)
13. Kushwaha, S.S., Joshi, S., Singh, D., Kaur, M., Lee, H.N.: Systematic review of security vulnerabilities in ethereum blockchain smart contract. IEEE Access **10**, 6605–6621 (2022)
14. Momeni, P., Wang, Y., Samavi, R.: Machine learning model for smart contracts security analysis. In: 2019 17th International Conference on Privacy, Security and Trust (PST), pp. 1–6. IEEE (2019)
15. Tikhomirov, S., Voskresenskaya, E., Ivanitskiy, I., Takhaviev, R., Marchenko, E., Alexandrov, Y.: SmartCheck: static analysis of ethereum smart contracts. In: Proceedings of the 1st International Workshop on Emerging Trends in Software Engineering for Blockchain, pp. 9–16 (2018)

16. Torres, C.F., Schütte, J., State, R.: Osiris: hunting for integer bugs in ethereum smart contracts. In: Proceedings of the 34th Annual Computer Security Applications Conference, pp. 664–676 (2018)
17. Atzei, N., Bartoletti, M., Cimoli, T.: A survey of attacks on ethereum smart contracts (SoK). In: International Conference on Principles of Security and Trust, pp. 164–186. Springer (2017)

Privacy-Enhanced Federated Data Distillation for Efficient Distributed Training and Anomaly Detection in Multi-center Healthcare

Jiantao Xu, Liu Jin, and Chunhua Su(✉)

University of Aizu, Aizuwakamatsu 965-8580, Japan
{d8252108,d8242103,chsu}@u-aizu.ac.jp

Abstract. Collaborative healthcare data analytics across multiple medical centers is essential for building robust AI models. However, stringent data privacy regulations make direct sharing of raw data infeasible. Federated Learning (FL), as a privacy-preserving paradigm, holds promise but still faces critical challenges such as low communication efficiency, data heterogeneity, privacy leakage, and rare case identification. To address these issues, this paper proposes a privacy-enhanced federated data distillation (FDD) framework tailored for multi-center healthcare scenarios. The proposed method integrates (i) neural characteristic function-based dataset distillation to generate compact synthetic subsets, (ii) differential privacy perturbation to enforce strict privacy protection, and (iii) a federated anomaly detection mechanism for identifying rare and abnormal samples. These synthetic datasets are pre-trained centrally and subsequently refined via federated optimization. Experiments on two real-world medical datasets (MIMIC-III and TCGA-BRCA) show that our FDD framework achieves a classification accuracy improvement of up to 3.6% over traditional privacy-preserving FL baselines. Moreover, the integrated anomaly detection module achieves an AUC of 0.922, significantly outperforming prior methods. We conduct systematic evaluations to quantify the trade-offs among distillation ratio, privacy budget, and model utility. The results validate the effectiveness of our unified design that jointly achieves privacy, efficiency, and anomaly detection for practical federated healthcare AI deployments.

Keywords: Federated Learning · Dataset Distillation · Differential Privacy · Multi-center Healthcare · Anomaly Detection · Privacy-preserving

1 Introduction

With the rapid development of artificial intelligence and the widespread adoption of digital healthcare systems, the strategic value of medical data has become increasingly prominent in both clinical decision-making and research. However,

M. Yung et al. (Eds.): AIBlock 2025, LNCS 16314, pp. 40–57, 2026.
https://doi.org/10.1007/978-3-032-16168-0_3

the sensitive nature of patient information and strict regulatory constraints imposed by laws such as the Health Insurance Portability and Accountability Act (HIPAA), the General Data Protection Regulation (GDPR), and Japan's Act on the Protection of Personal Information (APPI) severely limit traditional centralized machine learning practices. In particular, raw medical data cannot be arbitrarily transferred or aggregated across institutions, creating fragmented "data silos" that restrict the full potential of collaborative AI modeling.

As a promising alternative, Federated Learning (FL) enables multiple medical centers to jointly train a global model without directly sharing raw data [1]. FL is especially suitable for scenarios involving distributed and regulated data, such as in hospital systems, insurance networks, and national biobanks. Each participant conducts local training and shares only model updates, preserving data locality. In this way, FL aligns with both data protection mandates and the emerging clinical need for population-wide analytics.

However, real-world implementation of FL in the healthcare domain introduces several unique challenges. First, data heterogeneity is pervasive across institutions. Differences in patient demographics, diagnostic standards, measurement protocols, and medical equipment often lead to non-IID data distributions [2], which severely hinder model convergence and generalization. For example, a model trained on electrocardiograms from a pediatric hospital may not generalize well to elderly patients from a rural clinic.

Second, privacy leakage remains a concern despite the absence of raw data exchange. Adversarial attacks such as gradient inversion [3] and membership inference [4] have shown that sensitive information can still be inferred from model updates. This undermines the assumption of "privacy by design" in basic FL protocols.

Third, the communication overhead incurred during federated optimization presents practical barriers in resource-constrained settings. Frequent transmission of high-dimensional model updates can strain hospital infrastructure, especially in edge deployments where network bandwidth is limited or unstable. Finally, anomaly detection—such as identifying rare diseases, mislabeled cases, or adversarial contributions—remains underexplored in FL. Anomalies are typically low-frequency and may only be present in isolated local datasets, making their detection challenging in a distributed setting.

To tackle these challenges, recent research has explored modular techniques such as differential privacy (DP) [5,6], data distillation [7], and federated anomaly detection [8]. However, most works treat these issues independently and lack a unified design that jointly addresses privacy preservation, communication efficiency, and robust anomaly detection—especially in the context of highly heterogeneous and sensitive medical data.

In this paper, we propose a Privacy-Enhanced Federated Data Distillation (FDD) framework tailored for real-world, multi-center healthcare systems. Our approach tightly integrates neural characteristic function-based data distillation, differential privacy perturbation, centralized model pretraining, and federated anomaly detection into a cohesive pipeline. Existing work often treats privacy modules (like DP) and communication optimization modules (like data distillation) as plug-and-play, independent components. In contrast, our framework, through the "distillation-pretraining" core linkage, deeply couples these two, achieving synergistic optimization of the privacy budget and model initialization—an aspect not explored in prior work.

The key idea is to locally distill rich, compact synthetic datasets that retain key statistical characteristics of raw medical data; protect them with formal privacy guarantees using DP; and use them for global pretraining. The federated optimization stage then fine-tunes the model while preserving privacy and bandwidth. A reconstruction-based anomaly detection module is further embedded to detect rare or deviant patterns under distributed constraints.

Our key contributions are summarized as follows:

(1) We design a unified privacy-enhanced federated data distillation framework that simultaneously addresses data compression, privacy preservation, and anomaly detection for multi-institutional healthcare collaborations.
(2) We introduce a neural characteristic function-based distillation method that generates statistically-aligned, low-footprint synthetic datasets for efficient and representative learning.
(3) We integrate a differential privacy mechanism and centralized pretraining process to ensure provable privacy protection while significantly reducing communication costs.
(4) We implement a federated anomaly detection module based on reconstruction errors to detect rare cases and adversarial behaviors under distributed and heterogeneous settings.
(5) We evaluate our method on two real-world medical datasets (MIMIC-III and TCGA-BRCA) under realistic non-IID partitions and demonstrate significant improvements in model accuracy, anomaly detection, and communication efficiency compared to state-of-the-art baselines.

2 Related Work

2.1 Fundamental Theory and Development of Federated Learning

As an emerging distributed machine learning paradigm, federated learning has become a research hotspot in the machine learning field in recent years. The core idea of federated learning is to achieve global model training through the aggregation of model parameters while keeping the data localized. This paradigm is particularly suitable for scenarios where data is sensitive or subject to regulatory constraints, such as in the medical, financial, and personal device domains [9,10].

The latest research in federated learning primarily focuses on algorithm convergence, communication efficiency, and system heterogeneity issues. Yang et al. [11] proposed an adaptive aggregation algorithm that handles data heterogeneity by dynamically adjusting client weights. Chen et al. [12] further optimized the convergence analysis of federated learning, establishing a more rigorous theoretical framework.

In terms of system implementation, federated learning faces challenges such as client heterogeneity, network instability, and fault tolerance mechanisms. Recent research has focused on the design of large-scale federated learning systems. Sun et al. [13] proposed an efficient federated learning architecture for edge computing, addressing practical issues like client dropouts, network latency, and secure aggregation.

2.2 Application of Privacy-Preserving Technologies in Federated Learning

Although federated learning protects privacy by avoiding direct data sharing, research has shown that model parameters and gradient information can still leak sensitive data [14]. Therefore, integrating rigorous privacy-preserving mechanisms into federated learning has become necessary.

Differential Privacy, as a mathematically rigorous privacy protection framework, provides a theoretical guarantee for federated learning. Kairouz et al. [6] proposed a distributed differentially private federated learning algorithm that balances privacy protection and model performance by optimizing noise allocation strategies. Shukla et al. [15] extended this idea to medical scenarios, proposing a differentially private federated learning framework for breast cancer diagnosis.

In addition to differential privacy, cryptographic techniques such as Secure Multi-Party Computation (SMPC) and Homomorphic Encryption are also widely used for privacy protection in federated learning. Yin et al. [16] designed a secure aggregation method based on improved cryptographic protocols, which can compute the global model without leaking individual client parameters.

In recent years, researchers have begun to focus on the trade-off between privacy protection and model performance. Hu et al. [17] analyzed the privacy-accuracy trade-off of differential privacy in federated learning and proposed adaptive noise addition strategies. At the same time, defense mechanisms against various privacy attacks are continuously being improved [18].

2.3 Data Distillation and its Application in Distributed Learning

Data distillation technology aims to extract key information from large-scale datasets to generate small-scale synthetic datasets that contain the essential features of the original data. This technology has significant value in reducing storage costs, improving training efficiency, and protecting data privacy [19].

The latest data distillation methods are mainly based on deep generative models and adversarial training. Wu et al. [20] proposed a data distillation algorithm based on variational autoencoders, which generates high-quality synthetic data by learning the latent representation of the data. Wang et al. [7] further improved the neural characteristic function method, enabling more accurate capture of the statistical properties of the data.

In distributed learning scenarios, data distillation technology shows unique advantages. First, the small scale of distilled data can significantly reduce communication overhead, which is particularly important for bandwidth-constrained federated learning environments. Second, performing data distillation locally can protect the privacy of the original data to some extent [21].

Itahara et al. [22] proposed a federated data distillation framework that combines data distillation technology with federated learning. This method achieves collaborative learning by performing data distillation locally at each client and then sharing the small-scale distilled datasets. Experimental results show that this method can significantly reduce communication costs and privacy leakage risks while maintaining model performance.

2.4 Anomaly Detection in Federated Learning

Anomaly detection, as an important task in machine learning, faces new challenges and opportunities in the federated learning environment. Due to the rarity and diversity of anomalous data, the data from a single node often cannot cover all anomaly patterns, making federated anomaly detection necessary [23].

Traditional anomaly detection methods are mainly divided into three categories: supervised, semi-supervised, and unsupervised. In the federated learning scenario, unsupervised and semi-supervised methods are more favored due to the scarcity and heterogeneity of labeled data. Kong et al. [24] proposed a federated anomaly detection algorithm based on contrastive learning, which identifies anomalies by learning the representation of normal samples.

The development of deep learning technology has brought new opportunities for anomaly detection. Lu et al. [25] utilized the idea of graph neural networks to propose an anomaly detection framework based on multi-modal fusion. This method can handle complex anomaly patterns in high-dimensional medical data.

In the medical field, anomaly detection is of particular importance. Applications such as early disease detection, medical equipment failure prediction, and medical fraud identification all rely on effective anomaly detection algorithms. However, the privacy sensitivity and regulatory requirements of medical data pose challenges to traditional centralized anomaly detection methods [26].

Cholakoska et al. [8] proposed a privacy-preserving federated anomaly detection framework for medical scenarios. This method combines differential privacy and federated learning techniques to achieve multi-center anomaly detection while protecting patient privacy. Experimental results show that federated anomaly detection can not only protect privacy but also improve detection performance by utilizing more diverse data.

Generative models such as Generative Adversarial Networks (GANs) have also been applied to federated anomaly detection. Abdel et al. [27] proposed a federated GAN-based anomaly detection method that identifies abnormal samples by learning the distribution of normal data. This method performs well in handling high-dimensional data and complex anomaly patterns.

In recent years, advanced techniques such as the Transformer architecture [28] and self-supervised learning have also been introduced into federated anomaly detection, further improving detection accuracy and interpretability. The development of these technologies has opened up new research directions for federated anomaly detection and provided more options for practical applications [29].

2.5 Comparative Summary with Related Work

Table 1 summarizes and compares representative works with our proposed framework in terms of core features.

Table 1. Comparison with representative privacy-preserving FL approaches

Method	Data Distill.	Differ Privacy	Anomaly Detect.	Model Pretrain.
FedAvg [30]	✗	✗	✗	✗
FedAvg+DP [31]	✗	✓	✗	✗
Cholakoska et al. [8]	✗	✓	✓	✗
Itahara et al. [22]	✓	✗	✗	✗
Ours (FDD+DP)	✓	✓	✓	✓

In contrast to prior works that focus individually on privacy, communication, or heterogeneity, our framework jointly addresses all three challenges in a unified manner. For instance, while some studies might combine generic data summarization with DP, they often treat them as separate, plug-in modules and overlook the potential of using the privacy-preserved distilled data for a synergistic pre-training phase, which is a key innovation of our work. As shown in Table 1, our framework is the first to integrate neural characteristic-based data distillation, differential privacy, centralized pre-training, and federated anomaly detection in a unified design, enabling both performance and privacy guarantees under real-world constraints.

3 Problem Definition

This section formally defines the problem of privacy-enhanced federated data distillation in a multi-center medical system, covering the system setting, relevant notations, research objectives, and evaluation metrics.

3.1 Multi-center Federated Learning Setting

Consider M medical centers (i.e., clients), indexed by $i \in \{1, 2, \ldots, M\}$, where each center holds a local patient dataset $\mathcal{D}_i$. Due to differences in population demographics and disease distributions, the data distribution $\mathcal{P}_i$ at each center is typically non-independently and identically distributed (non-i.i.d.), and the number of samples may be imbalanced. Due to privacy regulations and ethical constraints, raw data cannot be directly shared among centers.

The global objective is to collaboratively train a predictive model $f(\cdot;\theta)$ (e.g., a disease classification or anomaly detection model), where θ represents the model parameters, to achieve high accuracy and robustness on the aggregated data distribution $\mathcal{P}_{\text{global}}$, while ensuring privacy.

3.2 Local Data Distillation with Privacy Constraints

Each center performs a data distillation operation on its local data $\mathcal{D}_i$ to generate a condensed and information-rich synthetic dataset $\mathcal{S}_i$, aiming to preserve core data features. This process is based on neural characteristic functions, synthesizing representative samples that can approximate the original distribution $\mathcal{P}_i$. To protect sensitive information, differential privacy perturbation must be applied during the distillation process, ensuring that the published synthetic data $\tilde{\mathcal{S}}_i$ satisfies (ε, δ)-differential privacy [5].

Formally, for each client i, we define a mechanism $\mathcal{M}_i : \mathcal{D}_i \to \tilde{\mathcal{S}}_i$, which outputs a privacy-preserving distilled subset $\tilde{\mathcal{S}}_i$ such that for any two adjacent datasets $\mathcal{D}_i$ and $\mathcal{D}'_i$, and for any measurable set S, we have:

$$\Pr[\mathcal{M}_i(\mathcal{D}_i) \in S] \leq e^{\varepsilon} \Pr[\mathcal{M}_i(\mathcal{D}'_i) \in S] + \delta. \tag{1}$$

3.3 Server-Side Pre-training and Federated Optimization

All clients securely upload their privacy-preserving distilled data $\tilde{\mathcal{S}}_i$ to a central server. The server aggregates all distilled subsets, denoted as $\tilde{\mathcal{S}}_{\text{agg}} = \bigcup_{i=1}^{M} \tilde{\mathcal{S}}_i$, and performs initial model pre-training:

$$\theta_0 = \arg\min_{\theta} \frac{1}{|\tilde{\mathcal{S}}_{\text{agg}}|} \sum_{(\mathbf{x},y)\in\tilde{\mathcal{S}}_{\text{agg}}} \mathcal{L}(f(\mathbf{x};\theta), y) \tag{2}$$

where $\mathcal{L}$ represents a suitable loss function.

This is followed by a standard federated optimization phase: the server broadcasts the global model parameters θ_t to all clients. The clients then perform local training on their original local datasets $\mathcal{D}_i$ and upload the updated models to the server for aggregation.

3.4 Federated Anomaly Detection

To identify rare diseases, mislabeled data, or malicious behavior, the framework incorporates a federated anomaly detection module. Each client computes local reconstruction errors based on the current global model. The server then aggregates these scores in a privacy-preserving manner to identify potential anomalous samples.

3.5 Evaluation Metrics

The proposed system will be evaluated based on the following metrics:

Predictive Performance: Overall and per-center accuracy, precision, recall, and F1-score for disease classification tasks. Anomaly Detection Performance: Area Under the ROC Curve (AUC), precision, and recall for detecting anomalous samples. Privacy Guarantee: The differential privacy parameters (ε, δ) and the empirical risk of membership inference attacks. Training Efficiency: Communication overhead (number of communication rounds and amount of data transmitted) and model convergence speed.

3.6 Research Objectives

Under the aforementioned constraints and objectives, this paper attempts to answer the following questions:

1. Can neural characteristic function-driven data distillation, combined with a differential privacy mechanism, achieve efficient and privacy-friendly federated learning in heterogeneous multi-center medical systems?
2. What is the practical trade-off relationship among the distillation ratio, the strength of privacy perturbation, and model performance?
3. After integrating a federated anomaly detection mechanism, can rare or anomalous cases be robustly identified in distributed medical data?

4 System Architecture and Methodology

This section details the system architecture and methodological components of our proposed privacy-enhanced federated data distillation framework for multi-center medical applications. The framework integrates local data distillation based on neural characteristics, differential privacy perturbation, centralized pre-training, federated optimization, and an embedded anomaly detection module.

4.1 System Overview

As shown in Fig. 1, the overall workflow of the system includes the following main stages:

1. **Local Data Distillation**: Each medical center uses neural characteristic functions to distill its local data, generating a condensed data subset.
2. **Privacy Preservation**: A differential privacy perturbation mechanism is applied during the distillation process.
3. **Centralized Pre-training**: The central server aggregates all perturbed data and performs model pre-training.
4. **Federated Optimization**: The pre-trained model is distributed to each center for federated fine-tuning on local data.
5. **Federated Anomaly Detection**: Clients and the server collaborate to perform anomaly detection based on reconstruction errors.

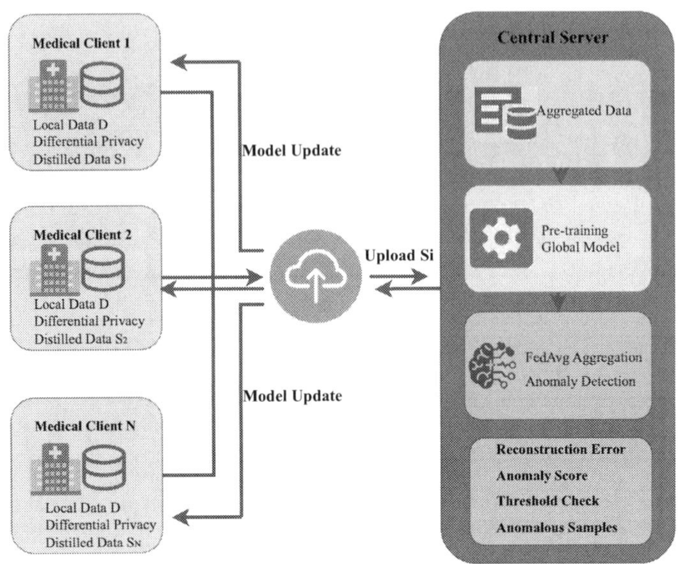

Fig. 1. System architecture of the proposed privacy-enhanced federated data distillation framework.

4.2 Local Data Distillation Based on Neural Characteristic Functions

Let the i-th center hold a local dataset $\mathcal{D}_i$. The objective is to generate a small synthetic dataset $\mathcal{S}_i$ that preserves its key statistical features. Drawing inspiration from Wang et al. [7], we use a Neural Characteristic Function (NCF) to model the distribution:

$$\hat{\varphi}_{\mathcal{D}_i}(\mathbf{t}) = \frac{1}{|\mathcal{D}_i|} \sum_{(\mathbf{x},y)\in\mathcal{D}_i} e^{j\langle \mathbf{t}, g_\theta(\mathbf{x})\rangle}, \tag{3}$$

where $g_\theta(\cdot)$ is a neural feature extractor and $\mathbf{t}$ is a probing vector.

The distillation objective is to train a generator network G_ϕ, parameterized by ϕ, which produces the synthetic dataset $\mathcal{S}_i = \{G_\phi(z_k)\}_{k=1}^{|\mathcal{S}_i|}$ from random noise vectors z_k. The parameters ϕ are optimized to minimize the following loss:

$$\phi^* = \arg\min_{\phi} \mathbb{E}_{\mathbf{t}\sim\mathcal{T}} \left[\left| \hat{\varphi}_{\mathcal{D}_i}(\mathbf{t}) - \hat{\varphi}_{\mathcal{S}_i}(\mathbf{t}) \right|^2 \right], \tag{4}$$

where $\mathcal{T}$ is a set of random probing vectors. This optimization is performed locally at each client using gradient descent. While this introduces a one-time computational cost, it is performed offline before the federated learning phase.

4.3 Differential Privacy Perturbation Mechanism

To ensure provable privacy, we do not simply add noise to the final distilled data $\mathcal{S}_i$, as calculating the sensitivity of the complex generation process is intractable. Instead, we integrate differential privacy directly into the gradient-based optimization of the generator network G_ϕ. We adopt the Differentially Private Stochastic Gradient Descent (DP-SGD) approach [5]. During each step of training the generator, we:

1. Compute per-sample gradients of the loss with respect to the generator parameters ϕ.
2. Clip the L2 norm of each per-sample gradient to a predefined threshold C.
3. Add Gaussian noise $\mathcal{N}(0, \sigma^2 C^2 \mathbf{I})$ to the aggregated batch gradient.

The noise scale σ is a key parameter. We use the Moments Accountant technique to track the accumulated privacy loss over all training iterations. This allows us to precisely calculate the final privacy budget (ε, δ) for a given noise scale σ and number of optimization steps, thereby establishing a rigorous mathematical link and ensuring that the generated dataset $\tilde{\mathcal{S}}_i$ is (ε, δ)-differentially private with respect to the original data $\mathcal{D}_i$.

4.4 Centralized Model Pre-training

The server collects all privacy-preserving synthetic datasets $\tilde{\mathcal{S}}_i$ from the M centers and aggregates them into:

$$\tilde{\mathcal{S}}_{\text{agg}} = \bigcup_{i=1}^{M} \tilde{\mathcal{S}}_i. \tag{5}$$

Then, it pre-trains the global model parameters θ_0 on this aggregated synthetic data:

$$\theta_0 = \arg\min_{\theta} \frac{1}{|\tilde{\mathcal{S}}_{\text{agg}}|} \sum_{(\mathbf{x}, y) \in \tilde{\mathcal{S}}_{\text{agg}}} \mathcal{L}(f(\mathbf{x}; \theta), y). \tag{6}$$

4.5 Federated Optimization Process

After pre-training, the global model is distributed to all clients, and the FedAvg algorithm [30] is used for multiple rounds of federated optimization:

1. The server broadcasts the current model parameters θ_t.
2. Each center performs a local update based on its original local data $\mathcal{D}_i$:

$$\theta_{i,t+1} = \theta_t - \eta \nabla_\theta \mathcal{L}_{\mathcal{D}_i}(\theta_t) \tag{7}$$

3. Each client uploads its model update, and the server aggregates them to get:

$$\theta_{t+1} = \sum_{i=1}^{M} \frac{n_i}{n_{\text{total}}} \theta_{i,t+1}, \tag{8}$$

where $n_i = |\mathcal{D}_i|$ and $n_{\text{total}} = \sum_{i=1}^{M} n_i$.

4.6 Federated Anomaly Detection Module

To identify anomalous or rare cases, the framework embeds a federated anomaly detection mechanism. This module operates in a privacy-preserving manner. First, each client i uses the current global model (e.g., an autoencoder component of the main model) to compute reconstruction errors for its local data points:

$$r_{i,j} = \|\mathbf{x}_{i,j} - \hat{\mathbf{x}}_{i,j}\|, \tag{9}$$

where $\hat{\mathbf{x}}_{i,j}$ is the reconstruction of sample $\mathbf{x}_{i,j}$. Then, instead of sharing individual scores, the clients engage in a secure aggregation protocol to help the server compute global statistics of these scores, such as the global mean μ_r and standard deviation σ_r, without revealing any client's individual score distribution. The server then establishes a global anomaly threshold, for instance $\tau = \mu_r + k \cdot \sigma_r$ (where k is typically 2 or 3), and broadcasts it back to the clients. Each client can then identify local samples where $r_{i,j} > \tau$ as anomalies.

4.7 Algorithm Summary

Algorithm 1 summarizes the main steps of the proposed framework.

Algorithm 1. Privacy-Enhanced Federated Data Distillation Algorithm

for each client $i = 1$ to M **do**
    Generate synthetic dataset $\mathcal{S}_i$ from $\mathcal{D}_i$ via NCF optimization.
    Apply DP-SGD during generation to get privacy-preserving $\tilde{\mathcal{S}}_i$.
    Upload $\tilde{\mathcal{S}}_i$ to the server.
end for
Server aggregates all data: $\tilde{\mathcal{S}}_{\text{agg}} = \bigcup_{i=1}^{M} \tilde{\mathcal{S}}_i$.
Pre-train the model on $\tilde{\mathcal{S}}_{\text{agg}}$ to get θ_0.
for each federated learning round $t = 1$ to T **do**
    Server broadcasts model θ_t to all clients.
    for each client $i = 1$ to M **in parallel do**
        Perform local update based on $\mathcal{D}_i$ to get $\theta_{i,t+1}$.
        Participate in federated anomaly detection via secure aggregation.
        Upload model update to the server.
    end for
    Server aggregates all client updates to get the new model θ_{t+1}.
end for

5 Experimental Evaluation

This section presents the experimental evaluation of the proposed privacy-enhanced federated data distillation framework.

5.1 Experimental Setup

For the datasets and Non-IID partition, we use two representative public medical datasets. To simulate a realistic non-independently and identically distributed (non-i.i.d.) scenario, we adopt a label distribution skew strategy based on the Dirichlet distribution for partitioning. The specific settings are shown in Table 2. **MIMIC-III**: An electronic health record database containing information on intensive care unit (ICU) patients. We selected the in-hospital mortality prediction task. **TCGA-BRCA**: The breast cancer dataset from The Cancer Genome Atlas, containing gene expression and clinical data. The task is to classify tumor subtypes based on gene expression data.

Table 2. Data partitioning overview for multi-center setting ($M = 10$ clients)

Dataset	Total Samples	Task	Partition Strategy	Client Sample Range
MIMIC-III	42,000	Mortality Prediction	Dir. ($\alpha = 0.5$)	2,100–6,500
TCGA-BRCA	1,100	Subtype Classification	Dir. ($\alpha = 0.5$)	50–180

For the Comparison Methods, we compare our proposed method with the following baselines: **FedAvg** [30]: The standard Federated Averaging algorithm, without any privacy enhancement or data distillation. **FedAvg+DP** [31]: Applies differential privacy noise to the client's local gradient updates. **FDD (Ours, w/o DP)**: Our proposed federated data distillation framework, but without applying differential privacy perturbation, used to evaluate the effect of distillation itself. **Random Subsampling+DP**: Uses random sampling instead of neural characteristic functions for data selection, combined with differential privacy, to validate the superiority of our distillation strategy.

For the implementation Details and hyperparameters, the experiments were run in a consistent environment, with key hyperparameter settings as shown in Table 3. We repeated all reported results 5 times with different random seeds and report the mean and standard deviation.

Hardware Environment: NVIDIA Tesla V100 GPU, Intel Xeon Gold 6248 CPU, 256 GB RAM. **Software Environment**: Python 3.8, PyTorch 1.10, CUDA 11.1.

5.2 Main Experimental Results

First, for the evaluation of predictive performance and communication efficiency, Table 4 shows the classification accuracy, total communication rounds, and total data transfer volume for each method on the two datasets. For statistical comparison, we performed a paired t-test between our method and the best-performing baseline (FedAvg+DP). The p-values were all less than 0.01, indicating that our performance improvement is statistically significant.

Table 3. Key experimental hyperparameter settings

Parameter	Value
Total Federated Learning Rounds (T)	100
Local Training Epochs	5
Optimizer	Adam
Learning Rate (η)	0.001
Batch Size	32
Differential Privacy δ	10^{-5}
Default Distillation Ratio	5%

Table 4. Comparison of accuracy, communication cost, and privacy (ε) in classification tasks (Mean ± Std. Dev.).

Method	ε	MIMIC-III		TCGA-BRCA	
		Acc. (%) ↑	Comm. (MB) ↓	Acc. (%) ↑	Comm. (MB) ↓
FedAvg	∞	83.2 ± 0.4	1250	78.5 ± 1.1	180
FedAvg+DP	1.0	75.9 ± 0.8	1660	72.1 ± 1.5	235
RandSub+DP	1.0	76.8 ± 0.7	95	72.9 ± 1.8	15
FDD (w/o DP)	∞	81.9 ± 0.5	95	77.1 ± 1.2	15
FDD+DP (Ours)	1.0	79.5 ± 0.6	95	75.6 ± 1.3	15

The experimental results clearly show that our FDD+DP method achieves significantly higher model accuracy than traditional FedAvg+DP while providing the same strict privacy protection ($\varepsilon = 1.0$). More importantly, because data distillation greatly compresses the amount of uploaded data, our method reduces the total communication overhead by more than an order of magnitude, which is crucial for resource-constrained edge computing environments.

Then, for the evaluation of anomaly detection performance, on the TCGA dataset, we evaluated anomaly detection performance by injecting synthetic rare gene mutation samples. For this experiment, we designated 2% of the samples in the test set as anomalies. These were synthetically generated by introducing rare gene expression patterns not present in the training distribution, simulating novel mutations. Figure 2 shows the Receiver Operating Characteristic (ROC) curves for different methods. Our method (FDD+DP) demonstrated the best performance in identifying these rare anomalies, achieving an AUC value of 0.922, significantly higher than other baseline methods. This is because data distillation preserves the core distributional features of the data, allowing the boundary of the normal pattern to be learned more clearly, thus making it easier to identify deviant samples.

For the trade-off analysis of distillation ratio, to investigate the impact of key parameters, we show how model performance varies with the distillation ratio in Fig. 3. It can be seen that when the privacy budget is fixed ($\varepsilon = 1.0$),

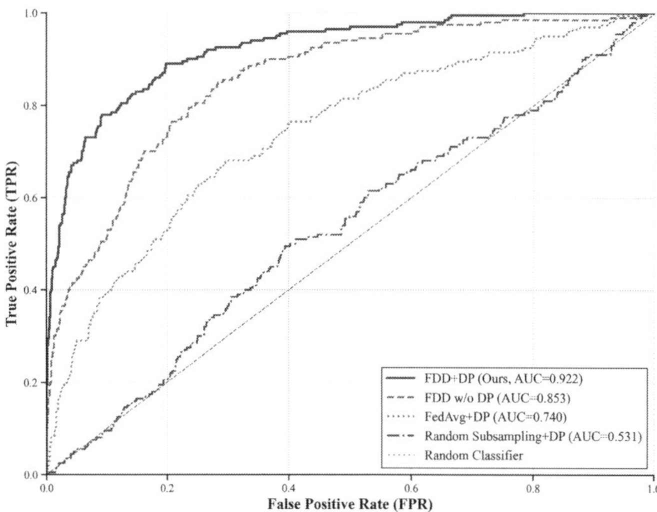

Fig. 2. Comparison of ROC curves for anomaly detection on the TCGA dataset. The x-axis is the False Positive Rate (FPR), and the y-axis is the True Positive Rate (TPR). Our method (FDD+DP, solid blue line) achieves the highest Area Under the Curve (AUC), indicating superior overall performance in identifying rare cases. (Color figure online)

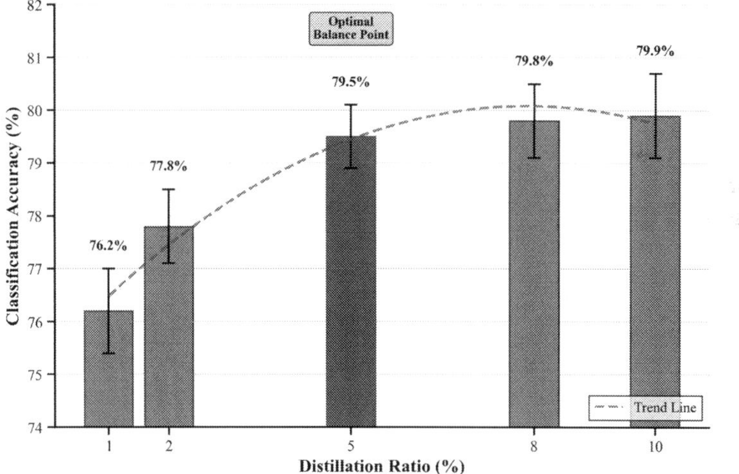

Fig. 3. The effect of different distillation ratios on classification accuracy.

increasing the distillation ratio from 1% to 10% improves model accuracy, but with diminishing marginal returns. This suggests that a 5% distillation ratio is a good balance point.

This figure provides practitioners with an intuitive basis for selecting appropriate parameters based on the privacy and performance requirements of their specific application scenarios.

5.3 Ablation Study

To verify the necessity of each core component in our framework, we conducted an ablation study. As shown in Table 5, removing any key module results in a significant performance drop, demonstrating the integrity of our design. **Without Centralized Pre-training**: The convergence speed is significantly slower (communication rounds increase by about 40%), and the final accuracy decreases, proving that the good initialization provided by pre-training is crucial. **Without Neural Feature Distillation**: Accuracy drops significantly, indicating that our NCF-based distillation method can more effectively capture the essence of the data. **Without Differential Privacy**: Although accuracy is highest, it sacrifices privacy protection and cannot meet medical application requirements.

Table 5. Ablation results on MIMIC-III ($\varepsilon = 1.0$, distill ratio = 5%)

Setting	Acc. (%) ↑	Rounds to Converge ↓	AUC ↑
Full (FDD+DP)	79.5	48	0.89
No Pre-training	77.2	67	0.85
Random Distillation	76.8	49	0.83
No DP (FDD only)	81.9	43	0.91

6 Discussion

Through comprehensive experiments, this study has demonstrated the effectiveness and superiority of our proposed privacy-enhanced federated data distillation framework in multi-center medical applications. The experimental results are not only statistically significant but also provide deep insights into several important aspects of the system.

We have achieved a balance between privacy protection, model performance, and communication efficiency. Compared to traditional federated learning (FedAvg) and simple privacy-enhancing methods (FedAvg+DP), our framework first uses local data distillation based on neural characteristic functions to compress large-scale, heterogeneous raw data into small-scale, information-rich synthetic datasets. This step not only drastically reduces the communication burden but also creates the conditions for effective privacy protection. Second, applying differential privacy during the distillation process and using the resulting data for server-side pre-training provides a robust starting point for the subsequent federated fine-tuning. Our ablation study clearly quantifies the contribution of each component, confirming that the pre-training and distillation strategies are key to improving performance.

A crucial aspect of our framework is the trade-off between communication efficiency and local computation. While our method significantly cuts down on data transmission, the local data distillation phase introduces a one-time computational cost at each client. For well-resourced medical centers, this upfront cost is generally acceptable. However, for extremely resource-constrained edge devices, the computational demand of distillation itself could become a new bottleneck. This highlights a potential limitation and an important direction for future research, such as exploring more lightweight distillation algorithms or adaptive strategies that balance distillation complexity with device capabilities.

Despite the promising results, this study has some limitations. The framework's performance under extreme data heterogeneity (e.g., when local datasets have disjoint label sets) could be further improved. Additionally, optimizing the allocation of the privacy budget across the distillation and federated training phases remains an open and challenging research question.

7 Conclusion

This paper addresses the challenges of privacy, efficiency, and performance in collaborative learning with multi-center medical data by proposing and implementing a privacy-enhanced federated data distillation framework. The framework innovatively integrates neural characteristic function-driven data distillation, differential privacy protection, server-side pre-training, and federated optimization. Comprehensive experimental evaluations show that, compared to existing baseline methods, our framework significantly improves model predictive accuracy and anomaly detection capabilities while ensuring strict privacy and reducing communication overhead by more than an order of magnitude.

Through experimental analysis, we have quantified the trade-off relationship between distillation ratio, privacy budget, and model performance. Through ablation studies, we have verified the effectiveness and robustness of each component of the system. This research offers a practical and efficient solution for collaborative data analysis in the medical field. Our work complements existing federated learning studies by bridging the gaps between data privacy, communication efficiency, and robust anomaly detection. Instead of offering isolated improvements, it presents a cohesive, end-to-end solution where data distillation and privacy preservation are deeply coupled with the learning process through a synergistic pre-training phase. This design is tailored for practical deployment in sensitive, distributed healthcare environments, thereby advancing the applicability of collaborative AI in medicine.

Acknowledgments. This work was partially supported by JSPS Grant-in-Aid for Scientific Research (C) 23K11103.

References

1. Li, T., Sahu, A.K., Talwalkar, A., Smith, V.: Federated learning: challenges, methods, and future directions. IEEE Signal Process. Mag. **37**(3), 50–60 (2020)
2. Vajrobol, V., Aggarwal, N., Baranwal, P., Saxena, G.J., Pundir, A., Singh, S.: Navigating bias and ensuring fairness in federated learning: an in-depth exploration of data distribution, IID, and non-IID challenges. Federated Intell. Syst. Healthc. Pract. Guide, 253–291 (2025)
3. Geiping, J., Bauermeister, H., Dröge, H., Moeller, M.: Inverting gradients-how easy is it to break privacy in federated learning? In: Advances in Neural Information Processing Systems, vol. 33, pp. 16,937–16,947 (2020)
4. Carlini, N., et al.: Extracting training data from large language models. In: 30th USENIX Security Symposium (USENIX Security 21), pp. 2633–2650 (2021)
5. Abadi, M., Chu, A., Goodfellow, I., et al.: Deep learning with differential privacy. In: Proceedings of the 2016 ACM SIGSAC Conference on Computer and Communications Security, pp. 308–318 (2016)
6. Kairouz, P., et al.: Advances and open problems in federated learning. Found. Trends® Mach. Learn. **14**(1–2), 1–210 (2021)
7. Wang, S., et al.: Dataset distillation with neural characteristic function: a minmax perspective. In: Proceedings of the Computer Vision and Pattern Recognition Conference, pp. 25570–25580 (2025)
8. Cholakoska, A., Pfitzner, B., Gjoreski, H., Rakovic, V., Arnrich, B., Kalendar, M.: Differentially private federated learningfor anomaly detection in ehealth networks. In: Adjunct Proceedings of the 2021 ACM International Joint Conference on Pervasive and Ubiquitous Computing and Proceedings of the 2021 ACM International Symposium on Wearable Computers, pp. 514–518 (2021)
9. Rieke, N., Hancox, J., Li, W., et al.: The future of digital health with federated learning. NPJ Digital Med. **3**(1), 1–7 (2020)
10. Li, L., Fan, Y., Tse, M., Lin, K.Y.: A review of applications in federated learning. Comput. Ind. Eng. **149**, 106854 (2020)
11. Yang, Q., Liu, Y., Chen, T., Tong, Y.: Federated machine learning: concept and applications. ACM Trans. Intell. Syst. Technol. (TIST) **10**(2), 1–19 (2019)
12. Chen, H., Wang, H., Long, Q., Jin, D., Li, Y.: Advancements in federated learning: models, methods, and privacy. ACM Comput. Surv. **57**(2), 1–39 (2024)
13. Sun, L., Wu, J.: A scalable and transferable federated learning system for classifying healthcare sensor data. IEEE J. Biomed. Health Inform. **27**(2), 866–877 (2022)
14. Rao, B., Zhang, J., Wu, D., Zhu, C., Sun, X., Chen, B.: Privacy inference attack and defense in centralized and federated learning: a comprehensive survey. IEEE Trans. Artif. Intell. (2024)
15. Shukla, S., Rajkumar, S., Sinha, A., Esha, M., Elango, K., Sampath, V.: Federated learning with differential privacy for breast cancer diagnosis enabling secure data sharing and model integrity. Sci. Rep. **15**(1), 13061 (2025)
16. Yin, X., Zhu, Y., Hu, J.: A comprehensive survey of privacy-preserving federated learning: a taxonomy, review, and future directions. ACM Comput. Surv. (CSUR) **54**(6), 1–36 (2021)
17. Hu, K., Gong, S., Zhang, Q., Seng, C., Xia, M., Jiang, S.: An overview of implementing security and privacy in federated learning. Artif. Intell. Rev. **57**(8), 204 (2024)

18. Li, H., Ge, L., Tian, L.: Survey: federated learning data security and privacy-preserving in edge-internet of things. Artif. Intell. Rev. **57**(5), 130 (2024)
19. Yu, R., Liu, S., Wang, X.: Dataset distillation: a comprehensive review. IEEE Trans. Pattern Anal. Mach. Intell. **46**(1), 150–170 (2023)
20. Wu, C., Wu, F., Lyu, L., Huang, Y., Xie, X.: Communication-efficient federated learning via knowledge distillation. Nat. Commun. **13**(1), 2032 (2022)
21. Gong, X., et al.: Ensemble attention distillation for privacy-preserving federated learning. In: Proceedings of the IEEE/CVF International Conference on Computer Vision, pp. 15076–15086 (2021)
22. Itahara, S., Nishio, T., Koda, Y., Morikura, M., Yamamoto, K.: Distillation-based semi-supervised federated learning for communication-efficient collaborative training with non-IID private data. IEEE Trans. Mob. Comput. **22**(1), 191–205 (2021)
23. Zhang, C., Yang, S., Mao, L., Ning, H.: Anomaly detection and defense techniques in federated learning: a comprehensive review. Artif. Intell. Rev. **57**(6), 150 (2024)
24. Kong, X., et al.: Federated graph anomaly detection via contrastive self-supervised learning. IEEE Trans. Neural Netw. Learn. Syst. (2024)
25. Lu, Y., Yang, T., Zhao, C., Chen, W., Zeng, R.: A swarm anomaly detection model for IoT UAVs based on a multi-modal denoising autoencoder and federated learning. Comput. Ind. Eng. **196**, 110454 (2024)
26. Li, X., Xiong, Z., Lian, Z., Liu, Y.: Federated learning with dataset distillation. In: arXiv preprint arXiv:2104.05637 (2021)
27. Abdel-Basset, M., Moustafa, N., Hawash, H.: Privacy-preserved generative network for trustworthy anomaly detection in smart grids: a federated semisupervised approach. IEEE Trans. Industr. Inf. **19**(1), 995–1005 (2022)
28. Vaswani, A., Shazeer, N., Parmar, N., et al.: Attention is all you need. In: Advances in Neural Information Processing Systems, vol. 30 (2017)
29. Raza, A., Tran, K.P., Koehl, L., Li, S.: Anofed: adaptive anomaly detection for digital health using transformer-based federated learning and support vector data description. Eng. Appl. Artif. Intell. **121**, 106051 (2023)
30. McMahan, B., Moore, E., Ramage, D., Hampson, S., y Arcas, B.A.: Communication-efficient learning of deep networks from decentralized data. In: Artificial Intelligence and Statistics, pp. 1273–1282. PMLR (2017)
31. Geyer, R.C., Klein, T., Nabi, M.: Differentially private federated learning: a client level perspective. In: arXiv preprint arXiv:1712.07557 (2017)

A Dual-Chain Architecture for Secure and Interoperable Lifelong Learning Certification

Hang Zheng[1], Wenjie Li[1], and Jiageng Chen[1,2](✉)

[1] School of Computer Science, Hubei Provincial Key Laboratory of Artificial Intelligence and Smart Learning, Central China Normal University, Wuhan 430079, People's Republic of China

[2] School of Central China Normal University Wollongong Joint Institute, Central China Normal University, Wuhan 430079, People's Republic of China

jiageng.chen@ccnu.edu.cn

Abstract. Existing blockchain-based certification systems face a fundamental trade-off between the public verifiability of public blockchains and the data privacy of consortium blockchains. This paper proposes a novel dual-chain architecture that resolves this dilemma by decoupling the attestation process from the verification process. On a permissioned consortium blockchain, trusted institutions validate credentials via internal consensus and then collectively sign a verification package using a threshold BLS signature scheme; this signature serves as a secure attestation for the cross-chain anchoring of the credential's data on a public blockchain. Here, learners can use zero-knowledge proofs(ZKPs) to prove specific attributes of their credentials without revealing sensitive data. Performance evaluation demonstrates the system's capacity to handle large-scale institutional needs, achieving up to 92.1 TPS, and our security analysis confirms its robustness against forgery and privacy leaks. This work provides a robust technical foundation for an interoperable lifelong learning ecosystem where trust is established through verifiable, multi-party cryptographic consensus.

Keywords: Lifelong learning · Dual-chain architecture · Privacy preserving

1 Introduction

The ongoing digital transformation of education and the rise of the knowledge economy necessitate a flexible and trustworthy system for lifelong learning certification. Individuals now accumulate a diverse portfolio of credentials beyond traditional degrees, including professional certifications, micro-credentials, and skill badges from various online and offline providers. However, managing, verifying, and sharing these heterogeneous records in a secure, interoperable, and privacy-preserving manner remains a significant challenge, creating friction between learners, educational institutions, and employers [10].

M. Yung et al. (Eds.): AIBlock 2025, LNCS 16314, pp. 58–75, 2026.
https://doi.org/10.1007/978-3-032-16168-0_4

Blockchain technology offers a promising foundation for a decentralized and immutable record-keeping system. Current solutions, however, typically rely on a single type of blockchain, leading to a fundamental architectural dilemma. To understand this, we must first distinguish between the two predominant models: public blockchains (e.g., Ethereum [7]) are fully decentralized and permissionless, meaning anyone can read the ledger and validate transactions. Consortium blockchains (e.g., Hyperledger Fabric [1]) are permissioned, restricting access to a pre-approved group of entities, which allows for greater control, privacy, and performance [15].

This distinction creates a critical trade-off for educational certification. On one hand, using a public blockchain provides true public verification: any third party, such as a global employer or another university, can independently and permissionlessly query the chain to confirm that a certificate hash is valid and has not been revoked. However, this comes at the cost of privacy. The on-chain transaction itself—linking a learner's wallet address to an institution's—is public, permanently revealing sensitive metadata about who received a credential from where and when. This lack of privacy for sensitive educational data is a major barrier to adoption. On the other hand, a consortium blockchain can protect this sensitive data by keeping all records, including certificate details and transaction metadata, private within a trusted circle of institutions. But this approach sacrifices public verification, creating a closed ecosystem or a blockchain silo. Storing a certificate hash on a consortium blockchain is only meaningful to its members, rendering it unverifiable to the outside world. While some solutions expose this data via proprietary APIs or QR codes, these methods merely create a web front-end to a centralized data source. The trust anchor remains the institution hosting the service, not the blockchain itself. This approach fails to provide the persistent, censorship-resistant, and truly decentralized verification that a public ledger offers. If the institution's servers go offline, verification becomes impossible.

To resolve this impasse, this paper proposes a novel dual-chain architecture that is realized through cross-chain technology [11]. This technology acts as a secure bridge, transferring essential verification data (such as cryptographic commitments to credentials) from the private, permissioned environment of the consortium blockchain to the open, permissionless environment of the public blockchain. Our framework thus synergistically combines a consortium blockchain for trusted data issuance and management with a public blockchain for universal verification. Even with this architecture, a deeper privacy challenge persists: learners need to prove specific attributes of their credentials without being forced to disclose the entire credential's contents, and without unnecessarily revealing their identity during initial verification steps.

The main contributions of this work are threefold:

1. **A balanced architecture for privacy and public verification:** We propose and implement a dual-chain system that resolves the inherent dilemma of single-chain solutions, achieving both data confidentiality on a consortium blockchain and universal verifiability on a public blockchain.

2. **Fine-grained privacy in public interactions:** On the public blockchain, we design a protocol that protects both credential data privacy (allowing learners to prove facts about their credentials via ZKPs without revealing them) and identity privacy during the verification process between learners and employers.
3. **Distributed and trusted issuance on the consortium blockchain:** We establish a robust issuance mechanism that leverages the consortium blockchain's permission management and a multi-party consensus protocol (via threshold signatures) to ensure certificate integrity and prevent fraudulent issuance from a single point of failure.

The remainder of this paper is organized as follows: Sect. 2 discusses related work. Section 3 provides the necessary technical preliminaries. Section 4 presents the system model and threat model. Section 5 details our proposed protocols. Section 6 presents our performance evaluation and security analysis. Finally, Sect. 7 concludes the paper.

2 Related Work

The application of blockchain in education has evolved significantly. To situate our contribution, we analyze representative works along key dimensions: their underlying architecture, their model for data and metadata privacy, and their support for public verifiability, selective disclosure, and issuance governance. A summary of this analysis is presented in Table 1.

Several prominent solutions leverage public blockchains to achieve universal accessibility. The Blockcerts [2] open standard and the Lifelong Learning Passport (LLP) [9] project proposed by Gräther et al. both utilize public ledgers. Their primary strength is providing robust, permissionless public verifiability. However, they only offer a partial privacy model. While sensitive credential content is kept off-chain, the on-chain transaction permanently and publicly links the issuer's address to the recipient's, exposing critical metadata and creating significant privacy risks.

In contrast, systems built on consortium blockchains prioritize confidentiality. EduCTX [14] and Cerberus [13] utilize permissioned networks, offering a strong solution for data and metadata privacy. This architectural choice, however, creates nuanced challenges for public verification. While some systems like EduCTX offer no public-facing verification mechanism, others like Cerberus provide partial support by exposing a public API. This API-based approach, while offering accessibility, relies on trusting the institution's centralized server and is fundamentally different from the persistent, decentralized trust provided by a public ledger.

Beyond this core trade-off, existing systems show varying levels of support for advanced features. For selective disclosure, systems like Cerberus offer what can be described as coarse-grained disclosure. Their role-based access control models allow a learner to choose whether to share an entire document, such as a full degree certificate or a complete transcript. This model is fundamentally different from the fine-grained disclosure enabled by our ZKP-based protocol. Our system does not require sharing the document at all; instead, a learner can generate a cryptographic proof of a specific fact (e.g., "my GPA is above 3.5" or "I have completed the required course") without revealing any other information from the credential. This provides a far stronger guarantee of data minimization and privacy. In terms of issuance governance, the consensus and permission management in systems like EduCTX, Cerberus, and the conceptualized LLP offer a degree of multi-party control, which can be considered partial decentralization. Our work enhances this by using a threshold signature scheme to distribute trust cryptographically.

In summary, our dual-chain architecture is unique in that it is the only approach that provides full support for both data privacy and public verifiability. Furthermore, by integrating advanced cryptographic protocols, it offers superior capabilities for both selective disclosure and issuance governance.

Table 1. Comparison of representative certification systems

System	Architecture	P1	P2	P3	P4
Blockcerts [2]	PB	◐	●	○	○
LLP [9]	PB	◐	●	○	◐
EduCTX [14]	CB	●	○	○	◐
Cerberus [13]	CB	●	◐	◐	◐
Our Work	**PB+CB**	●	●	●	●

Note: PB: Public Blockchain; CB: Consortium Blockchain;
●: Full Support; ◐: Partial Support; ○: No Support;
P1: Data & Metadata Privacy; P2: Public Verifiability;
P3: Selective Disclosure; P4: Issuance Governance;

3 Preliminaries

Cryptography provides core support for our blockchain-based certification system. This section introduces the key cryptographic techniques that serve as the building blocks for our protocol, defining their core algorithms and their specific roles within our system.

3.1 Hash Functions

A cryptographic hash function, $H(\cdot)$, is a one-way function that maps an input of arbitrary size to a fixed-size output.

- $y \leftarrow H(x)$: Computes a fixed-length hash value y from an input data string x.

Role in Our System: Hash functions create compact, unique identifiers for credentials, which are anchored on-chain for immutable and efficient verification.

3.2 Pedersen Commitment

A pedersen commitment scheme allows a party to commit to a value while keeping it hidden, with the properties of being perfectly hiding and computationally binding [12].

- $C \leftarrow \text{Commit}(v, r)$: Generates a commitment C from a value v and a random blinding factor r.

Role in Our System: Learners use Pedersen commitments to commit to sensitive credential attributes before proving facts about them with zero-knowledge proofs.

3.3 Bulletproofs

Bulletproofs are a concise, non-interactive zero-knowledge proof (NIZK) system [6].

- $\pi \leftarrow \text{ProofPrv}(C, info)$: Generates a proof π for a statement about the value in commitment C, based on public information $info$.
- $\{0, 1\} \leftarrow \text{ProofVrf}(\pi, C, info)$: Verifies that the proof π correctly corresponds to the public statement $info$, which includes the commitment C. It outputs 1 if the proof is valid, and 0 otherwise.

Role in Our System: We employ Bulletproofs to allow learners to prove facts about their credentials without revealing the underlying data.

3.4 ElGamal Encryption

The ElGamal encryption scheme is an asymmetric cryptosystem [8].

- $(pk, sk) \leftarrow \text{ElGKeyGen}()$: Generates a public key pk and a secret key sk.
- $c \leftarrow \text{ElGEnc}(m, pk)$: Encrypts a message m with a public key pk to produce a ciphertext c.
- $m \leftarrow \text{ElGDec}(c, sk)$: Decrypts a ciphertext c with a secret key sk to recover the original message m.

Role in Our System: Proof packages from learners are encrypted with the verifier's public key to ensure confidentiality during transmission over public channels.

3.5 Boneh-Boyen Signatures (BBS)

BBS is a short digital signature scheme providing data integrity and authenticity [3].

- $(pk, sk) \leftarrow \text{BBKeyGen}()$: Generates a public key pk and a secret key sk.
- $\sigma \leftarrow \text{BBSign}(sk, m)$: Computes a signature σ on a message m using a secret key sk.
- $\{0, 1\} \leftarrow \text{BBVer}(pk, m, \sigma)$: Verifies a signature σ on a message m using the corresponding public key pk.

Role in Our System: Issuing bodies use BBS to sign original credentials, and learners use it to sign the ZKP packages they generate, ensuring authenticity.

3.6 BLS Threshold Signatures

A (t, n) threshold BLS signature scheme enables collective signing by a group of participants [4,5].

- $\sigma_i \leftarrow \text{BLSSign}(sk_i, M)$: Computes a partial signature σ_i on a message M using a party's secret key share sk_i.
- $\sigma \leftarrow \text{Aggregate}(\{\sigma_i\}_{i \in S}, t)$: Combines a set of at least t partial signatures $\{\sigma_i\}_{i \in S}$ into a single threshold signature σ.
- $\{0, 1\} \leftarrow \text{BLSVer}(pkc, M, \sigma)$: Verifies the combined signature σ on the message M using the collective public key pkc.

Role in Our System: This scheme underpins our distributed governance model, ensuring a credential's verification data is approved for cross-chain transfer only after achieving a multi-party consensus.

4 System Model and Threat Model

4.1 System Model

Our proposed dual-chain architecture involves several key entities, each with distinct roles and responsibilities. The interactions between these participants define the lifecycle of a digital credential in our system. The high-level interaction between these entities is illustrated in Fig. 1.

- **Learner:** The owners and subjects of the credentials. Learners manage their digital certificates and, upon request from a Verifier, generate zero-knowledge proofs to demonstrate their qualifications without revealing underlying sensitive data.
- **Issuing Body(IB):** Entities such as universities, online platforms, or professional organizations that are authorized to create and cryptographically sign credentials after assessing a learner's capabilities.

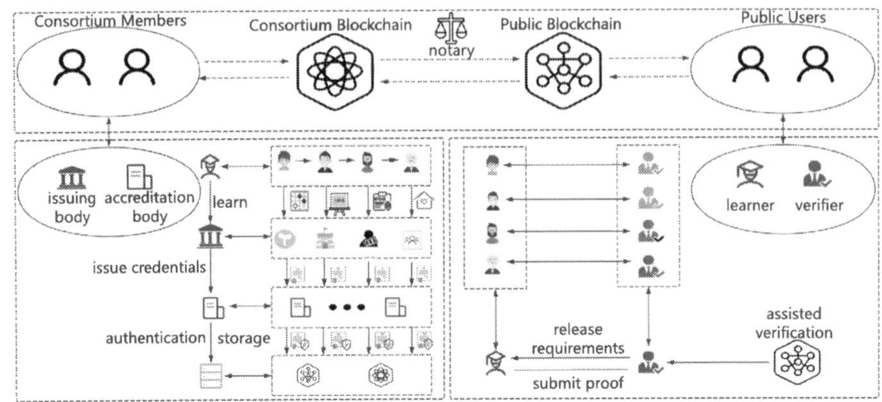

Fig. 1. The proposed dual-chain system architecture

- **Accreditation Body(AB):** A set of trusted, permissioned nodes that form the consortium blockchain. Their primary role is to validate credentials submitted by IBs and participate in the multi-party consensus protocol (via threshold signatures) to approve verification packages for cross-chain transfer.
- **Verifier:** Entities such as employers or university admissions offices. Verifiers request proof of qualifications from Learners and interact with the public blockchain and the learner's ZKP to validate the authenticity and specific attributes of a credential.
- **Notary:** A set of trusted nodes responsible for cross-chain communication. They monitor the consortium blockchain for approved verification packages and securely relay them to the public blockchain for universal access.

4.2 Threat Model

We analyze the security of our protocol under a standard adversary model, tailored to our blockchain context. We define the adversary's capabilities and our core trust assumptions as follows:

1. **Network Adversary:** The adversary has full control over the network, meaning they can read, intercept, delay, or block any messages transmitted over public channels.
2. **Computationally Bounded:** The adversary is a probabilistic polynomial-time (PPT) machine. They cannot break the underlying cryptographic primitives (e.g., discrete logarithm problem, collision-resistance of hash functions) in polynomial time.
3. **Participant Corruption:** The adversary may corrupt and fully control certain participants, including Learners, Issuing Bodies, and Verifiers, thereby obtaining any secret keys they hold.

4. **Trusted Notaries:** The Notary nodes responsible for cross-chain operations are assumed to be honest and trusted to faithfully execute the protocol.
5. **Threshold Trust for Accreditation Bodies:** For the n Accreditation Bodies forming the consortium, we assume a (t, n) threshold trust model. The adversary can corrupt at most $t-1$ ABs. The security of our multi-party consensus holds as long as at least t ABs remain honest.
6. **Secure Channels:** We assume that secure channels (e.g., authenticated and encrypted via TLS) are available for direct communication between honest parties when required, although interactions with the blockchains themselves are public.

5 Proposed Protocol

This section presents the detailed cryptographic protocols that underpin our dual-chain architecture. We first provide a high-level overview of the entire workflow and then delve into the formal specification of each protocol phase.

5.1 Overall Workflow

The overall workflow of our protocol, as illustrated in Fig. 2, consists of three distinct phases: trusted issuance and storage on the consortium blockchain, attested cross-chain relay, and fine-grained privacy-preserving verification on the public blockchain.

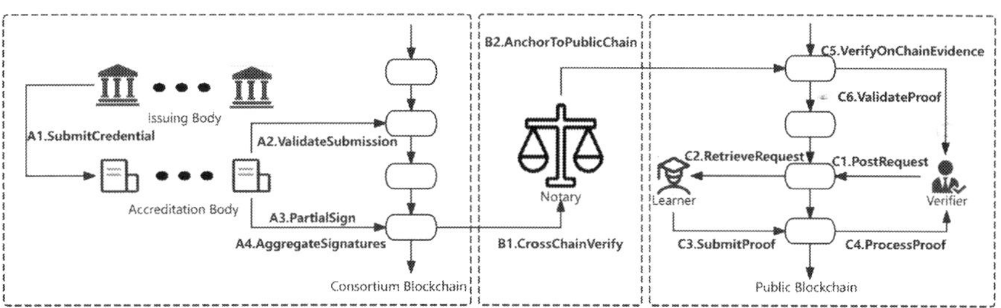

Fig. 2. Overall protocol workflow

Phase 1: Trusted Issuance and Storage on the Consortium Blockchain. The lifecycle of a credential begins on the permissioned consortium blockchain. In SubmitCredential(A1), an IB cryptographically signs a newly created credential and submits it to the Accreditation Bodies (ABs) for validation. In ValidateSubmission(A2), the ABs verify the IB's signature and the credential's content. For scalability, the full credential data is stored in a permissioned off-chain repository (e.g., IPFS), while its hash and key metadata are recorded on the consortium blockchain ledger. Following this, PartialSign(A3) begins, where each participating AB creates a partial threshold signature on the core verification package (containing the credential hash and learner's public key). Finally, in AggregateSignatures(A4), these partial signatures are combined into a single, collective threshold signature, representing the consortium's official approval of the on-chain record.

Phase 2: Attested Cross-Chain Relay. This phase is handled by trusted Notaries. In CrossChainVerify(B1), a Notary monitors the consortium blockchain, retrieves the approved verification package and its collective signature, and validates it. Then, in AnchorToPublicChain(B2), the Notary submits this package to a smart contract on the public blockchain, presenting the collective signature as cryptographic proof of the data's origin and integrity.

Phase 3: Fine-Grained Privacy-Preserving Verification. The final phase is a sophisticated, privacy-preserving interaction. The process starts with PostRequest(C1), where a Verifier might publish a requirement, such as needing proof of a"GPA above 3.5". After RetrieveRequest(C2), the Learner performs SubmitProof(C3) by generating a hybrid zero-knowledge proof package, which is then signed and encrypted for the Verifier. In ProcessProof(C4), the Verifier accesses the package and securely obtains the claimed certificate hash and the Learner's public key. Following this, in VerifyOnChainEvidence(C5), the Verifier uses this data pair to query the public blockchain and retrieve the corresponding anchored record. The workflow concludes with ValidateProof(C6), where the Verifier checks the zero-knowledge proof against the public information to validate the learner's claim with mathematical certainty.

5.2 Detailed Protocol Specification

Certificate Data Structure. To formalize our protocol, we first define the core data object, the digital certificate cert. Its structure, containing all relevant information for issuance and verification in Fig. 3.

This structured format allows the entire cert object to be hashed for integrity checks, while providing clear logical separation between public-facing metadata and sensitive attributes that are candidates for zero-knowledge proofs.

Auxiliary Algorithms. In addition to the core cryptographic primitives, we define several auxiliary algorithms to simplify the description of our main protocols. The first three are helper algorithms for setting up the threshold signature scheme.

- $(N, t) \leftarrow \text{TGen}(pp)$: This algorithm takes the public parameters pp as input and defines the threshold signature scheme's settings, outputting the total number of participants N and the required signature threshold t.

Certificate	
— *Core Metadata* —	
ID	`urn:uuid:c7362350-192b-4788-82b1-3e8f85a8b23b`
Type	`GraduationCertificate`
Issuance Date	`2025-01-01`
— *Issuer & Subject Information* —	
Issuer ID	`did:uni:Tsinghua`
Subject PK	$bbpk_x$ (The Learner's Public Key)
Subject Name	Bob
— *Credential Content (Sensitive Attributes)* —	
Degree	Bachelor of Science, Computer Science
GPA	3.8
Honors	Summa Cum Laude
— *Cryptographic Proof* —	
Issuer Signature	(Initially empty, to be populated with σ_i)

Fig. 3. Exemplar data structure of a digital certificate

- $(\{blspk_j, blssk_j\}_{j=1..n}) \leftarrow \text{DKGen}(N, t)$: This represents the Distributed Key Generation protocol executed by the n Accreditation Bodies. It takes the public parameters and threshold settings as input and outputs the individual secret key shares $blssk_j$ and public key shares $blspk_j$.
- $pkc \leftarrow \text{PKCombine}(\{blspk_j\}_{j=1..n})$: This algorithm, often part of the DKG protocol itself, combines the individual public key shares of all n ABs to compute the single collective public key pkc.

Furthermore, we define two abstract algorithms for interacting with the blockchains:

- $\text{PostPB}(tx)$: This algorithm allows any user to submit a transaction tx to the public blockchain.
- $\text{PostCB}(tx)$: This algorithm allows a consortium member to submit a message tx to the consortium blockchain.
- $\text{SubmitToABs}(tx)$: This algorithm allows a participant (e.g., an IB) to submit a message tx specifically to the Accreditation Bodies for validation and consensus.
- $(\hat{\sigma}, did_{CB}) \leftarrow \text{CheckPB}(hash_x, bbpk_x)$: This algorithm queries the public blockchain for an attested package corresponding to the pair $(hash_x, bbpk_x)$ and returns the associated collective signature $\hat{\sigma}$ and the consortium's DID did_{CB}.

- $pkc \leftarrow$ CheckPKC(did_{CB}): This algorithm queries the on-chain consortium registry using a consortium's DID and returns its corresponding registered collective public key pkc.

System Initialization. Before the protocol can be executed, a one-time setup phase is required. This phase begins with the generation of global public parameters via the algorithm $pp \leftarrow \text{Setup}(1^\lambda)$. This algorithm takes a security parameter 1^λ as input and outputs the public parameters pp, collected in a tuple $pp = (p, \mathbb{G}, \mathbb{G}_T, e, g, \mathbb{G}_1, \mathbb{G}_2, \hat{e}, g_1, g_2)$. Here, p is the prime order of the cryptographic groups. The tuple $(\mathbb{G}, \mathbb{G}_T, e, g)$ defines the setting for the BLS signature scheme, where g is a generator of group $\mathbb{G}$ and $e : \mathbb{G} \times \mathbb{G} \rightarrow \mathbb{G}_T$ is a bilinear pairing map. Similarly, the tuple $(\mathbb{G}_1, \mathbb{G}_2, \mathbb{G}_T, \hat{e}, g_1, g_2)$ defines the setting for the BBS signature scheme, where g_1, g_2 are generators of groups $\mathbb{G}_1, \mathbb{G}_2$ respectively, and $\hat{e} : \mathbb{G}_1 \times \mathbb{G}_2 \rightarrow \mathbb{G}_T$ is the corresponding bilinear map. The public parameters pp are assumed to be implicitly available to all subsequent algorithms.

Following the setup, all participants generate their long-term cryptographic keys:

- $(bbpk_i, bbsk_i) \leftarrow \text{BBKeyGen}(pp)$: This algorithm generates a BBS signature key pair for each IB.
- $(bbpk_x, bbsk_x) \leftarrow \text{BBKeyGen}(pp)$: This algorithm generates a BBS signature key pair for each Learner.
- $(upk_x, usk_x) \leftarrow \text{ElGKeyGen}()$: This algorithm generates an ElGamal key pair for each Learner.
- $(upk_y, usk_y) \leftarrow \text{ElGKeyGen}()$: This algorithm generates an ElGamal key pair for each Verifier.
- $(N, t) \leftarrow \text{TGen}(pp)$: This algorithm generates the parameters for the threshold scheme, outputting the total number of participants N and the required signature threshold t.
- $(blspk_j, blssk_j) \leftarrow \text{DKGen}(N, t)$: The n Accreditation Bodies (ABs) execute this Distributed Key Generation protocol to obtain their individual BLS secret key shares $blssk_j$ and the single collective public key pkc.
- $pkc \leftarrow \text{PKCombine}(\{\mathsf{blspk}_j\}_{j \in \{1,N\}})$: This algorithm combines the individual public key shares of all n ABs to compute the single collective public key pkc, which is used to verify aggregated threshold signatures.

All resulting public keys are assumed to be registered in a publicly accessible directory.

Consortium Blockchain Protocol. This protocol formalizes the procedures on the consortium blockchain, corresponding to steps A1-A4 in our workflow diagram. The process is initiated when an IB signs and submits a new credential for validation. The Accreditation Bodies (ABs) then execute a two-stage consensus protocol. In the first stage (A1-A2), they validate the credential's authenticity and content, resulting in an approved record on the consortium ledger. In the second stage (A3-A4), they collaboratively generate a collective threshold signature on the core verification package. This signature acts as a single, tamper-proof attestation from the entire consortium, proving the credential's validity and making it ready for cross-chain relay. The detailed protocol is presented in Fig. 4.

Cross-Chain Protocol This protocol, corresponding to steps B1-B2, acts as a secure bridge between the consortium and public blockchains and is performed by a trusted Notary. The Notary's primary role is to transfer the attested verification package from the private, permissioned environment to the public, permissionless one.

First, the Notary retrieves the package $(M, \hat{\sigma})$ from the consortium blockchain and performs the crucial verification step (B1) by checking the collective signature σ_c against the consortium's public key pkc. If the signature is valid, the Notary proceeds to the relay step (B2). To support a multi-consortium ecosystem, the Notary submits the package $(M, \hat{\sigma})$ to the public blockchain's smart contract along with the unique Decentralized Identifier (DID) of the source consortium, did_{CB}. The smart contract then creates a verifiable, on-chain record linking the consortium's identity to the data it has attested. This allows any public verifier to first use did_{CB} to look up the correct consortium and its public key pkc, and then verify the credential, enabling a scalable and interoperable system. The detailed protocol is presented in Fig. 5.

CrossChainVerify$(M, \hat{\sigma}, pkc)$:

- If BLSver$(pkc, M, \hat{\sigma}) = 0$, then return $\perp$.

AnchorToPublicChain$(M, \hat{\sigma}, did_{CB})$:

- PostPB$(M, \hat{\sigma}, did_{CB})$.

- A trusted Notary executes these protocols sequentially. It runs AnchorToPublicChain(B2) only after CrossChainVerify(B1) returns 1 (success).

Fig. 4. Formal protocol for issuance and consensus on the consortium blockchain

Public Blockchain Protocol. This final protocol formalizes the privacy preserving verification process on the public blockchain, corresponding to steps C1-C6 in our workflow. The interaction is initiated by a Verifier, who posts an abstract requirement without knowing any specific learner. In response, a Learner can generate and submit a cryptographic proof of their qualifications, which the Verifier can then comprehensively validate.

The process begins when a Verifier publishes a request (C1-C2). This request is abstract, defining the required attribute, $Need$ (e.g., GPA), and an acceptable value range (a,b) (e.g., [3.5, 4.0]). A Learner, holding a certificate with a specific value need for that attribute (e.g., their actual GPA of 3.8), generates a hybrid zero-knowledge proof package (C3). This package contains two main components: a hash preimage proof (π_{hash}) to prove ownership of the certificate hash $hash_x$,

SubmitCredential($cert_x, bbsk_i$):

- $hash_x \leftarrow$ H($cert_x$).
- $\sigma_i \leftarrow$ BBSign($bbsk_i, hash_x$).
- SubmitToABs($cert_x, hash_x, \sigma_i$).

ValidateSubmission($bbpk_i, hash_x, \sigma_i$):

- If BBVer($bbpk_i, hash_x, \sigma_i$) $= 0, then\ return\ \perp$.
- PostCB($hash_x, \sigma_i$).

PartialSign($hash_x, bbpk_x, blssk_j$):

- $M \leftarrow (hash_x, bbpk_x)$.
- $\hat{\sigma}_j \leftarrow$ BLSSign($blssk_j, M$).
- PostCB($M, \hat{\sigma}_j$).

AggregateSignatures($M, \{\hat{\sigma}_j, blspk_j\}_{j \in S}$):

- If $|S| < t$, then return $\perp$.
- For each $j \in S$:
  - If BLSver($blspk_j, M, \hat{\sigma}_j$) $= 0$, then discard $\hat{\sigma}_j$.
- Let S' be the set of valid partial signatures.
- If $|S'| < t$, return $\perp$.
- $\hat{\sigma} \leftarrow$ Aggregate($\{\hat{\sigma}_j\}_{j \in S'}, t$)
- PostCB($M, \hat{\sigma}$).

- SubmitCredential(A1) is executed by an IB.
- ValidateSubmission(A2) is executed by each AB (AB_j) upon receiving a submission.
- PartialSign(A3) is executed by each participating AB after successful content consensus.
- AggregateSignatures(A4) is executed by the consortium blockchain's smart contract logic.

Fig. 5. Formal protocol for cross-chain relay

and a range proof (π_{need}) to prove that their secret value need satisfies the public range (a,b). The entire package is then signed by the learner and encrypted for the verifier before being submitted to the public blockchain.

Upon retrieving and decrypting the package (C4), the Verifier embarks on a multi-step validation process (C5-C6). First, after verifying the learner's signature, the verifier obtains the learner's public key $bbpk_x$ and the certificate hash $hash_x$. The verifier then uses the data pair $(hash_x, bbpk_x)$ to query the public blockchain. This query retrieves the attested package previously anchored by the Notary, which contains the collective signature $\hat{\sigma}$ and the source consortium's identifier, did_{CB}. Next, the verifier uses did_{CB} to look up the consortium's collective public key pkc from the on-chain public registry. Finally, the verifier conducts a comprehensive validation: checking the consortium's collective signature $\hat{\sigma}$, and verifying both zero-knowledge proofs, π_{hash} and π_{need}. If all checks pass, the verifier is convinced of the learner's claim wchecks pass, the verifier is convinced of the learner's claim without ever learning the learner's actual GPA. The detailed protocol is presented in Fig. 6.ithout ever learning the learner's actual GPA. The detailed protocol is presented in Fig. 6.

6 Performance and Security Analysis

In this section, we evaluate the performance of our proposed system to demonstrate its feasibility for real-world application and provide an informal analysis of its key security properties.

6.1 Performance Evaluation

We evaluated the performance of the core logic on the consortium blockchain, which represents the most computationally intensive part of the issuance and consensus process.

Experimental Setup. Our evaluation simulates a lifelong learning certification environment for a large-scale institution, Central China Normal University (CCNU), which serves nearly 40,000 students. In this simulation, the 30+ faculties of CCNU act as IBs, while university-level administrative offices form the ABs. The experiment was conducted on a virtual machine with a 6-core processor and 8GB RAM, running a Hyperledger Fabric v2.5.9 network.

Throughput Analysis. We focused on the key performance metric of Throughput (TPS) for the three core consensus protocols on the consortium blockchain: ValidateSubmission (A2), PartialSign (A3), and AggregateSignatures (A4). To provide an intuitive understanding of this capacity, we translate our measured throughput into a daily processing capability. As illustrated in Fig. 7, the system achieves a peak throughput of up to 92.1 TPS. This translates to a theoretical capacity of processing nearly 8 million ($92.1 \times 86,400$) certification events per day. This capacity far exceeds the needs of our target scenario, easily handling peak loads such as issuing certificates for all 40,000 students of CCNU on a single day. It is important to note that these results were achieved in a resource-constrained virtual environment. Theoretically, the system's performance is horizontally scalable and can be further enhanced by deploying it on more powerful, dedicated hardware infrastructure, indicating its suitability for even larger, multi-institutional ecosystems.

Client-side and Public Blockchain Performance. For the public-facing components, performance is determined by two factors. Firstly, the client-side cryptographic operations. Based on established benchmarks for the Bulletproofs library, generating and verifying a zero-knowledge proof for a typical credential attribute occurs at the millisecond level, ensuring a smooth and responsive user experience. Secondly, the on-chain operations. Their speed is entirely dependent on the specific public blockchain platform chosen. Our architecture is flexible

PostRequest$(a, b, Need, upk_y)$:

- $req \leftarrow (a, b, Need)$.
- PostPB(req, upk_y).

RetrieveRequest(req, upk_y):

- $(a, b, Need) \leftarrow req$.
- return $(a, b, Need)$.

SubmitProof$(a, b, Need, cert_x, bbpk_x, bbsk_x, upk_y)$:

- $need \leftarrow cert_x[Need]$.
- $hash_x \leftarrow \mathrm{H}(cert_x)$.
- $r_{hash} \leftarrow \mathrm{random}(), r_{need} \leftarrow \mathrm{random}()$.
- $C_{hash} \leftarrow \mathrm{Commit}(hash_x, r_{hash}), C_{need} \leftarrow \mathrm{Commit}(need, r_{need})$.
- $\pi_{hash} \leftarrow \mathrm{ProofPrv}(C_{hash}, hash_x), \pi_{need} \leftarrow \mathrm{ProofPrv}(C_{need}, a, b, Need)$.
- $M_{proof} \leftarrow (\pi_{hash}, \pi_{need}, C_{hash}, C_{need}, hash_x)$.
- $\sigma_p \leftarrow \mathrm{BBsign}(bbsk_x, M_{proof})$.
- $M_{proofinfo} \leftarrow (M_{proof}, \sigma_p, bbpk_x)$.
- $C_{proofinfo} \leftarrow \mathrm{ELGEnc}(M_{proofinfo}, upk_y)$.
- $PostPB(C_{proofinfo})$.

ProcessProof$(C_{proofinfo}, usk_y)$:

- $M_{proofinfo} \leftarrow \mathrm{ElGDec}(C_{proofinfo}, usk_y)$.
- $(M_{proof}, \sigma_p, bbpk_x) \leftarrow M_{proofinfo}$.
- return $(M_{proof}, \sigma_p, bbpk_x)$

VerifyOnChainEvidence$(M_{proof}, \sigma_p, bbpk_x)$:

- If BBver$(bbpk_x, M_{proof}, \sigma_p) = 0$, then return $\perp$.
- $(\pi_{hash}, \pi_{need}, C_{hash}, C_{need}, hash_x) \leftarrow M_{proof}$.
- $(\hat{\sigma}, did_{CB}) \leftarrow CheckPB(hash_x, bbpk_x)$.
- $pkc \leftarrow CheckPKC(did_{CB})$.
- If BLSver$(pkc, (hash_x, bbpk_x), \hat{\sigma}) = 0$, then return $\perp$.
- return $(\pi_{hash}, \pi_{need}, C_{hash}, C_{need}, hash_x)$.

ValidateProof$(\pi_{hash}, \pi_{need}, C_{hash}, C_{need}, hash_x, a, b, Need)$:

- If ProofVrf$(\pi_{hash}, C_{hash}, hash_x) = 0$, then return $\perp$.
- If ProofVrf$(\pi_{need}, C_{need}, a, b, Need) = 0$, then return $\perp$.

- Verifier: Initiates the protocol by executing PostRequest (C1). After a learner responds, the verifier validates the proof by sequentially executing ProcessProof (C4), VerifyOnChainEvidence (C5), and ValidateProof (C6).
- Learner: Observes a verifier's demand by executing RetrieveRequest (C2) and responds by executing SubmitProof (C3).

Fig. 6. Formal protocol for privacy-preserving verification on the public blockchain

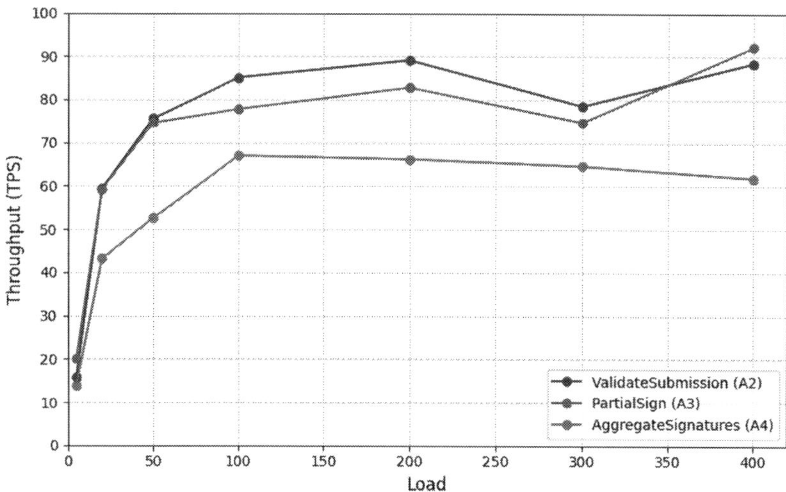

Fig. 7. Throughput performance of the system's core consensus operations.

and can be deployed on any platform that meets the required security and performance trade-offs for the given application.

6.2 Security Analysis

While a formal security proof is beyond this paper's scope, we argue our protocol's security based on its cryptographic design, which achieves the following properties:

- **Certificate Authenticity and Integrity.** Authenticity is guaranteed by the IB's initial BBS signature, which must be verified by the consortium. Integrity is ensured because all subsequent operations rely on the certificate's immutable hash, making any tampering immediately detectable during verification.
- **Distributed Trust and Non-Repudiation.** The protocol mitigates central authority risk via a (t, n) threshold BLS signature scheme. A credential's verification data is only approved for cross-chain transfer after achieving consensus from at least t ABs. This prevents fraudulent attestations by minority colluders and provides a non-repudiable proof of the consensus event itself.
- **Learner Privacy and Selective Disclosure.** Privacy is preserved at two levels. Content privacy is achieved with zero-knowledge proofs (Bulletproofs), allowing learners to prove facts (e.g., "GPA $>$ 3.5") without revealing the credential's data. Transmission privacy is ensured by encrypting the proof package with ElGamal, protecting it from network eavesdroppers.
- **Issuance Event Privacy.** Unlike public-chain systems that permanently link issuer and recipient addresses, our design shields this metadata. All

issuance events occur on the private consortium blockchain. The verification package relayed to the public chain is handled by a Notary and does not contain information that would reveal the original issuer or the specific time of issuance.
- **Ownership and Forgery Resistance.** Ownership is proven by cryptographic means, not just data possession. The verification package publicly binds a certificate's hash ($hash_x$) to a learner's public key ($bbpk_x$). To use the credential, the owner must sign any claim with the corresponding secret key ($bbsk_x$). An adversary who only has the certificate data cannot forge this signature and is thus prevented from impersonating the legitimate owner.

7 Conclusion

This paper proposed and evaluated a novel dual-chain architecture to resolve the fundamental conflict between data privacy and public verifiability in lifelong learning certification. By integrating a permissioned consortium blockchain for trusted issuance with a public blockchain for universal access, and employing zero-knowledge proofs and threshold signatures, our system achieves a robust balance of security, privacy, and usability. Performance results confirm the architecture's efficiency for large-scale deployments, while our security analysis demonstrates its resilience against key threats such as credential forgery and learner impersonation.

Acknowledgments. The corresponding author of this paper is Jiageng Chen. This work is financially supported by National Natural Science Foundation of China under Grant No. 12441102 and self-determined research funds of CCNU from the colleges' basic research and operation of MOE under Grant No. CCNU24ai010.

Declaration of Competing Interest. The authors declare that they have no known competing financial interests or personal relationships that could have appeared to influence the work reported in this paper.

References

1. Androulaki, E., et al.: Hyperledger fabric: a distributed operating system for permissioned blockchains. In: Proceedings of the Thirteenth EuroSys Conference, pp. 1–15 (2018)
2. Blockcerts: Blockcerts: Open standard for blockchain credentials (2021). https://www.blockcerts.org/. Accessed 1 Jan 2025
3. Boneh, D., Boyen, X.: Short signatures without random oracles. In: Cachin, C., Camenisch, J.L. (eds.) Advances in Cryptology - EUROCRYPT 2004. EUROCRYPT 2004. LNCS, vol. 3027, pp. 56–73. Springer, Berlin, Heidelberg (2004). https://doi.org/10.1007/978-3-540-24676-3_4

4. Boneh, D., Gentry, C., Lynn, B., Shacham, H.: Aggregate and verifiably encrypted signatures from bilinear maps. In: Biham, E. (ed.) EUROCRYPT 2003. LNCS, vol. 2656, pp. 416–432. Springer, Heidelberg (2003). https://doi.org/10.1007/3-540-39200-9_26
5. Boneh, D., Lynn, B., Shacham, H.: Short signatures from the weil pairing. In: Boyd, C. (ed.) Advances in Cryptology — ASIACRYPT 2001. ASIACRYPT 2001. LNCS, vol. 2248, pp. 514–532. Springer, Berlin, Heidelberg (2001). https://doi.org/10.1007/3-540-45682-1_30
6. Bünz, B., Bootle, J., Boneh, D., Poelstra, A., Wuille, P., Maxwell, G.: Bulletproofs: short proofs for confidential transactions and more. In: 2018 IEEE Symposium on Security and Privacy (SP), pp. 315–334. IEEE (2018)
7. Buterin, V.: A next-generation smart contract and decentralized application platform. White Paper (2014). https://ethereum.org/en/whitepaper/. Accessed 1 Jan 2025
8. ElGamal, T.: A public key cryptosystem and a signature scheme based on discrete logarithms. IEEE Trans. Inf. Theory **31**(4), 469–472 (1985)
9. Gräther, W., Kolvenbach, S., Ruland, R., Schütte, J., Torres, C., Wendland, F.: Blockchain for education: lifelong learning passport. In: Proceedings of 1st ERCIM Blockchain workshop 2018. European Society for Socially Embedded Technologies (EUSSET) (2018)
10. Nørgård, R.T.: Theorising hybrid lifelong learning. Br. J. Edu. Technol. **52**(4), 1709–1723 (2021)
11. Ou, W., Huang, S., Zheng, J., Zhang, Q., Zeng, G., Han, W.: An overview on cross-chain: mechanism, platforms, challenges and advances. Comput. Netw. **218**, 109378 (2022)
12. Pedersen, T.P.: Non-interactive and information-theoretic secure verifiable secret sharing. In: Feigenbaum, J. (ed.) Advances in Cryptology — CRYPTO '91. CRYPTO 1991. LNCS, vol. 576, pp. 129–140. Springer, Berlin, Heidelberg (1992). https://doi.org/10.1007/3-540-46766-1_9
13. Tariq, A., Haq, H.B., Ali, S.T.: Cerberus: a blockchain-based accreditation and degree verification system. IEEE Trans. Comput. Soc. Syst. **10**(4), 1503–1514 (2022)
14. Turkanović, M., Hölbl, M., Košič, K., Heričko, M., Kamišalić, A.: Eductx: a blockchain-based higher education credit platform. IEEE Access **6**, 5112–5127 (2018)
15. Yaga, D., Mell, P., Roby, N., Scarfone, K.: Blockchain technology overview. arXiv preprint arXiv:1906.11078 (2019)

Activating Value of Data-Driven Digital Assets: A Survey

Jianbo Gao[1], Liangqi Lei[1], Ziyue Shen[1], Zhengkang Fang[1], Shuo Wang[1], Tianxiu Xie[1], Jing Yu[2], and Keke Gai[1](✉)

[1] School of Cyberspace Science and Technology, Beijing Institute of Technology, Beijing 100081, China
{3120235247,3120245873,3220242027,3220245312, 3120215214,3120215672,gaikeke}@bit.edu.cn

[2] School of Information Engineering, Minzu University of China, Beijing 100081, China
jing.yu@muc.edu.cn

Abstract. The role of digital assets in realizing the value of data has become increasingly prominent in recent years. However, the demand for the value circulation of digital assets has become increasingly urgent. This survey investigates the latest technical solutions across digital asset authentication and distribution domains, revealing that ownership ambiguity and application circulation obstruct data-driven digital assets from activating value. Based on the investigation results, we propose a *authentication, authorization, and application* technical framework to achieve secure and reliable value circulation of digital assets. These findings lay a theoretical foundation for achieving digital asset sharing and trading.

Keywords: Digital Asset · Value Circulation · Data Authorization · Data-driven · Model Identity · Copyright Protection

1 Introduction

In the era of artificial intelligence, data is the new oil [2] and is gradually becoming an indispensable strategic resource. However, the use of data within individuals or a single enterprise forms a data value island [48], which cannot fully realize the full value of the data. Transforming data into data assets is an effective solution. The circulation of data assets enables multi-party collaboration to participate in the value development of various data [21,67]. New data can be generated during this process to achieve data value appreciation [38].

However, there are still two challenges in the current value circulation of digital assets. Ambiguous ownership of digital assets is an obstacle. Digital assets cannot confirm their ownership through their own identification [9,39,65], which is different from physical assets. This leads to disputes over ownership, management, and usage rights. There are difficulties in the application of digital assets. Digital assets are limited by the level of trust between entities [6,8] and concerns

M. Yung et al. (Eds.): AIBlock 2025, LNCS 16314, pp. 76–93, 2026.
https://doi.org/10.1007/978-3-032-16168-0_5

about privacy breaches [11,59,71,74]. This stifles the value flow across organizations, industries, and countries, ultimately limiting the potential economic benefits of digital assets. Therefore, addressing these obstacles is the foundation for achieving the value circulation of digital assets.

To bridge these critical gaps, we conduct a comprehensive investigation for the authentication [12,61,66] and distribution of the digital asset [14,44,72]. We have two significant findings on the basis of the investigation. (i) Existing ownership source mechanism relies on encryption technology and lacks inherent binding with the asset itself, which is not conducive to the rapid and secure circulation of data assets [49]. (ii) Existing data circulation method cannot dynamically adapt to the usage scenarios of multi participant or multi data asset collaboration. Based on the above findings, we propose a digital asset value circulation framework, *Authentication, Authorization, and Application (AAA) Framework*. Our framework effectively addresses the challenges of asset ownership ambiguity and application circulation, laying a theoretical foundation for achieving digital asset sharing and trading. The main contributions are twofold:

- This survey integrates the relevant developments in the value circulation of digital asset, covering ownership authentication and distribution. The findings of this work reveal the technical trilemma that hinders the value circulation of digital assets.
- Based on our investigation, we propose a technical framework for the value circulation of digital assets. This framework lays the technological foundation for the high-speed digital asset market.

The remaining structure of this survey is as follows. Section 2 introduces the concepts of digital asset value circulation. Section 3 investigates researches in the authentication of digital assets. A review of digital asset distribution is presented in Sect. 4. Technical framework is given in Sect. 5. Conclusions are given in Sect. 6.

2 Data-Driven Digital Asset

2.1 Digital Asset

Digital assets [46] refer to data resources that can bring economic benefits or other types of value. They are owned or controlled by individuals, businesses, or organizations. They exist in various forms [67], including databases, documents, images, audio, videos, etc. The value of digital assets [30,37] is reflected in the direct economic benefits, such as selling data for economic value. But it also reflected in indirect value, such as improving decision-making efficiency, optimizing business processes, and enhancing customer satisfaction.

There are significant differences between digital assets and traditional assets in multiple aspects, mainly reflected in their form, character, and value circulation. Digital assets usually exist in electronic form, such as documents, images, audio, or video etc. However, traditional assets have physical entities or clear monetary value representations, including physical assets and financial assets. In terms of replicability, digital assets can be infinitely replicated at low cost without compromising the quality of the original copies, and can be accessed and used by multiple users simultaneously. It makes digital assets highly shareable. However, trading or sharing traditional assets with others led the original owner to lose ownership. The value of digital assets often needs to be discovered through complex processing, while traditional assets usually directly generate economic benefits. Digital assets do not follow traditional depreciation rules. Certain types of data may become more valuable over time, but they may also become outdated. In contrast, traditional assets have a clear useful life and are depreciated according to accounting standards. Compared to traditional assets that only involve legal provisions such as property law and contract law, digital assets have more complex copyright, privacy, and data protection regulations, especially in cross-border transmission and personal information protection.

2.2 Value of Data-Driven Digital Assets

The value of digital assets is the quantified expression of economic benefits or other forms of benefits brought about directly or indirectly. The most direct understanding of data assets is that they can bring economic benefits to their holders, including sales of data analysis results, the use of data to improve products or services, and profits obtained by increasing sales. In addition, data assets are an intangible strategic resource. Enterprises can utilize data assets to create value for themselves by supporting decision-making processes, optimizing resource allocation, predicting market trends, and identifying new business opportunities in the digital age. However, due to the unique character of digital assets, their valuation and pricing [38,68] are inherently complex.

The value assessment of data assets involves multiple dimensions, each with its specific key indicators. Accurate, complete, and highly relevant data can provide a more comprehensive perspective for specific analysis. Timely and easily accessible data helps to improve work efficiency for market changes or internal demands. Scarce and high-potential data resources often have higher value and can bring long-term value. Meanwhile, privacy-preserving and secure digital assets are the foundation for realizing value circulation. Taking into account the above indicators comprehensively can better quantify the true value of data assets. It is worth noting that the importance of each indicator may vary in different business scenarios, so it is necessary to flexibly adjust the evaluation indicators according to specific situations.

2.3 Activate Value of Data-Driven Digital Assets

The value circulation of data assets refers to the process in which data is created, exchanged, shared [21,41], and utilized [40]. This process not only promotes the effective allocation of data resources but also drives innovation, improves efficiency, and creates economic value.

Raw data collected from multiple sources, such as sensors, transaction records, social media, etc., is cleaned, converted, and stored, and finally transformed into digital assets. The value assessment of data assets can be based on the cost of acquiring or creating data, or by referring to the market price of similar data assets to determine their value, and calculating their present value based on the expected future economic benefits brought by the data. On-exchange trading is conducted through formal data exchanges, whereas off-exchange trading is a trading conducted directly between individuals or businesses. A sharing agreement is reached between organizations, allowing two or more parties to jointly use data resources. Various departments within the enterprise utilize data assets to improve business processes, optimize products and services. At the same time, data assets can also be provided to third-party partners or customers to achieve greater business value.

Through the above steps, data assets can flow between different entities. They unleash their potential value, and inject vitality into the development of the digital economy. With the advancement of technology and the improvement of regulations, the value circulation mechanism of data assets will become more mature and efficient.

3 Authorization of Digital Assets

3.1 Formalization of Authorization of Digital Assets

Authentication of data assets is a prerequisite for ensuring data security and enabling data flow. We formalize the verification framework for digital asset authentication as follows. The authentication scheme for digital asset ownership is defined by:

$$\mathsf{Authentication} = \langle \text{Train}, \text{Embed}, \text{Assess}, \text{Verify} \rangle \tag{1}$$

1. **Model Training** (Train)

$$\text{Train}(D, \text{Arc}[\cdot], \text{Enc}[\cdot], L) = \{\text{Enc}[W], \text{Dec}[W]\} \tag{2}$$

   where $D = \{x_d, y_d\}$ is the training dataset, L is the combined loss function, and $\text{Arc}[\cdot]$ represents the base architecture.
2. **Identifier Embedding** (Embed)

$$\text{Embed}(data, \text{Arc}[\cdot], \text{Enc}[\cdot], ID) = \text{Carrier}[ID] \tag{3}$$

3. **Quality Assessment** (Assess)

$$\text{Assess}(\text{Arc}[\cdot], M, \epsilon) = \{\text{True}, \text{False}\} \tag{4}$$

   with quality constraint:

$$\|M(\text{Carrier}[ID]) - M_{\text{original}}\| \leq \epsilon \tag{5}$$

4. **Ownership Verification** (Verify)

$$\text{Verify}(\text{Carrier}, ID, \text{Atk}, \text{Dec}[\cdot]) = \{\text{True}, \text{False}\} \tag{6}$$

The standardized authentication of data assets focuses on the identity of data assets. Authentication aims to ensure that data subjects are entitled to relevant rights, such as the right of ownership and the right of use. It clearly defines the attribution of data in circulation and utilization, which safeguards the rights and interests of data subjects. In the context of value transfer and circulation, data assets in the carrier object, transaction mode, the flow of the region presents new characteristics, data asset storage medium [43,45,73] from static data carriers to dynamic multimodal carriers, transaction mode [13,63] from peer-to-peer internal interactive transaction mode to multilevel network non-interactive transaction mode, the flow of the region [6] shifts from isolated storage to collaborative data sharing across departments, organizations and regions. Data security, on the other hand, focuses on data confidentiality and traceability. It ensures data integrity and availability in order to maintain data security and trustworthiness. These characteristics have brought new challenges to data asset transformation, identifier authorization, and ownership traceability.

In the untrustworthy domain, data carriers face data misuse [71], illegal tampering [74], privacy leakage [11], data poisoning [59]. Given the non-physical, replicable and processable characteristics, the transformation of data into tradable data assets with a high degree of identifiability and uniqueness faces difficulties.

For the identity marking authorization mechanism, under the zero-trust transaction mode of cross-network and cross-domain, the ownership of the same data observed in different domains is inconsistent, and the security objectives, protection objects, and authorization subjects of the different ownerships of the data carriers are different, and the separation of each ownership relies on the combination of the technical paths of the digital carriers' generation, circulation, transaction, and traceability of multiple parties, which makes it difficult to manage the ownerships at a fine granularity. For the traceability of data asset ownership, under the complex chain of cross-domain flow of data, it is difficult to guarantee the source of derivative data carriers and pan-intelligent derivative applications. The research proposed in this chapter aims to synthesize the data assets from three aspects: credible and usable identity, controllable ownership management, and manageable data sources.

3.2 Trusted and Usable Data Identity

Aiming at the problem that data exist in a special form and the ownership is difficult to be guaranteed due to the characteristics of non-physicality, replicability and processability, this part of the research establishes a digital assetization transformation model and researches on the technology of generating tradable digital assets with a high degree of identifiability and uniqueness. In view of the illegal tampering, privacy leakage, and data poisoning and other problems faced by data carriers in the untrustworthy domain, research on anti-identity mark removal technology and stable digital asset identifier fusion technology. Since digital assets are encapsulated digital assets containing identifiers, how to quantify the impact of perturbations on the initial encapsulated data carriers and accurately identify the identifiers of the data carriers is the main challenge for the generation of identity-stabilized digital asset carriers after replication, processing, processing, and attacks in the data circulation through the untrustworthy domain.

According to the watermarking characteristics, there are two main types of embedded watermarking methods: parameter embedded watermarking and trigger driven watermarking. Parameter embedded watermarking [9,39,65] is a technique that embeds specific copyright information into the parameters of a model to protect the owner's rights. The key lies in the fact that deep neural networks have multiple local optimal points during model training. Thus it is possible to transfer from one local optimum to another by modifying the parameters of the model with less functional degradation. At the same time, the redundancy of the model parameter space makes it possible to embed watermarking.

Parameter embedded watermarking is an intrusive solution. Watermarking involves embedding owner identity information or identifiers into parameters or functions of the model. The identifiers can be extracted and verified through specialized decoders or algorithms. The watermark consists of specific activation patterns that require specific keys for decryption and verification. The parameter embedded watermarking is inspired by multimedia digital watermarking techniques.

However, there are significant differences between model watermarking and traditional digital watermarking techniques. In digital watermarking techniques, the owner can only embed the watermark into the static content of the multimedia. In contrast, in deep neural network watermarking techniques, in addition to static content, owners can embed watermarks into the model's functionality. the representative approaches [42,54] are regularization techniques. The basic idea is to add a special regular function $\mathcal{L}_r$ to the original loss function $\mathcal{L}_0$. The watermark information (k, b) is embedded into the original model m by means of model fine-tuning or model retraining, so that the value obtained by the subsequent extraction function $E(k, W_p)$ is as close as possible to the validation information b. This can be defined as:

$$\min_{\boldsymbol{W}} \mathcal{L}_0(m(\mathbf{X}; \boldsymbol{W}), \mathbf{Y}) + \lambda \mathcal{L}_r\left(E\left(\mathbf{k}; W_p\right), \boldsymbol{b}\right) \tag{7}$$

where $W_p \in W$ refers to a particular set of vectorized parameters in W that are specifically used to extract watermark information. k refers to the secret key of the watermarking. λ is an adjustable parameter.

The watermarking regulariser can take the form of a binary cross-entropy function with the following expression:

$$\mathcal{L}_r\left(E\left(\mathbf{k}; W_p\right), \boldsymbol{b}\right) = \boldsymbol{b} \log(y_i) + (1 - \boldsymbol{b}) \log\left(1 - y_i\right)) \tag{8}$$

where

$$y_i = \sigma(kW_p) \tag{9}$$

and $\sigma(\cdot)$ denotes the sigmoid function. In the verification phase, the verification message b' corresponding to the model is extracted using the key matrix k. Through comparing with the verification message pair, if $dist(b', b) < \mathcal{E}$, it is proved that the extracted validation information is identified as the original embedded model watermark. $dist(\cdot)$ denotes the function evaluating the difference of the verification message and $\mathcal{E}$ is the predefined threshold.

Trigger-driven watermarking [3,22,25,35] is to add special paradigms or model backdoors or construct adversarial samples [26] during model training. To address the limitation that model-related parameters will be exposed during watermark extraction, some papers propose zero-bit watermarking to accommodate black-box scenarios [3,31,33,69]. These studies propose various methods for producing watermark images and labels, collectively referred to as the trigger set. This trigger set is employed to subtly adjust the decision boundary of the pre-trained model to incorporate the watermark. The presence of the watermark is ascertained by querying the distant model with the watermark images and applying a threshold to the accuracy on the trigger set. The technical basis for this is mainly adversarial samples and model backdoors.

Model Backdoor is an attack technique against machine learning models where an attacker can trick the model into producing incorrect output by injecting specific backdoor samples. The attack causes the model to trust pre-defined backdoor inputs, allowing the attacker to use the model with the backdoor to obtain pre-defined outputs in a subsequent testing or deployment phase. In the context of model watermarking, the model owner can introduce specific backdoor samples during the training phase of the model. These backdoor samples serve as a sign for verifying the ownership of the model. Under specific samples, the model presents predefined watermarking information. Model owner injects backdoor samples during the training phase. The validation phase uses the backdoor sample as a key. The ownership is verified by accessing the model's for querying.

The adversary incorporates the poisoned dataset $D_p = (X_p, Y_p)$ with the clean training set $D_c = (X_c, Y_c)$ of the model for training, causing the model to generate a backdoor. As for input samples with backdoor triggers, the model will classify the data into the target category y_i specified by the attacker without affecting the normal performance of the model. Taking the image as an example, the attacker adds a specific pattern or perturbation as a backdoor trigger ∇ to the original image x_i. The process is as follows:

$$x_i + \nabla = x_i \odot (1 - m) + \nabla \odot m \tag{10}$$

$\odot$ denotes element-wise product. m refers to image mask. m, x_i, ∇ are of the same size. The value of 1 means that the image pixel is replaced by the corresponding position c, and 0 means that the pixel remains unchanged. After the attacker attack can be expressed by the following equation:

$$\min \sum_{x \in X} \mathcal{L}(y_t, f_{w^*}(x + \nabla)) \tag{11}$$

X refers to All data from the sample input space. W^* denotes the parameters for model training using poisoned data. $\mathcal{L}(\cdot)$ is the loss function. The optimisation objective of the training process can be expressed as follows:

$$\min_{w} \sum_{(x_c,y_c)\in D_c,(x_p,y_p)\in D_p} \mathcal{L}(y_c, f_w(x_c)) + l(y_p, f_w(x_p)) \tag{12}$$

Model backdoor attacks can ensure the accuracy of benign test samples while identifying the trigger's predicted samples with attacker-specified labels. During the training process, the model owner injects backdoor samples into the model, serving as a key for identity verification. If the obtained accuracy is below a certain threshold, it proves that they are the owner of the model. Some approaches also employ black-box testing as a preliminary method for detecting model infringement. Once there is evidence of potential infringement, the suspected model is then handed over to authoritative parties for further investigation, utilizing white-box techniques to extract the model's identity information.

3.3 Controllable Ownership Management

Aiming at the problems of ownership conflict and fine-grained ownership management of data carriers observed in different domains under the zero-trust transaction mode of cross-network and cross-domain [23], this part of the research establishes the theory of componentized modeling of identity and ownership of data carriers, and researches the ownership separation method and fine-grained ownership management mechanism of data carriers in the aspects of permissionized data carrier generation, cross-domain authorization mechanism of carriers, and chained dynamic carrier authority management [19], etc. Based on these researches, cross-domain data identity unified modeling technology, identity tenure credible separation technology, to protect the right to privacy, the right to forget, the right to know at the same time, refine the right to use, quantify the ownership, standardize the right to exploration, determine the right to responsibility.

Since the security subject, protection object and authorization target of different tenures of data carriers are different, and the separation of each tenure relies on the combination of technical paths of generation, circulation, transaction and traceability of digital carriers, how to carry out credible segmentation and credible authorization of the tenures of digital assets is the main challenge of the fine-grained tenure management mechanism of data carriers. Some watermarking methods fuse watermarks with model components during distribution. These methods fine-tunes variational autoencoders to embed watermarks into all generated outputs. Passport-based watermarking involves adding a passport branch to the model or embedding passport layers into the model's structure. This approach ensures that unauthorized users without the correct passport cannot obtain correct inference results or modify the protected model. Fan et al. [18] proposes a new passport-based DNN ownership verification scheme to prevent ambiguity attack. The specific method is to add a Passport layer after the convolutional layer. The scale factor γ and bias offset term β both depend on the convolutional kernel W_p and the specified Passport P. It can be described by the following equation:

$$\mathbf{O}^l(\mathbf{X}_p) = \gamma^l \mathbf{X}_p^l + \beta^l = \gamma^l(\mathbf{W}_p^l * \mathbf{X}_c^l) + \beta^l, \tag{13}$$

$$\gamma^l = \mathrm{Avg}(\mathbf{W}_p^l * \mathbf{P}_\gamma^l), \quad \beta^l = \mathrm{Avg}(\mathbf{W}_p^l * \mathbf{P}_\beta^l), \tag{14}$$

In the equation, $*$ represents the convolution operation, l represents the layer number, X_p represents the input to the conveyor layer, and X_c represents the input to the convolutional layer. $O(\cdot)$ denotes the linear transformation of the output, while $\mathbf{P}_\gamma^l$ and $\mathbf{P}_\beta^l$ are passports used to derive the scaling factor and bias term.

3.4 Traceable Data Sources

Aiming at the problem that the source of derived data carriers is difficult to be guaranteed under the complex chain of cross-domain data flow, [12,32,61,66] focus on the traceability mechanism of derivatives of data carriers aims at the generation of potentially infringing derivatives, malicious digital twins and the illegal output of pan-derivative intelligent applications. Tree-ring [60] and ZoDiac [70] propose random seed modification watermarks, which show significant advantages in dealing with various processing attacks [4], which is beneficial for model management and tracing. Stable Signature [20] and FSwatermark [64] effectively integrate the watermark at the final generation stage. Further research is still required for investigating other permissions and implementing fine-grained tracing mechanisms.

Under the complex multi-level cross-domain network [34,47,53], all kinds of upper layer applications under the cross-domain network will integrate multiple data carriers to generate data carriers through intelligent computing [24,29,50].

Traceability is a core challenge for the credible traceability technology and regulatory mechanism of data carriers. Data validation focuses on the circulation of data, including its generation, use, transmission, and application in different scenarios [10]. Data security aims to prevent leakage, tampering, or loss, ensuring protection against unauthorized access, modification, or destruction [36]. Corroboration serves as the technical means, while security is the goal. Security issues arise at each stage of data circulation. Improving data security involves methods such as encryption [7], access control [27], and blockchain [62].

Authorization of Digital Assets is more of a legal issue that requires legal and instrumental support, including data protection laws and privacy regulations [52], which aim to ensure the legitimacy [28], privacy and security of data.

4 Intelligent Distribution of Digital Assets

Sharing digital assets is a very important topic in technology today. Researchers are trying to find better ways to move and share different kinds of digital items safely and quickly. In the past, people used centralized systems, but these systems often had problems like being slow or not very safe. However, new technologies like blockchain, distributed file systems, and AI-driven policy engines have brought many new tools to improve this process. In this part, we will look at some of the most important technological changes and how they help make digital asset sharing more efficient and smarter.

4.1 Efficient Distribution Mechanisms Through Schema Validation

It is very important to check whether a deal is allowed and if it has the right address. Zhu et al. [72] introduced a system called BCDB-A. This system makes transactions faster by checking them earlier and at the schema level. It removes bad transactions before they reach the more expensive parts of the system, like the consensus or execution stage. This helps reduce the system work.

When asset schemas and validation code are added, the system can check whether each transaction is in the correct form and follows the correct rules. For example, the system will stop the transfer before it goes any further when someone tries to send a Non-Transferable Asset (NTA). By stopping wrong actions early, the system saves time and works better overall. A system such as BigChainDB makes it extremely easy to manage assets across types of projects.

Concurrently the use of a model for the assets and code blocks for validation helps in verifying transactions based on the predetermined structural as well as semantic rules. Then, if the transfer type transaction is the kind of NTA (Non Transferable asset) assets, it must be destroyed at the beginning. This early error reduces consensus stage load and hence prevents excessive loading of the system. Bridging these mechanisms with existing solutions like BigChainDB shows that they can make asset management for different use-cases easier.

4.2 Policy-Embedded Asset Models

To better manage and control digital assets, some studies have proposed policy-embedded asset models. Anonymous [5] categorizes assets into Functional Assets (FA) and NTA. FA makes sure that no one can have more than one main health insurance policy at the same time. NTA, on the other hand, makes sure assets can't be transferred by default, so you don't need to add extra rules for access control. This design simplifies development processes and enhances system reliability by reducing runtime errors. It also makes it easier for developers because they can just set the rules directly instead of writing special functions to make sure everything follows the same guidelines.

Suppose that a person is not allowed to keep more than one copy of certain rights or special benefits. These kinds of rules can be clearly written into the system so that the computer can follow them automatically. It makes smart contracts easier to write and helps keep them simple and easy to manage.

To protect people's privacy, for example, to check data while it is still hidden without showing any personal information, we can use special ways of protecting data, like homomorphic encryption [8]. Using these methods can make digital asset systems more secure and faster.

4.3 Towards Reusable Smart Asset Constructs

Although smart contracts are flexible and can describe how assets should behave, some problems have been found. Nazir et al. [44] pointed out that smart contracts often have repeated code, are hard to reuse, and sometimes do not clearly explain what they do. To fix this problem, Cheng et al. [14] introduced a new smart asset framework. In this system, developers can use ready-made templates for assets and also set clear rules at the start. This lets programmers say things like "this item cannot be changed" or "only one person can own this," and the system will check those rules before anything happens. Developers no longer need to write many lines of code to stop illegal transfers. The system will stop it by itself. This reduces copying code and means there is less need to change it later.

Now, artificial intelligence is also helping with managing digital assets. By looking at old data, AI can find patterns and guess future trends. This helps people make better decisions about where to put their resources, as shown in AI and blockchain and other examples. For instance, machine learning can find how assets are used and give advice on how to use them better. When companies use AI in their management, they can become more efficient and react faster to changes in the market.

4.4 Interoperability Technologies Across Platforms

It is also very important to let digital assets work across different platforms. Being able to move and use digital items freely from one system to another is really useful. Ren et al. [49] explain how tools like HTLCs allow people to exchange digital assets across different blockchains without needing to trust someone else. Tools like distributed key management provide extra security features like group signatures and multi-signature wallets [15]. All these technologies help connect different systems and make them stronger. They allow digital assets to move safely and openly between platforms.

Decentralized exchanges, or DEXs, let people trade assets directly with each other instead of through big companies. Smart contracts handle the trades automatically based on set rules. The network checks that everything is done correctly. This kind of system gives users more freedom and makes them feel safer using digital assets [16]. As more and more digital items appear online, being able to connect different systems becomes even more important.

4.5 Security and Privacy Considerations

When dealing with digital assets, safety and privacy are very important, especially if the information is personal. One way to protect user privacy is called differential privacy. It allows useful analysis to be done without showing private details [17]. The practice of adding random numbers to data sets makes it easier to keep personal information private; you can't tell exactly who is in the data. In this way, it is still collecting a meaningful overall trend but not anyone's specific information. This will be of great interest in the financial and healthcare industries, which have to deal with high degree of regulatory requirements.

Zero-Knowledge Proofs (ZKPs) are a method of demonstrating something's truth without revealing any of the details of how it's true. ZKPs have successfully been integrated into different blockchain-based systems for improving privacy and confidentiality [51]. ZKPs allow people to make private payments within the Bitcoin network, and Zerocash does so. It keeps the details of the transactions hidden but still makes sure they're valid and legitimate. These cryptographic methods are really important for keeping digital assets safe and making sure everything follows the necessary laws and rules.

5 Technical Framework

We use the principle of *Authentication–Authorization–Application* to establish a technical framework for digital asset circulation based in Fig. 1. It addresses core challenges of ownership authentication, dynamic authorization, and cross-industry applications by integrating technical solution toolkits.

5.1 Authentication Module

Authentication module constructs a third-party ownership verification system for different entities, including data owner, operator, and user. Digital watermarking (DW) helps data owners embed decentralized identifiers (DID) tags into the original digital assets to create indelible identifiers. These DID tags represent globally unique identities, which can solve the problem of cross-platform ownership identification. Data operators use ZKP to verify the ownership of assets, ensuring that all operations do not expose sensitive data. Access permissions of data users are bound to asset hashes through blockchain smart contracts. They are stored immutably on a distributed ledger and form an undeniable source chain.

5.2 Authorization Module

Authorization module implements hierarchical authorization of permissions. Data ownership is granted to others by the data owner through watermarks and DID chains. Differential privacy (DP) and other forms of protection are used to comply with legal requirements [1] and ensure immutable owner control. Data operators using attribute based encryption (ABE) to finely control data management rights and dynamically decrypt data based on user attributes and policies defined by the logical tree. Data users get data usage rights through smart contracts. Entire authorization workflow triggers smart contracts to verify attributes, perform data anonymization, execute authorization policies, and publish verifiable credentials.

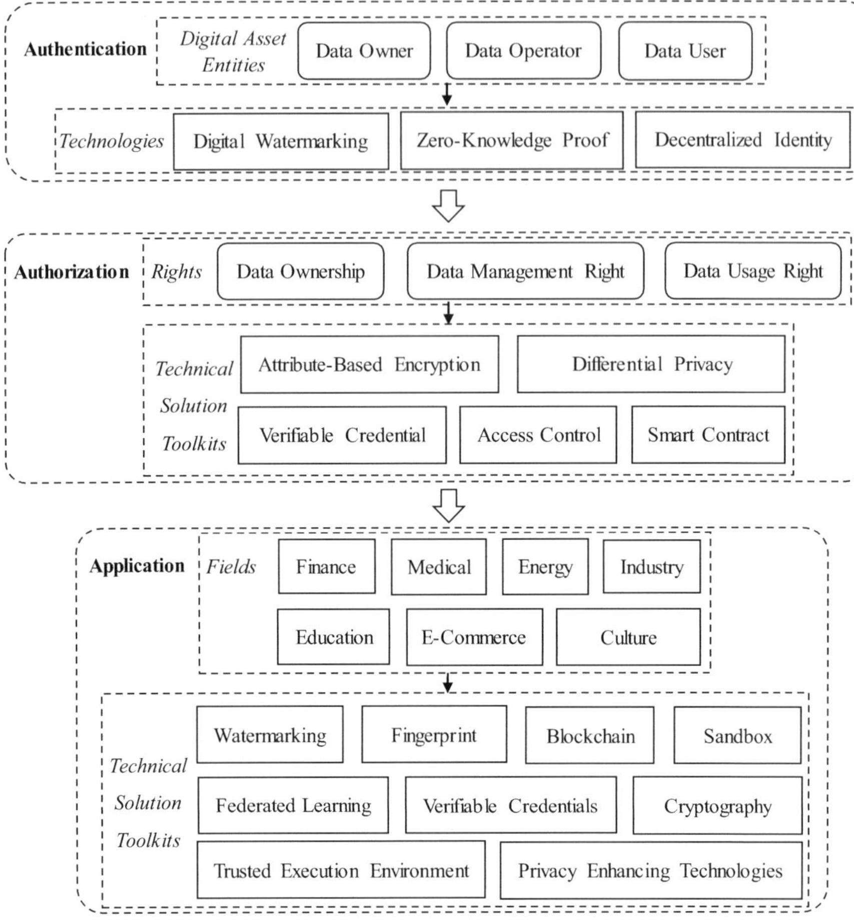

Fig. 1. Technical Framework of Digital Assets.

5.3 Application Module

The application module adopts sandboxes and domain specific toolkits, used in fields such as finance, healthcare, and industry. Federated Learning (FL) [55–58] enables cross-institutional economic model training without the need for raw data transmission. This process complies with data security laws in the financial sector. Medical genomic data can be processed in a trusted execution environment (TEE) and supplemented with DP to prevent patient information from being re-identified. Industrial equipment binds hardware MAC addresses to data hashes and achieves leak traceability through fingerprint recognition. Pre-execute watermark verification and policy checking in a sandbox environment, and output the value of digital assets. This value is quantified through Shapley value modeling and fed back in real-time to the asset pricing system.

5.4 Technical Integration and Innovations

The technical framework we proposed has three key innovations, including (i) we combine digital watermarking with ZKP to establish tamper-proof asset DID binding. We maintain content confidentiality and achieve provable ownership anchoring. (ii) We use DP and ABE dynamic strategies to achieve context-aware and restricted distribution of data assets. (iii) We deploy a sandbox with Shapley value feedback loop to optimize asset value circulation across industries.

This framework differs from static solutions in that it implements penetration policy control. Authorization constraints persist throughout the data asset circulation cycle. Its design of modular connectiondesign meets specific requirements. Our AAA framework has laid the technological foundation for the high-speed digital asset market by simultaneously addressing the issues of ownership ambiguity and low application circulation efficiency.

6 Conclusion

This survey has conducted a thorough review of the latest developments in digital asset authentication and distribution. We have summarized the key challenges in digital asset value circulation from multiple perspectives and explored possible solutions to overcome these issues. Based on this analysis, we propose a technical framework for digital asset value circulation, aiming to outline a clear path forward for future research and industry development.

Acknowledgments. This work is supported by the National Natural Science Foundation of China (Grant No.s U24B20146, 62372044), and Beijing Municipal Science and Technology Commission Project (Z241100009124008).

References

1. GDPR: General Data Protection Regulation — gdpreu.org. https://www.gdpreu.org/, Accessed 14 June 2025
2. The world's most valuable resource is no longer oil, but data. https://www.economist.com/leaders/2017/05/06/theworlds-most-valuable-resource-is-no-longer-oil-butdata, Accessed 14 June 2025
3. Adi, Y., Baum, C., Cisse, M., Pinkas, B., Keshet, J.: Turning your weakness into a strength: watermarking deep neural networks by backdooring. In: 27th USENIX Security Symposium (USENIX Security 18), pp. 1615–1631 (2018)
4. An, B., et al.: Benchmarking the robustness of image watermarks. arXiv preprint arXiv:2401.08573 (2024)
5. Anonymous: Smart asset modeling with policy-driven behavior. Symmetry **16**(1287), 1–15 (2024)
6. Asudeh, A., Nargesian, F.: Towards distribution-aware query answering in data markets. Proc. VLDB Endowment **15**(11), 3137–3144 (2022)
7. Atadoga, A., Farayola, O.A., Ayinla, B.S., Amoo, O.O., Abrahams, T.O., Osasona, F.: A comparative review of data encryption methods in the USA and Europe. Comput. Sci. IT Res. J. **5**(2), 447–460 (2024)

8. Back, A.: Bitcoins with homomorphic value(validatable but encrypted). Bitcointalk (2013)
9. Bansal, A., et al.: Certified neural network watermarks with randomized smoothing. In: International Conference on Machine Learning, pp. 1450–1465. PMLR (2022)
10. Bauer, A., et al.: Comprehensive exploration of synthetic data generation: a survey. arXiv preprint arXiv:2401.02524 (2024)
11. Bertran, M., Tang, S., Roth, A., Kearns, M., Morgenstern, J.H., Wu, S.Z.: Scalable membership inference attacks via quantile regression. Adv. Neural. Inf. Process. Syst. **36**, 314–330 (2023)
12. Bui, T., Agarwal, S., Yu, N., Collomosse, J.: Rosteals: Robust steganography using autoencoder latent space. In: Proceedings of the IEEE/CVF Conference on Computer Vision and Pattern Recognition, pp. 933–942 (2023)
13. Castro Fernandez, R.: Protecting data markets from strategic buyers. In: Proceedings of the 2022 International Conference on Management of Data, pp. 1755–1769 (2022)
14. Cheng, Y., et al.: A framework for reusable smart asset policies. In: Proceedings of IEEE ICWS, pp. 123–130 (2024)
15. Dagher, G.G., et al.: Provisions: privacy-preserving smart contracts for decentralized asset management. IEEE Trans. Serv. Comput. **11**(2), 346–359 (2018)
16. Dai, C.: Dex: A dapp for the decentralized marketplace. Blockchain Crypt. Curr. **95** (2020)
17. Dankar, F., Emam, K.: The application of differential privacy to health data. In: Proceedings of the 2012 Joint EDBT/ICDT Workshops, pp. 158–166 (2012)
18. Fan, L., Ng, K.W., Chan, C.S.: Rethinking deep neural network ownership verification: embedding passports to defeat ambiguity attacks. Adv. Neural Inf. Process. Syst. **32** (2019)
19. Feng, W., et al.: Aqualora: Toward white-box protection for customized stable diffusion models via watermark lora. arXiv preprint arXiv:2405.11135 (2024)
20. Fernandez, P., Couairon, G., Jégou, H., Douze, M., Furon, T.: The stable signature: rooting watermarks in latent diffusion models. In: Proceedings of the IEEE/CVF International Conference on Computer Vision, pp. 22466–22477 (2023)
21. Fernandez, R.C., Subramaniam, P., Franklin, M.J.: Data market platforms: trading data assets to solve data problems. Proc. VLDB Endow. **13**(11), 1933–1947 (2020). http://www.vldb.org/pvldb/vol13/p1933-fernandez.pdf
22. Gai, K., Wang, D., Yu, J., Wang, M., Zhu, L., Wu, Q.: Mfl-owner: ownership protection for multi-modal federated learning via orthogonal transform watermark. In: AAAI-25, Sponsored by the Association for the Advancement of Artificial Intelligence, February 25–March 4, 2025, Philadelphia, PA, USA, pp. 3049–3058. AAAI Press (2025). https://doi.org/10.1609/AAAI.V39I3.32313
23. Gai, K., Wang, Z., Yu, J., Zhu, L.: MUFTI: multi-domain distillation-based heterogeneous federated continuous learning. IEEE Trans. Inf. Forensics Secur. **20**, 2721–2733 (2025). https://doi.org/10.1109/TIFS.2025.3542246
24. Gal, R., et al.: An image is worth one word: Personalizing text-to-image generation using textual inversion. arXiv preprint arXiv:2208.01618 (2022)
25. Goldwasser, S., Kim, M.P., Vaikuntanathan, V., Zamir, O.: Planting undetectable backdoors in machine learning models. In: 2022 IEEE 63rd Annual Symposium on Foundations of Computer Science (FOCS), pp. 931–942. IEEE (2022)
26. Goodfellow, I.J., Shlens, J., Szegedy, C.: Explaining and harnessing adversarial examples. arXiv preprint arXiv:1412.6572 (2014)

27. Han, D., Zhu, Y., Li, D., Liang, W., Souri, A., Li, K.C.: A blockchain-based auditable access control system for private data in service-centric IoT environments. IEEE Trans. Industr. Inf. **18**(5), 3530–3540 (2021)
28. Hou, J., Qu, L., Shi, W.: A survey on internet of things security from data perspectives. Comput. Netw. **148**, 295–306 (2019)
29. Hu, E.J., et al.: Lora: Low-rank adaptation of large language models. arXiv preprint arXiv:2106.09685 (2021)
30. Koutroumpis, P., Leiponen, A.: Understanding the value of (big) data. In: Hu, X., et al. (eds.) 2013 IEEE International Conference on Big Data (IEEE BigData 2013), 6-9 October 2013, Santa Clara, CA, USA, pp. 38–42. IEEE Computer Society (2013). https://doi.org/10.1109/BIGDATA.2013.6691691
31. Le Merrer, E., Perez, P., Trédan, G.: Adversarial frontier stitching for remote neural network watermarking. Neural Comput. Appl. **32**, 9233–9244 (2020)
32. Lei, L., Gai, K., Yu, J., Zhu, L., Wu, Q.: Secure and efficient watermarking for latent diffusion models in model distribution scenarios. CoRR abs/2502.13345 (2025). https://doi.org/10.48550/ARXIV.2502.13345
33. Li, J., Yang, Y., Wu, Z., Vydiswaran, V., Xiao, C.: Chatgpt as an attack tool: Stealthy textual backdoor attack via blackbox generative model trigger. arXiv preprint arXiv:2304.14475 (2023)
34. Li, Y., Yu, J., Gai, K., Liu, B., Xiong, G., Wu, Q.: T2vindexer: a generative video indexer for efficient text-video retrieval. In: Proceedings of the 32nd ACM International Conference on Multimedia, MM 2024, Melbourne, VIC, Australia, 28 October 2024–1 November 2024, pp. 3955–3963. ACM (2024). https://doi.org/10.1145/3664647.3680673
35. Li, Y., Bai, Y., Jiang, Y., Yang, Y., Xia, S.T., Li, B.: Untargeted backdoor watermark: towards harmless and stealthy dataset copyright protection. Adv. Neural. Inf. Process. Syst. **35**, 13238–13250 (2022)
36. Li, Y., Wang, H., Barni, M.: A survey of deep neural network watermarking techniques. Neurocomputing **461**, 171–193 (2021)
37. Liang, F., Yu, W., An, D., Yang, Q., Fu, X., Zhao, W.: A survey on big data market: Pricing, trading and protection. IEEE Access **6**, 15132–15154 (2018). https://doi.org/10.1109/ACCESS.2018.2806881
38. Lin, J., Huang, Z., Tang, Y.: Pricing for data assets based on data quality, quantity and utility on the perspective of consumer heterogeneity. IEEE Trans. Knowl. Data Eng. **37**(6), 3641–3652 (2025). https://doi.org/10.1109/TKDE.2025.3551401
39. Luo, X., Zhan, R., Chang, H., Yang, F., Milanfar, P.: Distortion agnostic deep watermarking. In: Proceedings of the IEEE/CVF Conference on Computer Vision and Pattern Recognition, pp. 13548–13557 (2020)
40. Miao, Y., Gai, K., Yu, J., Tan, Y., Zhu, L., Meng, W.: Blockchain-empowered keyword searchable provable data possession for large similar data. IEEE Trans. Inf. Forensics Secur. **20**, 1374–1389 (2025). https://doi.org/10.1109/TIFS.2024.3516563
41. Miao, Y., Gai, K., Zhu, L., Choo, K.R., Vaidya, J.: Blockchain-based shared data integrity auditing and deduplication. IEEE Trans. Dependable Secur. Comput. **21**(4), 3688–3703 (2024). https://doi.org/10.1109/TDSC.2023.3335413
42. Nagai, Y., Uchida, Y., Sakazawa, S., Satoh, S.: Digital watermarking for deep neural networks. Int. J. Multimedia Inf. Retrieval **7**, 3–16 (2018)
43. Nagrecha, K., Kumar, A.: Saturn: An optimized data system for multi-large-model deep learning workloads. Proc. VLDB Endowment **17**(4) (2023)
44. Nazir, S., et al.: Challenges in blockchain-based digital asset management. J. Blockchain Res. **10**(2), 45–60 (2022)

45. Pei, J., Fernandez, R.C., Yu, X.: Data and ai model markets: opportunities for data and model sharing, discovery, and integration. Proc. VLDB Endowment **16**(12), 3872–3873 (2023)
46. Pei, J., Zhu, F., Cong, Z., Luo, X., Liu, H., Mu, X.: Data pricing and data asset governance in the AI era. In: Zhu, F., Ooi, B.C., Miao, C. (eds.) KDD '21: The 27th ACM SIGKDD Conference on Knowledge Discovery and Data Mining, Virtual Event, Singapore, August 14–18, 2021. pp. 4058–4059. ACM (2021). https://doi.org/10.1145/3447548.3470818
47. Qu, X., et al.: Visual-semantic decomposition and partial alignment for document-based zero-shot learning. In: Proceedings of the 32nd ACM International Conference on Multimedia, MM 2024, Melbourne, VIC, Australia, 28 October 2024–1 November 2024, pp. 4581–4590. ACM (2024). https://doi.org/10.1145/3664647.3680829
48. Ramakrishnan, R., et al.: Azure data lake store: A hyperscale distributed file service for big data analytics. In: Proceedings of the 2017 ACM International Conference on Management of Data, SIGMOD Conference 2017, Chicago, IL, USA, May 14–19, 2017, pp. 51–63. ACM (2017). https://doi.org/10.1145/3035918.3056100
49. Ren, L., et al.: Cross-chain technologies for interoperable digital assets. Sensors **23**(4114), 1–18 (2024)
50. Ruiz, N., Li, Y., Jampani, V., Pritch, Y., Rubinstein, M., Aberman, K.: Dreambooth: Fine tuning text-to-image diffusion models for subject-driven generation. In: Proceedings of the IEEE/CVF Conference on Computer Vision and Pattern Recognition, pp. 22500–22510 (2023)
51. Sasson, E., et al.: Zerocash: Decentralized anonymous payments from bitcoin. In: Proceedings of the 2014 IEEE Symposium on Security and Privacy, pp. 459–474 (2014)
52. Stojanov, R., Gramatikov, S., Mishkovski, I., Trajanov, D.: Linked data authorization platform. IEEE Access **6**, 1189–1213 (2017)
53. Tang, Y., et al.: Context-i2w: Mapping images to context-dependent words for accurate zero-shot composed image retrieval. In: Thirty-Eighth AAAI Conference on Artificial Intelligence, AAAI 2024, Thirty-Sixth Conference on Innovative Applications of Artificial Intelligence, IAAI 2024, Fourteenth Symposium on Educational Advances in Artificial Intelligence, EAAI 2014, February 20–27, 2024, Vancouver, Canada, pp. 5180–5188. AAAI Press (2024). https://doi.org/10.1609/AAAI.V38I6.28324
54. Uchida, Y., Nagai, Y., Sakazawa, S., Satoh, S.: Embedding watermarks into deep neural networks. In: Proceedings of the 2017 ACM on international Conference on Multimedia Retrieval, pp. 269–277 (2017)
55. Wang, S., Gai, K., Yu, J., Zhang, Z., Zhu, L.: Pravfed: practical heterogeneous vertical federated learning via representation learning. IEEE Trans. Inf. Forensics Secur. **20**, 2693–2705 (2025)
56. Wang, S., Gai, K., Yu, J., Zhu, L.: Bdvfl: Blockchain-based decentralized vertical federated learning. In: 2023 IEEE International Conference on Data Mining (ICDM), pp. 628–637. China (2023)
57. Wang, S., et al.: Rafls: Rdp-based adaptive federated learning with shuffle model. IEEE Trans. Dependable Secure Comput. **22**(2), 1181–1194 (2025)
58. Wang, S., Yu, J., Gai, K., Zhu, L.: Revfed: Representation-based privacy-preserving vertical federated learning with heterogeneous models. In: International Conference on Knowledge Science, Engineering and Management, pp. 386–397. Singapore (2024)

59. Wang, W., Feizi, S.: Temporal robustness against data poisoning. Adv. Neural. Inf. Process. Syst. **36**, 47721–47734 (2023)
60. Wen, Y., Kirchenbauer, J., Geiping, J., Goldstein, T.: Tree-ring watermarks: fingerprints for diffusion images that are invisible and robust. arXiv preprint arXiv:2305.20030 (2023)
61. Wen, Y., Kirchenbauer, J., Geiping, J., Goldstein, T.: Tree-rings watermarks: Invisible fingerprints for diffusion images. Adv. Neural Inf. Process. Syst. **36** (2024)
62. Wylde, V., et al.: Cybersecurity, data privacy and blockchain: a review. SN Comput. Sci. **3**(2), 127 (2022)
63. Xia, H., et al.: Equitable data valuation meets the right to be forgotten in model markets. Proc. VLDB Endowment **16**(11) (2023)
64. Xiong, C., Qin, C., Feng, G., Zhang, X.: Flexible and secure watermarking for latent diffusion model. In: Proceedings of the 31st ACM International Conference on Multimedia, pp. 1668–1676 (2023)
65. Yang, P., Lao, Y., Li, P.: Robust watermarking for deep neural networks via bi-level optimization. In: Proceedings of the IEEE/CVF International Conference on Computer Vision, pp. 14841–14850 (2021)
66. Yang, Z., Zeng, K., Chen, K., Fang, H., Zhang, W., Yu, N.: Gaussian shading: Provable performance-lossless image watermarking for diffusion models. In: Proceedings of the IEEE/CVF Conference on Computer Vision and Pattern Recognition, pp. 12162–12171 (2024)
67. Yiu, M.L., Assent, I., Jensen, C.S., Kalnis, P.: Outsourced similarity search on metric data assets. IEEE Trans. Knowl. Data Eng. **24**(2), 338–352 (2012). https://doi.org/10.1109/TKDE.2010.222
68. Yu, H., Zhang, M.: Data pricing strategy based on data quality. Comput. Ind. Eng. **112**, 1–10 (2017). https://doi.org/10.1016/J.CIE.2017.08.008
69. Zhang, J., et al.: Protecting intellectual property of deep neural networks with watermarking. In: Proceedings of the 2018 on Asia Conference on Computer and Communications Security, pp. 159–172 (2018)
70. Zhang, L., Liu, X., Martin, A.V., Bearfield, C.X., Brun, Y., Guan, H.: Robust image watermarking using stable diffusion. arXiv preprint arXiv:2401.04247 (2024)
71. Zhou, T., Luo, Y., Ren, S., Xu, X.: Nnsplitter: an active defense solution for DNN model via automated weight obfuscation. In: International Conference on Machine Learning, pp. 42614–42624. PMLR (2023)
72. Zhu, L., et al.: Towards a smart asset model for digital assets on blockchains. arXiv preprint arXiv:2406.00000 (2024)
73. Zhu, R., et al.: Pilotscope: steering databases with machine learning drivers. Proc. VLDB Endowment **17**(5), 980–993 (2024)
74. Zong, W., Chow, Y.W., Susilo, W., Baek, J., Kim, J., Camtepe, S.: Ipremover: a generative model inversion attack against deep neural network fingerprinting and watermarking. In: Proceedings of the AAAI Conference on Artificial Intelligence, vol. 38, pp. 7837–7845 (2024)

A Robust Stablizing Transformer with Deep Reinforcement Learning for Risk-Adjusted Equity Trading Strategies

Zhenjiang Chen[1], Jun Zheng[1], Pei-Gen Ye[1], Ning Shi[2], and Lishuang Pan[2(✉)]

[1] School of Cyberspace Science and Technology, Beijing Institute of Technology, Beijing, China
{3120221257,zhengjun,ypgmhxy}@bit.edu.cn

[2] Hebei Key Laboratory of IoT Blockchain Integration, Shijiazhuang University, Shijiazhuang, China
shining@sjzc.edu.cn, plshuang123@163.com

Abstract. With the development of financial markets, an increasing number of financial practitioners are engaging in stock trading activities. This trend not only enhances market vitality but also increases the uncertainty associated with portfolio risks faced by financial practitioners. This paper proposes a novel framework for risk-adjusted automated stock trading, based on the Stable Transformer model and the Proximal Policy Optimization (PPO) algorithm, to address challenges such as portfolio risks. First, a reinforcement learning environment for stock trading is constructed using historical stock trading data. Subsequently, an intelligent stock trading agent is designed using the Stable Transformer model with a shared feature extractor. Modifications are made to the original PPO algorithm to improve the training efficiency and stability of the agent, leveraging the network characteristics of the Stable Transformer. Experimental results demonstrate that this trading strategy surpasses other baseline models in its ability to mitigate portfolio risks in stock markets. Additionally, this trading strategy exhibits significant profitability, expanding the research frontiers of financial risk mitigation strategies.

Keywords: Portfolio Optimization · Stabling Transformer · Financial Risk · Reinforcement Learning

1 Introduction

In recent years, with the rapid development of financial technology (FinTech) and the evolution of machine learning methods, the application of deep reinforcement learning (DRL) in financial markets has attracted extensive attention from both academia and industry. Particularly, DRL has shown great potential in solving complex decision-making problems such as stock trading, asset

M. Yung et al. (Eds.): AIBlock 2025, LNCS 16314, pp. 94–109, 2026.
https://doi.org/10.1007/978-3-032-16168-0_6

allocation, and portfolio optimization. Compared to traditional rule-based or statistical models, DRL enables agents to learn adaptive policies through trial-and-error interactions with market environments, which is essential for handling the high volatility and non-stationarity of financial systems.

Several recent studies have demonstrated the feasibility and advantages of DRL in financial tasks. For instance, Liu et al. [1] proposed a comprehensive financial RL framework—FinRL—based on historical market data and the Stable-Baselines3 library. This framework supports various tasks, including single-stock trading, multi-asset portfolio management, and cryptocurrency analysis. Zou et al. [2] developed a trading agent by constructing cascaded LSTM-based Actor and Critic networks, trained with the Proximal Policy Optimization (PPO) algorithm, achieving competitive results in stock trading scenarios. Gao et al. [3] introduced the Stockformer model, which leverages multi-head self-attention mechanisms to encode market trends and utilizes the Soft Actor-Critic (SAC) algorithm [4] to optimize agent policies.

Despite these advances, several key challenges remain unsolved. First, traditional financial theories often rely on simplified assumptions (e.g., efficient markets, Gaussian returns), which are inconsistent with the chaotic and dynamic nature of real-world markets. Second, recurrent models such as LSTM, though widely used, often struggle to capture long-term dependencies and dynamic structural changes in high-frequency or noisy financial data. Third, while the Transformer architecture [5] has revolutionized fields such as natural language processing and time series modeling due to its powerful self-attention mechanism, its direct application to DRL tasks tends to result in training instability and poor generalization, particularly in environments with sparse or delayed rewards.

To address the above limitations, this paper proposes a novel stock trading strategy model that integrates the Stable Transformer [6]—a variant of Transformer designed for stable RL training—with the Proximal Policy Optimization (PPO) algorithm [7]. Specifically, we construct an RL trading environment using historical trading data from 32 randomly selected stocks in China's A-share market. A shared Stable Transformer-based feature extractor is used to construct the Actor and Critic networks of the agent, which allows effective modeling of long-term dependencies and inter-stock correlations. The PPO algorithm is then employed to enhance the convergence and stability of training.

The main contributions of this paper are summarized as follows:

- **Novel Architecture:** We design a Stable Transformer-based RL architecture tailored for financial time-series analysis, capable of modeling long-range temporal dependencies and complex interactions in stock markets.
- **Robust Policy Learning:** By integrating the PPO algorithm, we enhance training stability and policy robustness, which are critical for reinforcement learning in non-stationary and noisy environments such as stock trading.
- **Real-world Evaluation:** We evaluate our method on real-world historical data from the A-share market and conduct comprehensive experiments,

including ablation studies and comparisons with state-of-the-art DRL baselines.

- **Practical Insights:** Our study provides insights into how Transformer-based models can be effectively adapted and stabilized for reinforcement learning in financial contexts, bridging the gap between algorithmic finance and deep learning innovations.

2 Related Works

Deep Reinforcement Learning (DRL) has become a promising tool in quantitative finance due to its ability to model sequential decision-making under uncertainty. In the context of stock trading, DRL enables an agent to learn optimal trading strategies by interacting with a simulated or real market environment, where the agent continuously observes market states, takes trading actions (e.g., buy, sell, hold), and receives rewards based on profit, risk control, or portfolio performance.

Specifically, DRL has been widely applied to various financial tasks such as:

- **Single-stock trading:** Agents learn to maximize cumulative returns by making trading decisions for individual stocks based on price trends, technical indicators, or news signals.
- **Portfolio optimization:** DRL models can manage a group of assets dynamically by reallocating weights to balance risk and return over time.
- **Market making and arbitrage:** In high-frequency environments, DRL is used to develop policies for bid-ask spread control and exploiting price discrepancies across markets.
- **Risk-sensitive trading:** DRL frameworks incorporate reward shaping or constraints to minimize drawdowns, volatility, or Value at Risk (VaR).

Compared with traditional financial models based on static optimization or predefined rules, DRL is more flexible in handling non-stationary environments, multi-objective optimization, and large-scale data from multiple market sources.

2.1 Financial Reinforcement Learning

Research in recent years has extensively applied deep reinforcement learning methods to stock trading and portfolio management, driving advancements in areas such as portfolio optimization and financial risk management. For instance, [8] applied Deep Q-Networks (DQN) to portfolio management, significantly improving portfolio profitability while maintaining high computational efficiency. [9] proposed a hierarchical reinforcement approach to portfolio management, which incorporates two agents tasked with maximizing long-term profits and minimizing transaction costs, respectively. Alpha Stock [10], based on the Buying Winners and Selling Losers (BWSL) strategy, designed two optimization agents for purchasing selected winning assets and selling selected losing assets, using a cross-asset attention network to optimize the Sharpe ratio. Experimental analysis reveals that Alpha Stock tends to select stocks with long-term growth potential, low volatility, high intrinsic value, and undervalued market prices.

To address the dynamic nature of financial markets, [11] introduced multi-agent strategies, where each agent aims to optimize portfolios and minimize the potential adverse effects of systemic risks on portfolios. [12] proposed a multi-network model that integrates financial background information and asset states to predict economic health. Experimental results showed that the model outperforms baseline models even during financial recessions. DeepPocket [13], focused on the robustness of portfolio returns, represents asset relationships using an asset relationship graph, where nodes denote financial assets and edges signify interactions between assets. The asset relationship graph is encoded as state input for agents in an Actor-Critic algorithm. Experiments demonstrated that DeepPocket effectively mitigates market risk shocks during the COVID-19 pandemic.

2.2 Data-Driven Reinforcement Learning

Data-driven reinforcement learning refers to training reinforcement learning agents on collected datasets to learn corresponding policies. Offline reinforcement learning [14] is a method that learns policies from pre-collected static datasets without requiring real-time interaction with the environment. The core challenge of offline reinforcement learning lies in overcoming issues such as policy overestimation or suboptimal decision-making caused by data distribution shift. Common approaches include introducing policy constraints, uncertainty estimation, or value function regularization to restrict policy updates within the support range of the dataset. Offline reinforcement learning is particularly suited for scenarios where data collection costs are high or there are safety risks, such as robotic control, autonomous driving, and medical decision-making. Current research focuses on efficiently utilizing historical data while ensuring policy generalization and robustness.

Curriculum learning [15] is a machine learning paradigm inspired by the human learning process. Its core idea is to enhance model capabilities through an orderly training process that progresses from simple to complex and from easy to difficult. Typically, strategies such as task difficulty ranking, sample selection, or dynamic adjustment of learning objectives are employed to guide the model in first learning basic patterns in the data, before gradually tackling more complex patterns. This approach accelerates convergence, enhances generalization, and overcomes local optima, making it widely applicable in fields such as image classification, machine translation, and robotic control. Curriculum learning is especially effective in scenarios with significant task difficulty variation or imbalanced training data distributions. Current research priorities include automated curriculum design, task difficulty quantification, and the integration of dynamic curricula with meta-learning.

3 Methodology

This paper models the stock trading process as a Markov Decision Process (MDP), which consists of State, State Transition Equation, Action, and Reward. The Deep Reinforcement Learning (DRL) method collects trajectories through interactions between the agent and the environment, and the agent is trained using experience extracted from these trajectories. Stock data exhibit low signal-to-noise ratio and nonlinear time-series characteristics, making it difficult for a conventional MLP network to effectively capture the dynamic evolution of the stock market. To efficiently extract hidden information within stock time-series data, this paper proposes a DRL-based automated stock trading model utilizing GTrXL and PPO algorithms.

The proposed model employs GTrXL to extract stock time-series features from historical data, which are then fed into an agent constructed with an MLP network. The agent generates corresponding trading decisions, while the environment provides appropriate rewards and new states based on the agent's actions. To improve the stability and efficiency of the training process, this paper adopts the Proximal Policy Optimization (PPO) algorithm for agent training. The overall framework of the proposed model is illustrated in Figure 1.

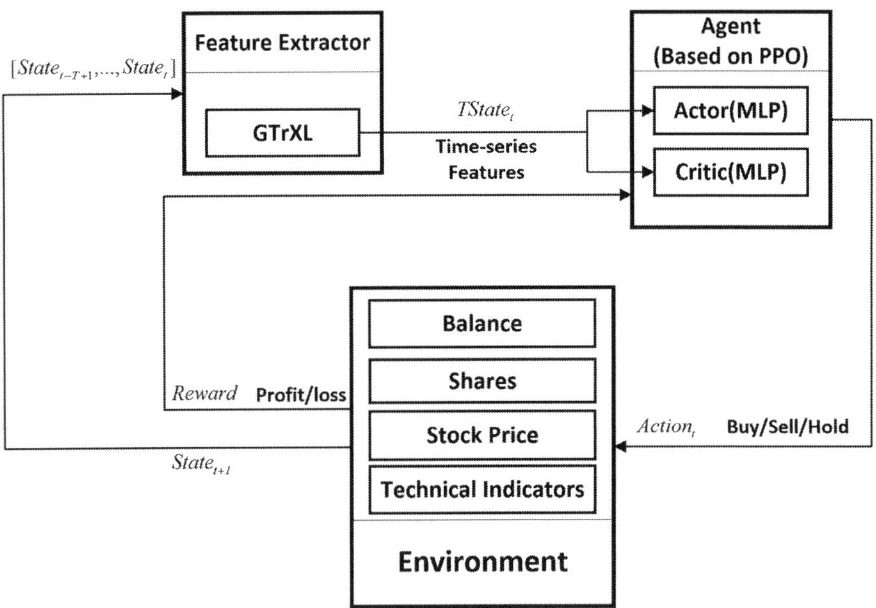

Fig. 1. Agent-environment interaction in reinforcement learning.

3.1 Environment for Stock Trading

To enhance the scalability of this study, a stock trading reinforcement learning environment was constructed based on the data-driven framework of OpenAI Gym [16]. The trading environment primarily includes attributes such as *state* space, *action* space, and *reward* function. The automated trading agent in this study focuses exclusively on 32 randomly selected stocks from the stock market.

3.1.1 State Space

To effectively utilize the Transformer model's capabilities for time series modeling and further enhance the effectiveness and robustness of the agent's stock trading strategies, the state of the agent is represented as a matrix S of shape 12×193. This matrix encapsulates the agent's observations over the past 12 days, where each observation is a 193-dimensional vector $[b_t, p_t, h_t, M_t, R_t, C_t, X_t]$, composed of the following components:

- $b_t \in \mathbb{R}_+$: Represents the account balance of the agent at time step t.
- $p_t \in \mathbb{R}_+^{32}$: Denotes the closing prices of 32 selected stocks at time step t.
- $h_t \in \mathbb{Z}_+^{32}$: Represents the quantities of shares held for each stock at time step t.
- $M_t \in \mathbb{R}^{32}$: Refers to the Moving Average Convergence Divergence (MACD) [17], a widely-used technical analysis indicator in stock, forex, and cryptocurrency markets. MACD calculates the dynamic relationship between two exponentially moving averages (EMA) of different periods, measuring the strength, direction, and potential turning points of price trends.
- $R_t \in \mathbb{R}_+^{32}$: Refers to the Relative Strength Index (RSI), a momentum oscillator used to quantify the speed and magnitude of asset price changes. RSI helps identify overbought or oversold market conditions, aiding in predicting short-term price reversal signals by calculating the relative strength of price increases versus decreases over a specific period.
- $C_t \in \mathbb{R}_+^{32}$: Refers to the Commodity Channel Index (CCI), initially developed for commodity markets but now widely applied in stocks, forex, and cryptocurrency. CCI measures the deviation of prices from their statistical average, identifying overbought or oversold conditions and potential trend reversals.
- $X_t \in \mathbb{R}^{32}$: Represents the Average Directional Index (ADX), used to quantify the strength of price trends rather than their direction. Stronger trends imply higher persistence of prices moving in a single direction.

3.1.2 Action Space

The action space is defined as a set of $2k + 1$ integers, represented as $\{-k, \ldots, -1, 0, 1, \ldots, k\}$, where k denotes the number of stocks the agent can buy or sell. Additionally, the action space satisfies the following conditions:

- The value of k is subject to an upper limit, denoted as $h_{\max}$.
- The total size of the action space is $(2k + 1)^{32}$.
- During the trading process, the action space is normalized to $[-1, 1]$.

3.1.3 Reward Function

This study defines the change in portfolio value resulting from the agent's action (e.g., buying or selling stocks) as the reward. Formally, it is expressed as:

$$\text{Return}_t(s_t, a_t, s_{t+1}) = \left(b_{t+1} + p_{t+1} \cdot h_{t+1}^{\top}\right) - \left(b_t + p_t \cdot h_t^{\top}\right) - c_t, \tag{1}$$

where c_t denotes the transaction cost.

3.2 Transformers Stabilization

The stock market is characterized by high volatility, low signal-to-noise ratio, and strong chaotic behavior. To enable the agent to learn the dynamic evolution patterns of the stock market and extract internal features of financial data, this study employs the Gated TransformerXL (GTrXL) model [6] to construct the stock trading agent. The agent's architecture, as illustrated in Fig. 2, consists of multiple Transformer blocks and Memory blocks. Each Transformer block comprises a relative multi-head self-attention mechanism (RMHA), a Gating Layer, Layer Normalization, and a Position-Wise Multi-Layer Perceptron (MLP). Based on the GTrXL model, a shared feature extractor is designed for both the Actor and Critic networks. The embedding vectors output by GTrXL are passed through a multi-layer perceptron to generate the agent's action commands and state value predictions. The shared feature extractor parameters enhance computational efficiency and training speed, ensuring that the Actor and Critic networks share the same feature space distribution. This design improves the accuracy of the agent's state value predictions and action execution.

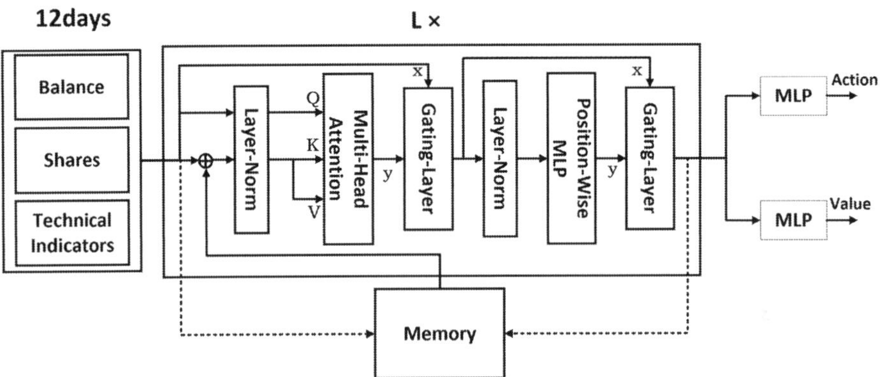

Fig. 2. Overview of Stablizing Transformer agent for stock trading. The dotted line represents memory storage.

The original Transformer model's multi-head self-attention mechanism (MHA) processes fixed-length time series as input, which limits the model's receptive field. Inspired by TransformerXL [18], this study incorporates memory components into each Transformer block. Specifically, for the l-th Transformer block, the fixed-length historical output (memory length set to 24 in this study) from the $(l-1)$-th Transformer block is fetched from the memory component. For the first Transformer block, historical states are used as memory. These memory components are concatenated with the current inputs of the l-th Transformer block along the temporal dimension to form a tensor, which undergoes layer normalization and linear projection to generate Key-Value pairs for RMHA. Meanwhile, the current inputs are directly projected via a linear layer to form Query vectors.

In the original Transformer model, absolute positional encoding is added to each token to preserve its positional information. However, the incorporation of memory modules in TransformerXL [18] preserves historical tokens, rendering absolute positional encoding incapable of representing relative positional relationships between current and historical tokens. To address this, RMHA employs relative positional encoding, which provides precise and effective representations of token-to-token relative positional relationships.

To ensure the Markov property of the reinforcement learning agent, the residual connections in the original Transformer model are replaced with gating units, further enhancing the stability of the training process.

Formally, for memory $M^{(l-1)}$ and input $E^{(l-1)}$ to the l-th GTrXL block, the computation process is as follows:

$$\begin{aligned}
\bar{Y}^{(l)} &= \text{RMHA}\left(\text{LayerNorm}\left(\left[\text{StopGrad}\left(M^{(l-1)}\right), E^{(l-1)}\right]\right)\right), \\
Y^{(l)} &= g_{\text{MHA}}^{(l)}\left(E^{(l-1)}, \text{ReLU}\left(\bar{Y}^{(l)}\right)\right), \\
\bar{E}^{(l)} &= f^{(l)}\left(\text{LayerNorm}\left(Y^{(l)}\right)\right), \\
E^{(l)} &= g_{\text{MLP}}^{(l)}\left(Y^{(l)}, \text{ReLU}\left(\bar{E}^{(l)}\right)\right)
\end{aligned} \tag{2}$$

The $g_{\text{MHA}}^{(l)}$ represents the gating unit, which is inspired by the Gated Recurrent Unit (GRU) structure. This component achieves performance comparable to that of Long Short-Term Memory (LSTM) networks while requiring fewer parameters. Furthermore, the superior properties of this gating mechanism eliminate the necessity of binding activation functions, enhancing both efficiency and simplicity.

The integration of this gating mechanism ensures stable and efficient learning processes within the Transformer architecture.Formally, the gating mechanism $g_{\text{MHA}}^{(l)}$ is defined as:

$$\begin{aligned}
r &= \sigma\left(W_r^{(l)} y + U_r^{(l)} x\right), \\
z &= \sigma\left(W_z^{(l)} y + U_z^{(l)} x - b_g^{(l)}\right), \\
\hat{h} &= \tanh\left(W_g^{(l)} y + U_g^{(l)} (r \odot x)\right), \\
g^{(l)}(x, y) &= (1 - z) \odot x + z \odot \hat{h}
\end{aligned} \tag{3}$$

Incorporating the Gated TransformerXL architecture [6] into our agent significantly enhances its ability to effectively handle the volatility and complexities of financial markets. This architecture possesses an extended receptive field for time series, making it particularly adept at processing long sequences. Such capabilities improve the agent's ability to predict stock price trends and generate corresponding trading decisions.

Moreover, the gating components in the Gated TransformerXL allow the model to retain critical historical information while discarding irrelevant data. This characteristic further enhances the effectiveness of the agent's trading strategies. The architecture's features greatly assist the agent in addressing the diverse challenges of stock markets, improving training stability, and strengthening the accuracy and robustness of trading strategies.

3.3 Proximal Policy Optimization

Due to the instability of the Transformer model in reinforcement learning training processes, this study adopts the Proximal Policy Optimization (PPO) algorithm [7] to further improve the training efficiency of the stock trading agent. PPO is a policy-gradient-based reinforcement learning algorithm that incorporates a probability ratio clipping mechanism to limit the magnitude of policy updates, thereby avoiding instability during training. The core idea of PPO is to ensure that the difference between the new and old policies remains within a controlled range (i.e., "proximal optimization"), balancing exploration and exploitation while ensuring sample efficiency. PPO combines the stability of Trust Region Policy Optimization (TRPO) with implementation simplicity and efficiency and is widely applicable to complex tasks in both continuous and discrete action spaces. The objective function of PPO is defined as:

$$L^{\mathrm{CLIP}}(\theta) = \mathbb{E}_t \left[\min\left(r_t(\theta)A_t, \operatorname{clip}\left(r_t(\theta), 1-\varepsilon, 1+\varepsilon\right) A_t\right)\right], \tag{4}$$

where θ denotes the parameters of the agent, $r_t(\theta) = \frac{\pi_\theta(a_t|s_t)}{\pi_{\theta_{\mathrm{old}}}(a_t|s_t)}$, s_t and a_t represent the state and action at time step t, ε is a hyperparameter defining the clipping threshold, and A_t refers to the advantage function.

Selecting PPO as the training algorithm for the stock trading agent enhances training stability and convergence, ensuring an effective training process. Additionally, to fully exploit the GTrXL architecture's capability for modeling time series and further leverage the potential of the relative multi-head self-attention mechanism (RMHA) and memory modules, this study introduces modifications to the PPO algorithm. Specifically, after collecting a complete trajectory, the experiences within the trajectory are sequentially traversed to train the agent. This training approach ensures the correctness of the operations performed by the GTrXL memory module and RMHA.

Furthermore, to further restrict the magnitude of parameter updates, the training iteration is terminated when the Kullback-Leibler (KL) divergence of the agent exceeds a predefined threshold. Training algorithm is as follow:

Algorithm 1. Proximal Policy Optimization For Financial GTrXL

Initialize Feature extractor parameters α,policy parameters θ, value function parameters ϕ

for each iteration **do**
  Collect a trajectory $\{(s_t, a_t, r_t, s_{t+1})\}$ by running policy π_θ
  Compute advantage estimates A_t using the value function $V_\phi(s_t)$
  total_KL $\leftarrow 0$ ▷ Initialize total KL as zero
  for each $\{(s_t, a_t, r_t, s_{t+1})\}$ in trajectory **do** ▷ Sequentially iterate through all experience
    Compute the probability ratio $r_t(\theta) = \frac{\pi_\theta(a_t|s_t)}{\pi_{\theta_{\text{old}}}(a_t|s_t)}$
    Define the clipped surrogate objective $L^{\text{CLIP}}(\theta)$ by equation 4
    Update policy parameters α and θ by maximizing $L^{\text{CLIP}}(\theta)$
    Update value function parameters α and ϕ by minimizing the error:

$$L^{\text{VF}}(\phi) = \frac{1}{2}\mathbb{E}_t\left[\left(V_\phi(s_t) - R_t\right)^2\right]$$

    Compute approximate KL divergence:

$$\text{approx\_KL} = \frac{1}{N}\sum_{i=1}^{N}\left(e^{log(r_t(\theta))} - 1 - log(r_t(\theta))\right)$$

    total_KL += approx_KL
  end for
  if total_KL exceeds threshold **then**
    Terminate the current iteration
  end if
end for
Return: α,θ,ϕ

In summary, this study comprehensively considers the stability and flexibility of the Proximal Policy Optimization (PPO) algorithm [7] and the Gated TransformerXL (GTrXL) architecture [6] for reinforcement learning tasks. By integrating these two methodologies and applying them to the stock trading domain, this research provides innovative approaches and techniques to address challenges such as portfolio risk management and stock trading.

4 Experiment

4.1 Experiment Setup

We select 32 stocks from the A-share market randomly, with the stock codes as follows: 601628, 600048, 600030, 600015, 601318, 600000, 601088, 600031, 601688, 601668, 601328, 603288, 600519, 600150, 601818, 600018, 600028, 600585, 600372, 601398, 601288, 601901, 600050, 601919, 600010, 601857, 000001, 600016, 600809, 601601, 600036, and 600104.

To evaluate the effectiveness of the proposed architecture, this study first constructs a stock trading agent training environment based on historical trading data. The training data is divided into two parts:

- **Training Data:** January 4, 2016, to August 16, 2020.
- **Testing Data:** August 17, 2020, to February 10, 2021.

All data were obtained from `www.resset.com`. The experiments were conducted on an Ubuntu 20.04 platform using an Intel Core i9-11900 CPU and an NVIDIA RTX 3080Ti GPU.

The training parameters of PPO are set as shown in the Table 1.

Table 1. Training parameters of PPO.

Parameter	Value
Reward Discount Factor	0.99
Loss Function Weight of Critic	0.5
Loss Function Weight of Distribution Entropy	0.01
Clip Range	0.1
Maximum of Gradient Truncation	0.5
Optimizer	Adam
TargetKL	0.06
Learning Rate	$1e-3$

4.2 Metrics for Portfolio Evaluation

- **Cumulative Return:** Cumulative Return is a core metric for measuring the total performance of an investment over a specific period. It is calculated as: Cumulative Return $= \frac{\text{Ending Value}}{\text{Starting Value}} - 1$.
- **Sharpe Ratio:** The Sharpe Ratio is a key metric for measuring risk-adjusted returns of a portfolio. It is calculated as:

$$\text{Sharpe Ratio} = \frac{R_p - R_f}{\sigma_p},$$

where R_p represents portfolio returns, R_f denotes the risk-free rate, and σ_p is the standard deviation of returns, representing risk. This ratio quantifies the excess return obtained for each unit of risk undertaken, with higher values indicating superior investment efficiency. It is commonly used to compare the performance of funds or strategies. However, its assumption of normally distributed returns limits its ability to evaluate extreme risks, necessitating complementary analysis with the Sortino Ratio.

- **Sortino Ratio:** The Sortino Ratio evaluates risk-adjusted returns, focusing on downside risk. It is calculated as:

$$\text{Sortino Ratio} = \frac{R_p - R_{\min}}{\sigma_{\text{down}}},$$

where $R_{\min}$ represents the minimum acceptable return, and σ_{down} denotes downside standard deviation (calculated only for negative deviations from the target return). Compared to the Sharpe Ratio, the Sortino Ratio penalizes only unfavorable fluctuations, aligning more closely with investors' loss-aversion preferences. It is especially suitable for evaluating strategies with asymmetric return distributions or those focused on tail risk control. However, its reliance on subjective thresholds for defining downside risks poses challenges.
- **Calmar Ratio:** The Calmar Ratio measures the relationship between portfolio returns and maximum drawdown as a risk-adjusted indicator. It is calculated as: $\text{Calmar Ratio} = \frac{\text{Annualized Return}}{\text{Maximum Drawdown}}$, where maximum drawdown refers to the largest loss from peak to trough in asset value over a given period (typically 36 months). This ratio emphasizes the erosion of returns due to extreme downside risks. Higher values indicate stronger performance under identical drawdowns, and it is frequently used to evaluate hedge funds or long-term investment strategies.

4.3 Experiment Result

In this study, we selected four widely used deep reinforcement learning (DRL) algorithms as baseline methods for comparison: Proximal Policy Optimization (PPO), Soft Actor-Critic (SAC), Twin Delayed Deep Deterministic Policy Gradient (TD3), and Deep Deterministic Policy Gradient (DDPG). These algorithms have been extensively applied to portfolio optimization tasks in financial domains and are representative of state-of-the-art DRL approaches.

SAC is an off-policy algorithm based on the maximum entropy framework. It is well-suited for handling uncertainty and volatility in financial markets due to its ability to balance exploration and exploitation in continuous action spaces.

TD3 enhances the DDPG algorithm by introducing three key improvements: twin Q-networks to reduce overestimation bias, delayed policy updates, and target policy smoothing. These modifications significantly improve the stability and performance of DRL agents in continuous control tasks.

DDPG is an actor-critic algorithm designed for high-dimensional continuous action spaces. It enables fine-grained adjustment of asset allocations, making it suitable for responding dynamically to market changes.

The choice of these baseline methods allows for a comprehensive evaluation of our proposed framework under a range of reinforcement learning strategies, validating its effectiveness in both risk control and return optimization.

In this study, we compare the proposed model with stock trading strategies constructed using reinforcement learning, including CLSTM-PPO [2], FinRL-SAC [4], TD3 [19], and DDPG [20]. The experimental results are shown in Table 2.

Table 2. Performance metrics comparison. The optimal results in the table are highlighted in bold, while the second-best results are underlined.

	Cumulative Return	Sharpe Ratio	Sortino Ratio	Calmar Ratio
CLSTM-PPO	0.025087	2.771206	4.776764	5.872052
FinRL-SAC	0.354094	2.72785	4.746541	9.690938
TD3	0.313112	2.688888	4.705256	9.103432
DDPG	<u>0.356320</u>	<u>2.830659</u>	<u>5.047212</u>	<u>11.052943</u>
Ours	**0.406146**	**3.169874**	**5.822360**	**16.355468**

The experimental results demonstrate that the trading strategy of the proposed model achieves superior returns compared to most existing models. Additionally, risk metrics indicate that the agent's trading strategy significantly outperforms other models in combating financial risks, enhancing portfolio robustness, and reducing financial risk. This provides investors with improved risk management strategies. Figure 3 illustrates the changes in the total asset value of various agents during the trading process.

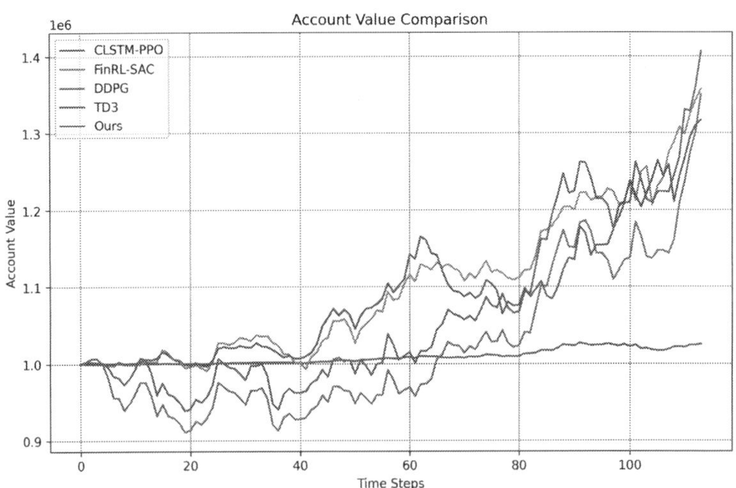

Fig. 3. Comparison of portfolio asset values across different automated stock trading frameworks.

4.4 Ablation Study

Table 3. Result of Ablation Experiment

	Cumulative Return	Sharpe Ratio	Sortino Ratio	Calmar Ratio
Ours:Without Memory	0.077511	2.443415	3.961612	4.387126
Ours:Without GRU	0.033471	0.858939	1.349193	1.08891
Ours:Without History	−0.004208	−0.836418	−1.190423	−0.888715
Ours	**0.406146**	**3.169874**	**5.822360**	**16.355468**

To validate the effectiveness of each component in the proposed architecture, ablation experiments were conducted with varying memory lengths, removal of gating units, and different historical data lengths. The experimental results are shown in Table 3. The results demonstrate that the memory module preserves essential information required for stock trading decision-making. Compared to residual connections, gating units further enhance the agent's ability to model time series data.

Furthermore, unlike methods such as FinRL-SAC [4], TD3 [19], and DDPG [20], which input only the current observation into the agent, this study inputs observations from the past 12 days into the agent. This approach significantly expands the model's receptive field, enabling it to extract auxiliary decision-making information from historical trading states and thereby improving the effectiveness and robustness of the agent's trading strategies.

5 Conclusion

This study constructs an automated stock trading agent using deep reinforcement learning and Transformer models. Specifically, the architecture leverages Gated TransformerXL (GTrXL) to build Actor and Critic networks through a shared feature extractor design. The Proximal Policy Optimization (PPO) algorithm [7] was modified to adapt to the structural characteristics of the GTrXL network.

This approach significantly enhances the agent's ability to model time series data in financial markets and uncover dynamic evolutionary patterns in stock market behavior. Furthermore, experimental results demonstrate that the proposed stock trading agent exhibits higher robustness and profitability compared to conventional reinforcement learning-based trading strategies. It effectively addresses various financial market risks, providing investors with valuable support in portfolio risk management and advancing the frontier of research in financial risk management.

Acknowledgement. This work was supported by the National Key Research and Development Program of China under Grant 2023YFC3305404, Major Project of Humanities and Social Sciences Research in Higher Education Institutions in Hebei Province (ZD202509) and Doctoral research Foundation of Shijiazhuang University (No. 18BS013).

References

1. Liu, X.-Y., et al.: Finrl: a deep reinforcement learning library for automated stock trading in quantitative finance. arXiv preprint arXiv:2011.09607 (2020)
2. Zou, J., Lou, J., Wang, B., Liu, S.: A novel deep reinforcement learning based automated stock trading system using cascaded LSTM networks. Expert Syst. Appl. **242**, 122801 (2024)
3. Gao, S., Wang, Y., Yang, X.: Stockformer: learning hybrid trading machines with predictive coding. In: IJCAI, pp. 4766–4774 (2023)
4. Haarnoja, T., Zhou, A., Abbeel, P., Levine, S.: Soft actor-critic: off-policy maximum entropy deep reinforcement learning with a stochastic actor. In: International Conference on Machine Learning, pp. 1861–1870. PMLR (2018)
5. Vaswani, A., et al.: Attention is all you need. In: Advances in Neural Information Processing Systems, vol. 30 (2017)
6. Parisotto, E., et al.: Stabilizing transformers for reinforcement learning. In: International Conference on Machine Learning, pp. 7487–7498. PMLR (2020)
7. Schulman, J., Wolski, F., Dhariwal, P., Radford, A., Klimov, O.: Proximal policy optimization algorithms. arXiv preprint arXiv:1707.06347 (2017)
8. Gao, Z., Gao, Y., Hu, Y., Jiang, Z., Su, J.: Application of deep q-network in portfolio management. In: 2020 5th IEEE International Conference on Big Data Analytics (ICBDA), pp. 268–275. IEEE (2020)
9. Wang, R., Wei, H., An, B., Feng, Z., Yao, J.: Commission fee is not enough: a hierarchical reinforced framework for portfolio management. arxiv 2020. arXiv preprint arXiv:2012.12620 (2012)
10. Wang, J., Zhang, Y., Tang, K., Wu, J., Xiong, Z.: Alphastock: a buying-winners-and-selling-losers investment strategy using interpretable deep reinforcement attention networks. In: Proceedings of the 25th ACM SIGKDD International Conference on Knowledge Discovery & Data Mining, pp. 1900–1908 (2019)
11. Lee, J., Kim, R., Yi, S.-W., Kang, J.: Maps: multi-agent reinforcement learning-based portfolio management system. arXiv preprint arXiv:2007.05402 (2020)
12. Benhamou, E., Saltiel, D., Ohana, J.-J., Atif, J.: Detecting and adapting to crisis pattern with context based deep reinforcement learning. In: 2020 25th International Conference on Pattern Recognition (ICPR), pp. 10050–10057. IEEE (2021)
13. Soleymani, F., Paquet, E.: Deep graph convolutional reinforcement learning for financial portfolio management-deeppocket. Expert Syst. Appl. **182**, 115127 (2021)
14. Levine, S., Kumar, A., Tucker, G., Fu, J.: Offline reinforcement learning: tutorial, review, and perspectives on open problems. arXiv preprint arXiv:2005.01643 (2020)
15. Wang, X., Chen, Y., Zhu, W.: A survey on curriculum learning. IEEE Trans. Pattern Anal. Mach. Intell. **44**(9), 4555–4576 (2021)
16. Brockman, G., et al.: OpenAI gym. arXiv preprint arXiv:1606.01540 (2016)
17. Chong, T.T.-L., Ng, W.-K., Liew, V.K.-S.: Revisiting the performance of MACD and RSI oscillators. J. Risk Financ. Manage. **7**(1), 1–12 (2014)

18. Dai, Z., Yang, Z., Yang, Y., Carbonell, J., Le, Q.V., Salakhutdinov, R.: Transformer-XL: attentive language models beyond a fixed-length context. arXiv preprint arXiv:1901.02860 (2019)
19. Fujimoto, S., Hoof, H., Meger, D.: Addressing function approximation error in actor-critic methods. In: International Conference on Machine Learning, pp. 1587–1596. PMLR (2018)
20. Lillicrap, T.P., et al.: Continuous control with deep reinforcement learning. arXiv preprint arXiv:1509.02971 (2015)

Keyword Searchable Data Integrity Auditing Protocol for Cloud-Assisted WBANs

Ying Miao(✉), Yihang Wei, Jianbo Gao, and Keke Gai

School of Cyberspace Science and Technology, Beijing Institute of Technology, Beijing 100081, China
yingmiao@bit.edu.cn

Abstract. Cloud computing has accelerated the implementation of wearable devices. Data is the core task of wearable devices, and ensuring the integrity of data in cloud-assisted wearable device systems is related to personal life and health issues. Therefore, it is even more important to check the integrity of data by category. In recent years, some data integrity schemes have been proposed. However, these schemes adopt Public Key Infrastructure and face some problems of large certificate management overhead, which are not suitable for mobile wearable device systems. For this reason, we propose a cloud-assisted wearable device data integrity audit protocol based on keywords. Specifically, we use identity-based cryptography to generate authenticators and design a keyword-based index to ensure that third-party auditors can directly check the integrity of data containing a certain keyword according to the keyword, which is beneficial to the protection of wearable system data integrity. Security proofs and experimental results show that the proposed scheme is secure and efficient.

Keywords: Keyword search · Data integrity auditing · Cloud storage · Wireless body area networks (WBANs)

1 Introduction

Cloud storage has greatly facilitated the development of wearable devices by providing a scalable and reliable platform for data storage and management [6]. Globally, the wearable technology market size was 120.15 billion dollars in 2023 and is expected to grow to 1695.46 billion dollars by 2032[1]. Wearable device data is of utmost importance as it provides valuable insights into an individual's health and fitness metrics, enabling personalized wellness strategies [7]. Furthermore, this data plays a crucial role in medical research and development, contributing to the advancement of healthcare solutions tailored to individual

[1] https://www.fortunebusinessinsights.com/wearable-technology-market-106000.

M. Yung et al. (Eds.): AIBlock 2025, LNCS 16314, pp. 110–123, 2026.
https://doi.org/10.1007/978-3-032-16168-0_7

needs. Protecting the integrity of wearable device data is crucial for maintaining the accuracy and reliability of health monitoring, ensuring that users and healthcare providers can trust the information for informed decisions.

Cloud-assisted *Wireless Body Area Networks* (WBANs) includes wearable devices like smartwatches, fitness trackers, and a *Cloud Server* (CS) for data storage, processing, and analysis. It comprises wearable sensors, a local communication module, and a cloud platform for data management and analytics [1]. Wearable devices can implement user identity authentication through identity-based cryptosystem to ensure that data owner who has been authorized can access the data collected by the devices [12,13]. In addition, by utilizing identity-based encryption technology, wearable devices can encrypt personal information during data outsourcing and storage to resist unauthorized access or leakage of data [15].

Integrity auditing protocol emerged to address the need for secure and reliable verification of data integrity in cloud storage environments. Originating from the challenges of ensuring data security and privacy in big data computing, integrity auditing protocols utilize cryptographic techniques to enable a *Third-Party Auditor* (TPA) to verify the integrity of data outsourced onto cloud without accessing the data itself, thus protecting sensitive information from unauthorized access or tampering. Up to now, the state of data integrity auditing protocols reflects ongoing efforts to address the challenges posed by data environments, such as data application [4,5,17,19], data privacy protection [20], data in decentralized enviornment [11,18], data in cloud-assisted WBANs [10,20].

However, these schemes encounter two issues. The first issue is that the majority of data integrity audit schemes for wearable devices are founded on the cryptographic of *Public Key Infrastructure* (PKI), which brings about enormous overhead from certificate management. Moreover, wearable device systems mostly adopt identity-based cryptosystems, direct adoption of existing schemes has low efficiency. Another issue is that, based on the characteristics of data collected by wearable devices, such as heart-rate-related data and blood-oxygen-related data, the absence of these data will make it impossible to make an accurate judgment of an individual's health condition. Thereby, it is crucial and necessary to ensure the integrity of a certain type of data. Hence, there is not yet a data integrity audit scheme that can simultaneously check a certain type of data.

In this paper, we put forward a keyword-searchable data integrity auditing protocol being applied in cloud-assisted WBANs. The main contributions are presented as follows:

- We utilize the concept of keywords and design keyword-based index tags, enabling the cloud server to directly search for data corresponding to keywords and verify the integrity of the data, which can check the integrity of data more accurately according to category attributes. The scheme enhances the efficiency of the wearable device system.
- Aiming at the management problem of data integrity verification certificates in existing wearable device systems, we use an identity-based cryptographic

system and design identity-based authentication tags, thus reducing the management overhead of certificates.
- We have carried out security proofs for our scheme and verified its feasibility through experimental comparisons. In terms of index generation and tag generation, our scheme does not differ much compared with existing schemes.

2 Related Work

In order to resist data loss and, Ateniese *et al.* [2] proposed the concept of *Provable Data Possession* (PDP), which was intended to verify the integrity of remotely stored data. Later, Juels and Kaliski [8] came up with the idea of *Proofs of Retrievability* (PoR), a mechanism that ensured both the integrity and retrievability of remote data. Subsequently, researchers investigated remote data integrity auditing from different perspectives [9]. Wang *et al.* [17] used attribute-based revocable signatures for IoT devices in cloud storage environments. The access policy control limited users' permissions to access shared data. Gudeme *et al.* [5] utilized data attributes to develop an authenticator, adopting a distinct public key instead of individual public keys for integrity verification. Ge *et al.* [4] took into account the limitation that when an attribute was revoked, the new ciphertext with the revoked access policy was unsuitable for data decryption. Zhang *et al.* [19] incorporated lattice-based attribute signatures to develop a lattice-based data integrity auditing scheme that supported revocation. Most of these schemes utilized attribute-based signatures. However, attribute-based signature operations entailed a substantial amount of computation, took a long time, and impacted system performance. Considering the unique features of wearable system data, ensuring the security of certain types of data is especially critical.

Zhang *et al.* [20] enabled conditional identity preservation in cloud-based WBANs, thereby protect the privacy for patients. Garg *et al.* [3] reduced the computational burden on the client side during the setup phase of the auditing protocol. Lin *et al.* [11] made use of a consortium chain to record the auditor's actions and authorized certain parties to examine the verification result issued by the auditor. Li *et al.* [14] applied a homomorphic authenticator to create a multifunctional data tag in order to optimize storage capacity. This design made it possible to carry out simultaneous data deduplication and auditing while ensuring security against a variety of potential attacks. Shen *et al.* [16] designed a keyword tag, which allowed the TPA to conduct verification whether the CS correctly preserved all files which contain the specific keyword. Nevertheless, the majority of these schemes were based on PKI and thus cannot be directly applied to wearable systems.

3 Preliminaries

Suppose $\mathbb{G}_1$ and $\mathbb{G}_2$ are two multiplicative cyclic groups, the order of the group is p, and g is a generator of $\mathbb{G}_1$. A bilinear map is a function $e : \mathbb{G}_1 \times \mathbb{G}_1 \rightarrow \mathbb{G}_2$ with the following characteristics:

- Bilinearity: Given any $u, v \in \mathbb{G}_1$ and $a, b \in \mathbb{Z}_q^*$, the equation $e(u^a, v^b) = e(u, v)^{ab}$ is satisfied.
- Computability: The algorithm that can compute the mapping e efficiently exists.
- Non-degeneracy: It is not the case that $e(g, g) = 1$.

Computational Diffie-Hellman (CDH) Problem
For arbitrary $x, y \in \mathbb{Z}_q^*$ that are unknown, when g, g^x and g^y are given as inputs, the output is $g^{xy} \in \mathbb{G}_1$. The assumption in group $\mathbb{G}_1$ is valid if it is impractical to resolve the CDH problem in $\mathbb{G}_1$ in a computationally way.

Discrete Logarithm (DL) Problem
For an unknown element x in $\mathbb{Z}_q^*$, if g and g^x are provided as inputs, then the output will be x. The discrete logarithm (DL) assumption is valid in $\mathbb{G}_1$ when it is difficult in a computationally way to resolve the DL problem within group $\mathbb{G}_1$.

4 System Model and Definitions

4.1 System Model

As shown in Fig. 1, the portable terminal periodically uploads data to the CS via a wireless access point. A third-party auditor, similar to a physician or an emergency medical service center, oversees the data and transmits health reports to the patient. Additionally, they are capable of analyzing the data and saving the diagnosis outcomes on the server. Patients or their guardians are able to obtain health information and diagnosis results from the cloud-based medical system.

4.2 Definition

Definition 1. *The keyword searchable data integrity auditing protocol comprises the following algorithms:*

1. $(param, msk) \leftarrow \mathsf{Setup}(1^\kappa)$ is carried out by the PKG. It needs to take a security parameter κ and gives out the master secret key msk and the system public parameter pp as outputs.
2. $sk_{ID} \leftarrow \mathsf{Extract}(param, msk, ID)$ is implemented by the PKG. Its inputs include the system public parameters $param$, the master secret key msk, and a user's identity ID. The user's private key sk_{ID} as outputs. The user conduct the correctness verification of sk_{ID}, and will only regard it as his own private key after it has passed the verification.
3. $\{SE_{w_k}\}_{k\in[1,K]} \leftarrow \mathsf{KeywordExtract}(\{F_i\}_{1\leqslant i\leqslant n})$ is executed by the user ID, uses the original files $\{F_i\}_{1\leqslant i\leqslant n}$ as its input. And it generates the file index sets SE_{w_k} related to the keywords $w_k (k \in [1, K])$ as outputs.

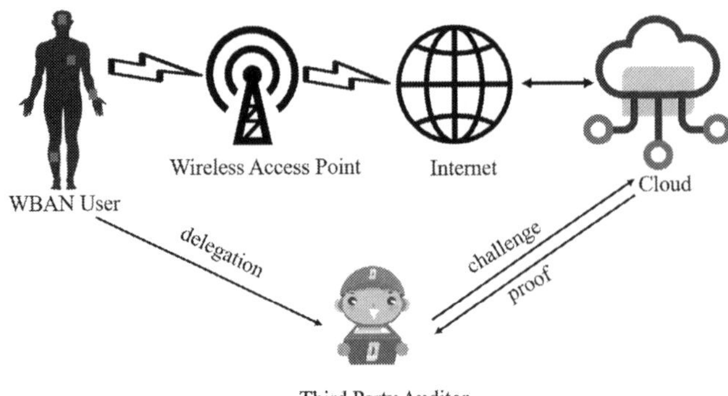

Fig. 1. The system model of MKPDP.

4. $\{tag_{w_k}\}_{w_k(k\in[1,K])} \leftarrow \mathsf{SearchIndex}(\{F_i\}_{1\leqslant i\leqslant n}, \{SE_{w_k}\}_{k\in[1,K]})$ is executed by user ID, uses the original files $\{F_i\}_{1\leqslant i\leqslant n}$ and the file index sets SE_{w_k} associated with the keywords $w_{k,k\in[1,K]}$ as inputs. It outputs the keyword tags tag_{w_k} for each $w_{k,k\in[1,K]}$.
5. $\{\phi_i, \{m_{i,j}\}_{j\in[1,s]}\}_{i\in[1,n]} \leftarrow \mathsf{AuthGen}(\{F_i\}_{1\leqslant i\leqslant n}, \{SE_{w_k}\}_{k\in[1,K]})$ is carried out by user ID, takes the original files $\{F_i\}_{1\leqslant i\leqslant n}$ and the file index sets SE_{w_k} as inputs. It produces authenticators ϕ_i for every file.
6. $Chal \leftarrow \mathsf{ChalGen}(\{w_k, SE_{w_k}\}_{k\in[1,K]})$ is executed by the TPA, uses the file index sets SE_{w_k} related to the keywords $w_{k,k\in[1,K]}$ as its input. And it generates the challenge information $Chal$ as the output.
7. $Proof \leftarrow \mathsf{ProofGen}(Chal, \{F_i\}_{1\leqslant i\leqslant n}, \{\phi_i\}_{1\leqslant i\leqslant n})$ is carried out by CS, takes the challenge $Chal$, the original files $\{F_i\}_{1\leqslant i\leqslant n}$, and the corresponding authenticators $\{\phi_i\}_{1\leqslant i\leqslant n}$ as inputs. It produces proof information $Proof$ as the output.
8. $true/false \leftarrow \mathsf{ProofVerify}(\{w_k, SE_{w_k}\}_{k\in[1,K]}, Proof)$ is executed by the TPA, uses the file index sets SE_{w_k} related to the keywords w_k $(k \in [1, K])$ and the proof information $Proof$ as inputs. It generates the verification result $true/false$ as the output.

4.3 Security Model

To establish the security model, we will describe a game that involves $\mathcal{C}$ (challenger) and $\mathcal{A}$ (adversary). This game serves to illustrate the potential threats from $\mathcal{A}$ in the proposed scheme. In this context, the DO is represented by $\mathcal{C}$, while the untrusted CS is act as $\mathcal{A}$. The game consists of several phases:

1. **Setup phase.** The $\mathcal{C}$ executes the Setup algorithm in order to acquire the master secret key msk, the system public parameters $param$, and subsequently transmits the public parameters $param$ to the $\mathcal{A}$.
2. **Query phase.** The $\mathcal{A}$ conducts some queries to the challenge $\mathcal{C}$.

- **Hash Queries:** The $\mathcal{A}$ conducts hash queries of $H_1 \sim H_3$. In response, the challenger generates the corresponding values and sends them to $\mathcal{A}$.
- **Extract Queries:** The $\mathcal{A}$ asks for the private key information corresponding to the identity ID. Subsequently, the $\mathcal{C}$ executes the *Extract* algorithm to create the private key sk_{ID} and subsequently transmits it to $\mathcal{A}$.
- **SearchIndex Queries:** The $\mathcal{A}$ makes a request for the index information pertaining to file F. In response, the $\mathcal{C}$ utilizes the *SearchIndex* algorithm to retrieve the index for file F and subsequently transmits these information to the $\mathcal{A}$.
- **AuthGen Queries:** The $\mathcal{A}$ submits a request for a target authenticators of the file F. As a result, the $\mathcal{C}$ begins by running the *Extract* algorithm to acquire the private key. After that, the $\mathcal{C}$ employs the *AuthGen* algorithm to create the authenticators for file F. Ultimately, the $\mathcal{C}$ transmits these authenticators information to the $\mathcal{A}$.
- **ProofGen Queries:** Upon the $\mathcal{A}$'s request for the poof pertaining to file F, the $\mathcal{C}$ proceeds to compute the required proof using the *ProofGen* algorithm. Once computed, this proof is conveyed to the $\mathcal{A}$.

3. **Challenge phase:** The $\mathcal{C}$ presents the challenge $Chal = (w_k, c, k_1, k_2)$ associate with user ID' to the $\mathcal{A}$. This challenge demands that the $\mathcal{A}$ supply a data integrity proof $Proof$.
4. **Forgery phase:** When the $\mathcal{A}$ gets the challenge from $\mathcal{C}$, it produces a proof $Proof$ for the data blocks specified by $Chal$ in response to $\mathcal{C}$. When the proof $Proof$ passes the verification carried out by $\mathcal{C}$ with a probability that is non-negligible, then it infers that the $\mathcal{A}$ successes in the aforementioned game under the following conditions:
   - The challenge information $Chal$ associated with the target identity ID' was not be asked earlier.
   - The private key which corresponds to the target identity ID' was not be previously queried.

Definition 2. *The proposed scheme ensures auditing soundness, provided that no probabilistic polynomial time (PPT) adversary $\mathcal{A}$ can prevail in the game with a significant probability.*

5 Proposed Scheme

(1) $(param, msk) \leftarrow$ Setup(1^κ)

- The PKG picks out two multiplicative cyclic groups, namely $\mathbb{G}_1$ and $\mathbb{G}_2$, both of which have a prime order q. Moreover, it selects an elements $g \in \mathbb{G}_1$, a bilinear mapping $e : \mathbb{G}_1 \times \mathbb{G}_1 \rightarrow \mathbb{G}_2$, a pseudorandom permutation $\psi : \mathbb{Z}_q^* \times \{0,1\}^s \rightarrow \mathbb{Z}_q^*$, and a pseudorandom function $\pi : \mathbb{Z}_q^* \times \mathbb{Z}_q^* \rightarrow \mathbb{Z}_q^*$.

- The PKG randomly picks a private element x from $\mathbb{Z}_q^*$, and then selects a number of elements $u, \mu', \mu_1, \cdots, \mu_l, g_2 \in \mathbb{G}_1$, together with cryptographic hash functions H_1, H_2, H_3 which map binary strings to elements within the cyclic group $\mathbb{G}_1$.
- The PKG calculates the public value g_1 in the form of g^x, and obtains the master secret key msk by computing g_2^x.
- The PKG announces the system parameters

$$param = (p, \mathbb{G}_1, \mathbb{G}_2, g_1, g_2, e, g, u, \mu', \mu_1, \ldots, \mu_l, H_1, H_2, H_3, \psi, \pi)$$

and retains the master secret key msk.

(2) $sk_{ID} \leftarrow$ Extract$(param, msk, ID)$

- When the PKG gets the user's identity which is denoted as $ID = (ID_1, \cdots, ID_l) \in \{0,1\}^l$, it randomly selects a value $r_{ID} \in \mathbb{Z}_q^*$ and calculates the user's private key $sk_{ID} = (sk'_{ID}, sk''_{ID})$ in the following way: $sk'_{ID} = g_2^x \times (\mu' \times \prod_{j=1}^{l} \mu_j^{ID_j})^{r_{ID}}$ and $sk''_{ID} = g^{r_{ID}}$. Afterwards, the PKG transmits this private key to the user identified by ID.
- User ID confirms the accuracy of the received private key sk_{ID} through examining if a specific equation holds true.

$$e(sk'_{ID}, g) = e(g_1, g_2) \times e(\mu' \times \prod_{j=1}^{l} \mu_j^{ID_j}, sk''_{ID}).$$

If the aforementioned equation is not satisfied, user ID will decline the private key sk_{ID}; otherwise, user ID will accept it.

(3) $\{SE_{w_k}\}_{k \in [1,K]} \leftarrow$ KeywordExtract$(\{F_i\}_{1 \leqslant i \leqslant n})$

Suppose there are n files in the CS, and the sum of keywords across all these files, which are denoted as $\{F_i\}_{1 \leqslant i \leqslant n}$. Every keyword is indicated by w_k, with k representing its sequence number.

- Before uploading all files to the CS, the user extracts certain keywords from every file $F_{i,i \in [1,n]}$. For every keyword $w_{k,k \in [1,K]}$, the user then constructs a file index set denoted SE_{w_k}. This set consists of the indices of all files which contains the keyword w_k. Initially, every file index set SE_{w_k} is initialized as empty. As each file F_i is processed, should F_i contain the keyword w_k, the user appends the index i of file F_i to the pertinent file index set SE_{w_k} linked with that keyword.
- The user sends the collection of keywords $\{w_k\}_{k \in [1,K]}$ together with their respective file index sets $\{SE_{w_k}\}_{k \in [1,K]}$ to the CS.

(4) $\{tag_{w_k}\}_{w_k (k \in [1,K])} \leftarrow$ SearchIndex$(\{F_i\}_{1 \leqslant i \leqslant n}, \{SE_{w_k}\}_{k \in [1,K]})$

- For each file $F_{i,i \in [1,n]}$, the user compiles a relevant keyword set $W_{F_i} = \{w_{b_1}, \cdots, w_{b_l}, \cdots, w_{b_t}\}$ $(l \in [1,t])$. Herein, $w_{b_l, b_l \in [1,K]}$ represents the l-th keyword in file F_i, and t denotes the overall number of keywords in that file. It should be noted that W_{F_i} encompasses all the keywords within file F_i, and the quantity of keywords may vary from file to file.

- For each file $F_{i,i\in[1,n]}$, the user calculates a hash value HF_i by taking the product of the outputs from applying a hash function H_1 to each keyword w_{b_l} in the keyword set W_{F_i} for that file. This computation is expressed as $HF_i = \prod_{l=1}^{t} H_1(w_{b_l})$, where w_{b_l} is a member of W_{F_i}. Afterward, the user computes the auxiliary information Ω_i for file F_i using the formula $\Omega_i = (HF_i \times H_2(FID_i))^{-r}$, where FID_i represents the identifier of file F_i.
- The user transmits the set of file information $\{FID_i, \Omega_i, W_{F_i}\}_{i\in[1,n]}$ to the CS and TPA respectively.

(5) $\{\phi_i, \{m_{i,j}\}_{j\in[1,s]}\}_{i\in[1,n]} \leftarrow$ AuthGen$(\{F_i\}_{1\leqslant i\leqslant n}, \{SE_{w_k}\}_{k\in[1,K]})$

- At first, the user splits each file $F_{i,i\in[1,n]}$ into some fixed number of data blocks, leading to the expression $F_i = \{m_{i,1}, \cdots, m_{i,j}, \cdots, m_{i,s}\}_{i\in[1,n]}$, in which $m_{i,j}$ indicates the j-th block in file F_i. After that, the user forms an index switch set $S_i = \{\theta_{i,j}\}_{i\in[1,n],j\in[1,s]}$, with each $\theta_{i,j}$ being defined as $(j, au_{i,j})$, where j represents for the block index of file F_i, $au_{i,j}$ represents the authenticator index of the same file.
- The user calculates the authenticator $\sigma_{i,j}$ for each data block $m_{i,j}$ (where $i \in [1,n]$ and $j \in [1,s]$) according to the formula $\sigma_{i,j} = g_2^x \times (\mu' \times \prod_{j=1}^{l} \mu_j^{ID_j})^{r_{ID}} \times (HF_i \times H_2(FID_i) \times H_3(au_{i,j}) \times u^{m_{i,j}})^r$, leveraging the authenticator index $au_{i,j}$. Afterwards, the set of authenticators for file F_i is specified as $\phi_i = \{\sigma_{i,j}, R = g^x\}_{j\in[1,s]}$, which denotes the authenticator set related to file $F_{i,i\in[1,n]}$.
- The user transmits $\{FID_i, \phi_i, \{m_{i,j}\}_{j\in[1,s]}\}_{i\in[1,n]}$ to the CS, and posts $\{FID_i, S_i\}_{i\in[1,n]}$ to the TPA.

(6) $Chal \leftarrow$ ChalGen$(\{w_k, SE_{w_k}\}_{k\in[1,K]})$
The task of TPA is to conduct the verification of files that contain a particular keyword w_k, it randomly picks random seeds $k_1, k_2 \in \mathbb{Z}_q^*$ and c data blocks to create a challenge. The TPA then constructs and transmits the challenge $Chal = \{w_k, c, k_1, k_2\}$ to the CS. For each $\alpha \in [1,c]$, it computes $j_1 = \psi_{k_1}(\alpha)$, and for each $i \in SE_{w_k}$, it calculates $v_{1ij} = \pi_{x_i}(j)$ where $x_i = \pi_{k_2}(i)$. This process results in a set $Q_1 = \{j = \psi_{k_1}(\alpha)\}_{\alpha\in[1,c]}$.
(7) $Proof \leftarrow$ ProofGen$(Chal, \{F_i\}_{1\leqslant i\leqslant n}, \{\phi_i\}_{1\leqslant i\leqslant n})$
when received the challenge $Chal$, the CS identifies all files which contains the specific keyword w_k using the file index set SE_{w_k}. The CS then generates specific challenge information: for each $\alpha \in [1,c]$, it computes $j_2 = \psi_{k_1}(\alpha)$, and for each $i \in SE_{w_k}$, it calculates $v_{2ij} = \pi_{x_i}(j)$ where $x_i = \pi_{k_2}(i)$. This process results in a set $Q_2 = \{j_2 = \psi_{k_1}(\alpha)\}_{\alpha\in[1,c]}$. Next, the CS constructs a proof $Proof = \{T, \mu, R\}$, where $T = \prod_{i\in SE_{w_k}} \prod_{j\in Q_2} \sigma_{i,j}^{v_{2ij}}$, and $\mu = \sum_{i\in SE_{w_k}} \sum_{j\in Q_2} v_{2ij} m_{i,j}$. Eventually, the CS transmits the proof $Proof$ together with the file index set SE_{w_k} related to the specific keyword w_k to the TPA.
(8) $true/false \leftarrow$ ProofVerify$(\{w_k, SE_{w_k}\}_{k\in[1,K]}, Proof)$

- After getting the proof $Proof$, the CS employs the set SE_{w_k} to find out all files which contains the specific keyword w_k. Next, the TPA goes on to ask for the switch set S_i for each file $F_{i,i\in SE_{w_k}}$. Through this process, TPA obtains the authenticator indexes $au_{i,j}$ corresponding to the challenged blocks $m_{i,j}$ (for $i \in SE_{w_k}$ and $j \in Q_1$).

- Utilizing the set of file information $\{FID_i, \Omega_i, W_{F_i}\}_{i\in[1,n]}$ and the authenticator indexes $au_{i,j}$ (where $i \in SE_{w_k}$ and $j \in Q$), the TPA executes the verification of the proof $Proof$.

$$\begin{aligned} & e(T \times \prod_{i\in SE_{w_k}} \prod_{j\in Q_1} \Omega_i^{v_{1ij}}, g) = e(g_1, g_2)^{\sum_{i\in SE_{w_k}} \sum_{j\in Q_1} v_{1ij}} \\ & \times e(\mu' \times \prod_{j=1}^{l} \mu_j^{ID_j}, g^{r_{ID}})^{\sum_{i\in SE_{w_k}} \sum_{j\in Q_1} v_{1ij}} \times \\ & e(\prod_{i\in SE_{w_k}} \prod_{j\in Q_1} H_3(au_{i,j})^{v_{1ij}} \times u^{\mu}, R) \end{aligned} \tag{1}$$

If the equation holds true, it implies that all files containing the specific keyword w_k are unaltered and still intact; conversely, if the equation does not hold, it suggests that these files have been altered or are no longer intact.

6 Security Analysis

Theorem 1. *The proof information cannot be forged without possessing the entire data.*

Proof. **Game 0:** Game 0 operates exactly as it is defined within security model. **Game 1:** Game 1 is nearly identical to Game 0, with just one crucial distinction. In the forged proof $Proof' = \{T', \mu', R\}$, the aggregated authenticator T' does not match the actual aggregated authenticator T. Consequently, within this game, the forged proof is able to pass the verification

$$\begin{aligned} & e(T' \times \prod_{i\in SE_{w_k}} \prod_{j\in Q_1} \Omega_i^{v_{1ij}}, g) = e(g_1, g_2)^{\sum_{i\in SE_{w_k}} \sum_{j\in Q_1} v_{1ij}} \\ & \times e(\mu' \times \prod_{j=1}^{l} \mu_j^{ID_j}, g^{r_{ID}})^{\sum_{i\in SE_{w_k}} \sum_{j\in Q_1} v_{1ij}} \\ & \times e(\prod_{i\in SE_{w_k}} \prod_{j\in Q_1} H_3(au_{i,j})^{v_{1ij}} \times u^{\mu'}, R). \end{aligned} \tag{2}$$

According to the verification

$$\begin{aligned} & e(T \times \prod_{i\in SE_{w_k}} \prod_{j\in Q_1} \Omega_i^{v_{1ij}}, g) = e(g_1, g_2)^{\sum_{i\in SE_{w_k}} \sum_{j\in Q_1} v_{1ij}} \\ & \times e(\mu' \times \prod_{j=1}^{l} \mu_j^{ID_j}, g^{r_{ID}})^{\sum_{i\in SE_{w_k}} \sum_{j\in Q_1} v_{1ij}} \\ & \times e(\prod_{i\in SE_{w_k}} \prod_{j\in Q_1} H_3(au_{i,j})^{v_{1ij}} \times u^{\mu}, R). \end{aligned} \tag{3}$$

It can be deduced that $\mu \neq \mu'$, otherwise $T = T'$, which would violate the aforementioned assumption. Let $\triangle\mu = \mu' - \mu$, if the adversay emerges victorious in the game, $\mathcal{C}$ can retrieve the CDH problem. That is, given a tuple $(g, g^\alpha, h) \in \mathbb{G}_1$, the $\mathcal{C}$'s objective is to retrieve h^α. The simulator chooses $x \in \mathbb{Z}_q^*$, and sets $g_1 = g^x$, $g_2 = h$ and the master secret key $msk = g_2^x$. Subsequently, the simulator defines $u = g_2^a g^b$, $h = g_2$ $R = g^r = (g^\alpha)^\chi$. By diving Eq. 2 by Eq. 3, we obtain $e(T'/T, g) = e(u^{\triangle\mu}, R) = e((g_2^a g^b)^{\triangle\mu}, (g^\alpha)^\chi)$. We can derive that $e(T' \times T^{-1} \times (g^\alpha)^{-\chi b\triangle\mu}, g) = e(h, g^\alpha)^{\chi a\triangle\mu}$. Consequently, it follows that $h^\alpha = (T \times T^{-1} \times (g^\alpha)^{-\chi b\triangle\mu})^{1/(\chi a\triangle\mu)}$. It is crucial to understand that the probability of the game failing is equal to the probability that the equation $\chi \times a \times \triangle\mu \equiv 0 \pmod p$ holds true. Since p is a large prime number, the likelihood of this equation being fulfilled is $1/p$, which is considered to be negligibly small. Consequently, this shows that the CDH problem can be solved with a probability of $1 - 1/p$, thus casting doubt on the CDH assumption which is infeasible to retrieve in a limited time.

Game 2: Game 2 is nearly identical to Game 1, with one key difference. In Game 2, if for any instance the aggregate message does not align with the expected value generated through $\mathcal{C}$, the $\mathcal{C}$ will declare a failure and terminate the process. Given a tuple $(g, h = g^\alpha) \in \mathbb{G}_1$, the aim is to ascertain the value of α. The simulator operates similarly to the challenger in Game 1, with a single difference: it selects $a, b \in \mathbb{Z}_q^*$ and sets $u = g_2^a g^b$, where $g_2 = h$. Following the logic of Game 1, we find that $T = T'$. Let $\triangle\mu = \mu - \mu'$. By employing the two verification equations, we deduce the equation that $u^\mu = u^{\mu'}$, which further implies $1 = u^{\triangle\mu} = (g_2^a g^b)^{\triangle\mu} = h^{a\triangle\mu} \times g^{b\triangle\mu}$. Moreover, it is guaranteed that $\triangle\mu \neq 0 \bmod p$, since $\mu' \neq \mu \bmod p$ would contradict our initial assumption. Consequently, we derive an instance solution of the DL problem to be $h = g^{-\frac{b\triangle\mu}{a\triangle\mu}} = g^{-\frac{b}{a}}$. However, the probability that a equals zero is merely $1/p$, which is insignificant since p represents a large prime number. Thus, we are able to retrieve the DL problem in a probability of $1 - 1/p$, thereby questioning the idea that the DL problem is resolved difficultly in a limited time. This implies that if there is a substantial difference in the $\mathcal{A}$'s probabilities of success between Game 2 and Game 3, the $\mathcal{C}$ can solve the DL problem.

7 Performance Evaluation

7.1 Theoretical Analysis

Assume there exist n documents, which incorporates K distinct keywords. These documents are segmented into s data blocks, with each block encompassing t_i keywords. Every keyword is associated with $|SE_{w_k}|$ documents.

Computation Overhead Comparison. The scheme primarily involves several types of computations: hash operations in group $H_{\mathbb{G}_1}$, exponentiation operations $Exp_{\mathbb{G}_1}$, multiplication operations $Mul_{\mathbb{G}_1}$ and $Mul_{\mathbb{Z}_q^*}$, and bilinear pairing operations $Pair$. During the auditing phase, the quantity of challenged data blocks per challenged document amounts to c. We conducted computational

Table 1. Computation Overhead

Phase	[16]	Our scheme
IndexGen	$\lvert W\rvert \times (t_i \times H_{\mathbb{G}_1} + t_i \times Mul_{\mathbb{G}_1} + Exp_{\mathbb{G}_1}) + K \times \lvert SE_{w_k}\rvert Mul_{\mathbb{G}_1}$	$\lvert W\rvert \times (t_i \times H_{\mathbb{G}_1} + (t_i + \lvert SE_{w_k}\rvert) \times Mul_{\mathbb{G}_1} + Exp_{\mathbb{G}_1})$
AuthGen	$n \times s \times (2H_{\mathbb{G}_1} + 2Exp_{\mathbb{G}_1} + 3Mul_{\mathbb{G}_1})$	$n \times s \times (H_{\mathbb{G}_1} + 4Mul_{\mathbb{G}_1} + Exp_{\mathbb{G}_1})$
ProofGen	$c \times \lvert SE_{w_k}\rvert \times Mul_{\mathbb{G}_1} + \lvert SE_{w_k}\rvert \times Mul_{\mathbb{Z}_q^*} + c \times Exp_{\mathbb{G}_1}$	$\lvert SE_{w_k}\rvert \times c \times Mul_{\mathbb{G}_1} + (\lvert SE_{w_k}\rvert \times c + 1)Mul_{\mathbb{Z}_q} + (\lvert SE_{w_k}\rvert \times c + 1)Exp_{\mathbb{G}_1}$
ProofVerify	$2 \times Pair + c \times \lvert SE_{w_k}\rvert \times Mul_{\mathbb{G}_1} + (2c+1) \times Exp_{\mathbb{G}_1}$	$4 \times Pair + (2c \times \lvert SE_{w_k}\rvert + l)Mul_{\mathbb{G}_1} + (2c \times \lvert SE_{w_k}\rvert + l + 2)Exp_{\mathbb{G}_1} + 2c \times \lvert SE_{w_k}\rvert \times Mul_{\mathbb{Z}_q^*}$

Table 2. Communication Overhead

Phase	[16]	Our scheme
DO → CS	$n \times \lvert F\rvert + (n \times s + n)\lvert\mathbb{G}_1\rvert + (1 + n \times K)\lvert\mathbb{Z}_q^*\rvert$	$n \times \lvert F\rvert + (n \times s + n)\lvert\mathbb{G}_1\rvert$
DO → TPA	$(s+1)\lvert\mathbb{Z}_q^*\rvert + s\lvert n\rvert$	$K(\lvert\mathbb{Z}_q^*\rvert + \mathbb{G}_1)$
TPA → CS	$(c+1)\lvert\mathbb{Z}_q^*\rvert + c\lvert n\rvert$	$3\lvert\mathbb{Z}_q^*\rvert + \lvert c\rvert$
CS → TPA	$K\lvert\mathbb{Z}_q^*\rvert + \lvert\mathbb{Z}_q^*\rvert + \lvert\mathbb{G}_1\rvert$	$\lvert\mathbb{Z}_q^*\rvert + 2\lvert\mathbb{G}_1\rvert$

comparison with scheme [16]. As listed in Table 1, before transmitting the file to the CS, the DO generates the index for each file. The computation overhead is $\lvert W\rvert \times (t_i \times H_{\mathbb{G}_1} + t_i \times Mul_{\mathbb{G}_1} + Exp_{\mathbb{G}_1}) + K \times \lvert SE_{w_k}\rvert Mul_{\mathbb{G}_1}$. The authenticator generation requires $n \times s \times (H_{\mathbb{G}_1} + 4Mul_{\mathbb{G}_1} + Exp_{\mathbb{G}_1})$. This does not differ significantly from the scheme [16]. The CS generates and sends the auditing evidence, referred to as Proof, to the TPA. The computational expense associated with the creation of this proof is $\lvert SE_{w_k}\rvert \times c \times Mul_{\mathbb{G}_1} + (\lvert SE_{w_k}\rvert \times c + 1)Mul_{\mathbb{Z}_q} + (\lvert SE_{w_k}\rvert \times c + 1)Exp_{\mathbb{G}_1}$. This result does not differ significantly from the scheme [16], mainly because we ensured security by adding random data. The TPA requires $4 \times Pair + (2c \times \lvert SE_{w_k}\rvert + l)Mul_{\mathbb{G}_1} + (2c \times \lvert SE_{w_k}\rvert + l + 2)Exp_{\mathbb{G}_1} + 2c \times \lvert SE_{w_k}\rvert \times Mul_{\mathbb{Z}_q^*}$ computation cost to conduct verification. This outcome incurs higher costs compared to scheme [16], due to our adoption of an identity-based cryptographic system.

Communication Overhead. Let F represent the size of fils, $\mathbb{G}_1$ represent the size of elements in $\mathbb{G}_1$, $\mathbb{Z}_q^*$ represent the size of elements in $\mathbb{Z}_q^*$, $\lvert n\rvert$ represent the size of elements in $[1, n]$. As listed in Table 2, data and its authenticators are uploaded into cloud, the communication overhead is $n \times \lvert F\rvert + (n \times s + n)\lvert\mathbb{G}_1\rvert$. Different from scheme [16], the index information is transfered to TPA, so the communication cost from DO to TPA is $K(\lvert\mathbb{Z}_q^*\rvert + \mathbb{G}_1)$. In our scheme, we adopt the way of transfering random seeds to CS in the challenge phase, the communication cost cost from TPA to CS is $3\lvert\mathbb{Z}_q^*\rvert + \lvert c\rvert$. This entails a lower overhead compared to scheme [16]. The CS transmits proof $Proof = \{T, \mu, R\}$ to TPA. The size of proof is $3|\mathbb{Z}_q^*|+|c|$. Scheme [16] needs extra keyword information.

7.2 Performance Comparison

Tests were performed using a Windows 10 computer featuring an Intel i7 processor operating at 2.5 GHz and equipped with 8GB of memory. To evaluate the efficiency of the proposed approach, essential parameters were established. Data sectors were configured to be 160 bits in size, and Type-A pairings with a group order of 160 bits were utilized. Moreover, the dimensions of elements within mathematical sets, including $\mathbb{Z}_q^*$ and $\mathbb{G}$, were uniformly se to 160 bits.

Figure 2 illustrated the time cost assessment encompassing indexing, authenticator generation, proof generation, and proof verification, contrasting the approach proposed in this paper with the scheme presented in [16]. As the scheme [16] incorporated a design element for the number of files within each keyword, it was a feature deemed unnecessary in our approach, so we standardized this aspect to a value of 1 in scheme [16] for a fair comparison of the two schemes' overheads. Figure 2(a) depicted the time cost associated with index generation. The number of keywords contained in each file varied from 10 to 100, increasing in increments of 10. As indicated by the figure, the time required increased with the number of keywords per file, and there was only a minor difference in overhead between the two schemes. Figure 2(b) illustrated the time cost for authenticator generation. The number of files linked to a keyword ranged from 100 to 1000, with increments of 100. The figure showed that the time increased with the number of data blocks in a file, and there was little difference in overhead between the two schemes. Figure 2(c) displayed the time cost for proof generation at $c = 300$ and 460. The number of files contained within a keyword ranged from 5 to 50, increasing by 5 each step. As evidenced by the figure, the time required for proof generation was directly proportional to the number of files per keyword and rose with the increase in the number of challenge blocks. Figure 2(d) represented the time cost for proof verification under the same conditions of $c = 300$ and $c = 460$. The trend for proof verification time mirrored that of Fig. 2(c), indicating a positive correlation with both the number of files contained in each keyword and the number of challenge blocks.

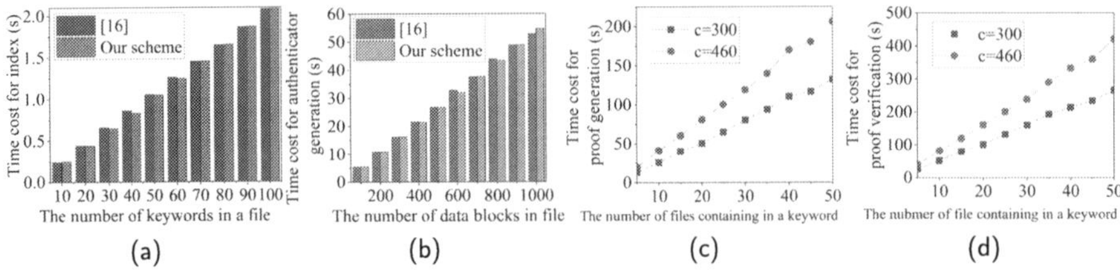

Fig. 2. The time expenditure for: (a) indexing, which varies with the quantity of distinct keywords within a file; (b) generating authenticators, which changes according to the number of data blocks in a file; (c) producing proofs, which fluctuates with the varying number of files associated with a keyword when c = 300 and 460; (d) verifying proofs, which also varies with the different number of files contained in a keyword under the conditions of c = 300 and 460.

8 Conclusion

We have proposed a keyword searchable data integrity auditing protocol designed for cloud-assisted WBANs. This scheme facilitates the qualitative inspection of wearable system data integrity, allowing for the retrieval of corresponding data through specific keywords by the CS, which then participates in the integrity verification process. The proposed approach enhances the protection of wearable system data integrity with greater accuracy. Moreover, considering that wearable devices are often closely linked to personal identity information, we have developed an authenticator utilizing an identity-based cryptographic system. This reduces the overhead associated with certificate management, making it more suitable for wearable systems. The feasibility of our proposed scheme has been demonstrated through rigorous security proofs and experimental validation.

References

1. Abidi, B., Jilbab, A., Mohamed, E.: Wireless body area networks: a comprehensive survey. J. Med. Eng. Technol. **44**(3), 97–107 (2020)
2. Ateniese, G., et al.: Provable data possession at untrusted stores. In: Proceedings of the 14th ACM Conference on Computer and Communications Security, pp. 598–609 (2007)
3. Garg, N., Bawa, S., Kumar, N.: An efficient data integrity auditing protocol for cloud computing. Futur. Gener. Comput. Syst. **109**, 306–316 (2020)
4. Ge, C., Susilo, W., Baek, J., Liu, Z., Xia, J., Fang, L.L.: Revocable attribute-based encryption with data integrity in clouds. IEEE Trans. Dependable Secure Comput. **19**(5), 2864–2872 (2021)
5. Gudeme, J., Pasupuleti, S., Kandukuri, R.: Attribute-based public integrity auditing for shared data with efficient user revocation in cloud storage. J. Ambient. Intell. Humaniz. Comput. **12**, 2019–2032 (2021)
6. Hajar, M., Al-Kadri, M., Kalutarage, H.: A survey on wireless body area networks: architecture, security challenges and research opportunities. Comput. Secur. **104**, 102211 (2021)

7. Jabeen, T., Ashraf, H., Ullah, A.: A survey on healthcare data security in wireless body area networks. J. Ambient. Intell. Humaniz. Comput. **12**(10), 9841–9854 (2021). https://doi.org/10.1007/s12652-020-02728-y
8. Juels, A., J. Kaliski, S.B.: PORs: proofs of retrievability for large files. In: Proceedings of the 14th ACM Conference on Computer and Communications Security, pp. 584–597 (2007)
9. Li, A., Chen, Y., Yan, Z., Zhou, X., Shimizu, S.: A survey on integrity auditing for data storage in the cloud: from single copy to multiple replicas. IEEE Trans. Big Data **8**(5), 1428–1442 (2020)
10. Li, Y., Zhang, F.: An efficient certificate-based data integrity auditing protocol for cloud-assisted WBANs. IEEE Internet Things J. **9**(13), 11513–11523 (2021)
11. Lin, Y., Li, J., Kimura, S., Yang, Y., Ji, Y., Cao, Y.: Consortium blockchain-based public integrity verification in cloud storage for IoT. IEEE Internet Things J. **9**(5), 3978–3987 (2021)
12. Narwal, B., Mohapatra, A.: A survey on security and authentication in wireless body area networks. J. Syst. Architect. **113**, 101883 (2021)
13. Nyangaresi, V.: Privacy preserving three-factor authentication protocol for secure message forwarding in wireless body area networks. Ad Hoc Netw. **142**, 103117 (2023)
14. Peng, L., Yan, Z., Liang, X., Yu, X.: SecDedup: secure data deduplication with dynamic auditing in the cloud. Inf. Sci. **644**, 119279 (2023)
15. Ramadan, M., Liao, Y., Li, F., Zhou, S., Abdalla, H.: IBEET-RSA: identity-based encryption with equality test over RSA for wireless body area networks. Mob. Netw. Appl. **25**, 223–233 (2020)
16. Shen, W., Gai, C., Yu, J., Su, Y.: Keyword-based remote data integrity auditing supporting full data dynamics. IEEE Trans. Serv. Comput. **17**(5), 2516–2529 (2023)
17. Wang, Y., Chen, C., Chen, Z., He, J.: Attribute-based user revocable data integrity audit for internet-of-things devices in cloud storage. Secur. Commun. Netw. **2020**(1), 8837456 (2020)
18. Zhang, Q., et al.: Efficient blockchain-based data integrity auditing for multi-copy in decentralized storage. IEEE Trans. Parallel Distrib. Syst. (2023)
19. Zhang, X., Liu, X., Liu, Q., Wang, J., Liu, X.: Revocable attribute-based data integrity auditing scheme on lattices. In: 2022 International Conference on Computer Science, Information Engineering and Digital Economy (CSIEDE 2022), pp. 383–396. Atlantis Press (2022)
20. Zhang, X., Zhao, J., Xu, C., Li, H., Wang, H., Zhang, Y.: CIPPPA: conditional identity privacy-preserving public auditing for cloud-based WBANs against malicious auditors. IEEE Trans. Cloud Comput. **9**(4), 1362–1375 (2019)

SA-aChain: A Blockchain Hybrid Architecture for Privacy-Preserving Alert Data Management

Xinzhuo Xia, Lei Xu(✉), KeKe Gai, and Liehuang Zhu

Beijing Institute of Technology, Haidian District, Beijing 100081, China
{3120241299,6120180029,gaikeke,liehuangz}@bit.edu.cn

Abstract. Alert aggregation plays an important role in intrusion detection. Traditionally, a centralized system is utilized to manage the massive alert data generated by various network security devices. However, such a system faces data tampering risks and cannot support cross-organization alert information sharing. To overcome the shortcomings of centralized alert management systems, in this paper we propose SA-aChain, a hybrid architecture which incorporates relational database into blockchain so as to enhance the online analytical processing performances of blockchain. Considering that alert data may contain sensitive information and cannot be directly stored on blockchain, the proposed architecture utilizes field-level encryption to secure sensitive data. And a dual-indexing scheme is designed to support ciphertext queries. More importantly, the proposed architecture adopts a hybrid storage structure which seamlessly combines encrypted tables with blockchain metadata. Simulation results show that, compared to existing hybrid architecture which does not provide privacy protection, SA-aChain has slightly higher storage overhead and query latency. The results demonstrate that SA-aChain balances well between privacy and efficiency, and is applicable to practical alert data management scenarios.

Keywords: Blockchain · Relational Database · Field-Level Encryption · Zero-Knowledge Proofs · Hybrid Storage

1 Introduction

In modern cybersecurity systems, various security devices deployed in the network, such as Intrusion Detection Systems (IDS) and Security Information and Event Management (SIEM), generate massive alert data [2,11]. These alert data describe attack behaviors such as scanning probes, SQL injection, privilege escalation, and data exfiltration, using critical attributes such as attack source, target, type, timestamp, and event priority [7]. The alert data are vital for analyzing cyberattack patterns, constructing attack chains, detecting advanced persistent threats (APTs) [10], and enhancing cybersecurity situational awareness [9].

To manage the alert data, current cybersecurity systems generally rely on centralized SQL or NoSQL databases. Though centralized databases can provide

M. Yung et al. (Eds.): AIBlock 2025, LNCS 16314, pp. 124–142, 2026.
https://doi.org/10.1007/978-3-032-16168-0_8

good online analytical processing (OLAP) services, they have several shortcomings. On one hand, centralized databases suffer from high tampering risks. The centralized storage model makes logs vulnerable to manipulation or deletion by attackers who breach the system, undermining incident tracing and forensics [1]. On the other hand, different databases are generally managed by different organizations. The systems built upon centralized databases struggle to support cross-organizational threat intelligence sharing, thereby creating detection silos.

Blockchain, a decentralized and distributed storage technology, offers core properties of immutability, transparency, traceability, and consensus validation, making it suitable for distributed data storage, transaction processing, and multi-party collaboration. Blockchain technology has demonstrated significant potential in applications such as credit assessment [12], supply chain traceability [26], and cross-border payments [19], etc. Currently, major database companies in industrial fields, such as IBM, SAP, and Oracle, are advancing blockchain database designs to manage on-chain data efficiently. However, their solutions primarily support SQL-like queries with limited functionality. Most of these solutions are restricted to non-encrypted data, and lack privacy-preserving mechanisms [17]. In academia, studies often replicate on-chain data to external databases but lack consistency checks for analytical tasks, compromising the security characteristics of blockchain [29]. Meanwhile, works on verifiable query [28] and data management mechanisms [25] for blockchains remain far from supporting full SQL operations. Existing verifiable query systems generally utilize zero-knowledge proofs (ZKPs) to handle only simple operations and often incur high latency for complex queries, which makes them unsuitable for real-time analysis.

Aforementioned approaches fail to balance SQL efficiency with sensitive data security, creating a privacy-performance trade-off. In order to fully provide SQL-based OLAP services, Wang *et al.* proposed aChain [24], a hybrid "blockchain + database" architecture that achieves data collaboration through deep coupling. However, aChain does not take into account the privacy of data. An implicit assumption of aChain is that all the data stored in the system are publicly accessible. While in the alert data management scenario which we study in this paper, the privacy issues must be handled carefully. Alert data generally contains information, such as attack payloads and IP addresses, that can be leveraged to infer private information about individuals. Directly storing such data in blockchain ledger or database will lead to privacy disclosure. Some previous studies have explored ZKPs and homomorphic encryption to address the privacy issue caused by blockchain transparency. Most of these studies are solutions based on generic blockchain frameworks like Hyperledger Fabric [3]. They face challenges such as high encryption overhead in smart contracts or incompatibilities between indexing mechanisms and blockchain storage, making it difficult to balance performance and privacy in practice.

To address the gaps between SQL-empowered blockchain and privacy-preserving blockchain, in this paper we propose SA-aChain (Security Augmented aChain), a hybrid architecture that enhances aChain's deeply coupled "blockchain + relational database" framework with four core innovations for secure and efficient alert data management. First, the proposed architecture introduces a four-layer framework for end-to-end sensitive data encryption, with layers linked via encryption metadata (EM) to ensure state continuity. Second, SA-aChain differentiates sensitive fields from non-sensitive fields in an alert record. Sensitive fields are encrypted using AES-GCM [6]. And SA-aChain adopts a dual-index design to improve query efficiency. Specifically, B+ trees are designed for plaintext queries, and Block Range Index (BRIN) indexes are designed for ciphertext range queries [21]. Third, SA-aChain adopts a three-phase protocol to reach consensus on transaction orders, enabling Merkle-proof read validation (anti-dirty read), integrity-checked write sets, and delta-compressed history logs. Finally, the hybrid storage engine of SA-aChain combines encrypted relational data with immutable blockchain metadata, while the query processor ensures General Data Protection Regulation (GDPR) compliance via automatic plaintext/ciphertext separation.

The remainder of this paper is structured as follows. Section 2 details the proposed architecture and mathematical models for encryption, indexing, and traceability. Section 3 deeply dives into the four layers of SA-aChain. In Sect. 4, we evaluate the performance of SA-aChain via simulations. Finally, we conclude our work in Sect. 5.

2 Architecture Overview

Inspired by aChain, in this paper we propose a hybrid architecture SA-aChain which combines blockchain with relational database. As shown in Fig. 1, when a client submits an SQL operation containing sensitive data (such as alert data insertion), the data flow first goes through the Data Preprocessing layer for SQL parsing, sensitive field identification, and encryption processing. Then, the Consistency layer globally orders the operations through a consensus protocol. Subsequently, the Data Management layer extracts EM and establishes data associations. Finally, the Hybrid Storage layer persistently stores the encrypted data and metadata in a relational database. All layers work collaboratively through a sophisticated metadata transmission mechanism to ensure that sensitive data undergoes full-lifecycle management in an encrypted state.

SA-aChain is designed to counter a Byzantine adversary model. In this model, malicious entities may attempt to leak sensitive data through cryptanalytic attacks on ciphertexts, tamper with transactions to falsify alert records, or infer patterns from metadata such as encryption parameters or query logs.

To address these threats, the architecture employs layered defenses. Field-level encryption mitigates data leakage: AES-GCM provides semantic security for fields requiring complete confidentiality, while OPE supports range queries on fields where order preservation is necessary. PBFT consensus, augmented with Merkle proofs, prevents tampering by ensuring transaction integrity and immutability. Additionally, strict binding of EM to ciphertexts blocks inference attacks by preventing adversaries from correlating encrypted data with real-world entities through auxiliary information.

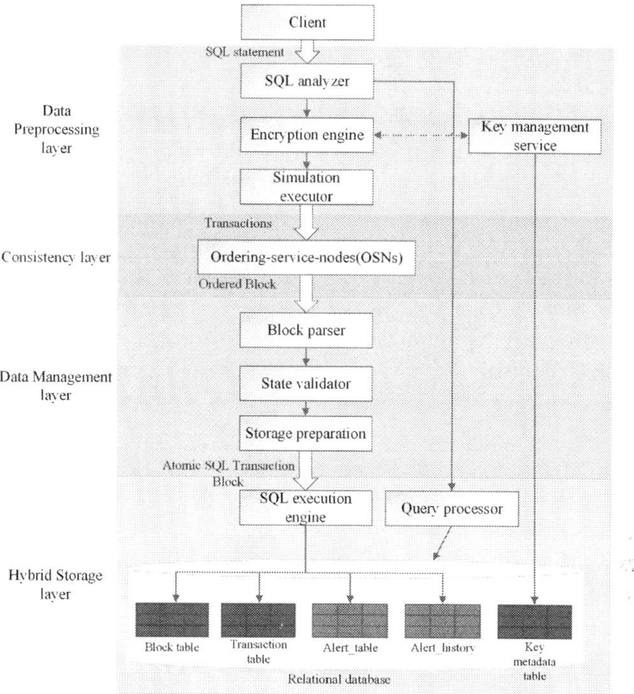

Fig. 1. A simple illustration of the proposed architecture.

Before introducing the components of each layer, we first describe the data model adopted by SA-aChain. The core data entity processed by SA-aChain is the alert record. The record is structurally represented as a 7-tuple:

$$Alert = (alert\_id, timestamp, severity, status, alarm\_type, source\_ip, content)$$

where *alert_id* is the unique identifier of the alert record, *severity* denotes the level of severity, *status* denotes the processing status, *alarm_type* denotes the type of the alert, *source_ip* denotes source IP address, and *content* describes the details of the alert. We refer to each tuple as a field. Some of the fields are non-sensitive, including alert_id, timestamp, severity, status, and alarm_type. These fields can be stored in plaintext format. Some fields are sensitive, including source_ip and content. These fields are subject to encryption protection. Such a data model enables full-lifecycle management of alert records, including create, read, update, and delete operations, through blockchain transactions. Notably, encryption operations remain transparent to upper applications.

The Data Preprocessing layer acts as a security gateway for blockchain SQL operations. Its core functions include identifying sensitive data, performing encryption transformations, rewriting SQL statements, and generating verifiable transaction proposals. The basic workflow of the Data Preprocessing layer is as follows. First, the SQL preprocessor receives raw SQL statements from clients. It parses the syntax to identify operation types (INSERT/DELETE/UPDATE/SELECT) and involved fields. Based on a predefined encryption policy metadata table, it marks sensitive fields and assigns encryption algorithms. Next, the Encryption engine takes plaintext values of sensitive fields, the algorithm mapping table, and the original SQL statement as input. It retrieves keys from the Key Management Service (KMS), encrypts each sensitive field with the specified algorithm, and generates EM containing parameters. The engine outputs two items, namely the rewritten SQL statement with ciphertexts and an EM set describing ciphertext-parameter associations. Finally, The Simulation Executor simulates the execution of the rewritten SQL on the node's local database. And the execution is converted to read-only queries for conflict checking. The engine generates three outputs, including a read set(rSet) recording data access versions, a write set(wSet) with state updates and bound EM, and query results for non-sensitive fields. Additionally, it creates a unique deterministic row_key to ensure state consistency. The final output is a signed transaction proposal, which is then sent to the Consistency layer.

The Consistency layer establishes a globally ordered sequence of encrypted SQL operations through Practical Byzantine Fault Tolerance (PBFT) consensus mechanism, ensuring deterministic execution across all nodes while maintaining cryptographic transparency. As the core ordering coordinator, Ordering Service Nodes (OSNs) process data through four sequential stages. First, the Transaction Receipt and Sanitization stage accepts signed transaction proposals from the Data Preprocessing layer. It ensures structural integrity via Elliptic Curve Digital Signature Algorithm (ECDSA) signature verification [13], while filtering abnormal transactions using heuristic rules. Next, the PBFT-based Total Ordering stage processes sanitized transactions through a PBFT pipeline [16]. This stage outputs a linearized transaction sequence. Then, the Self-Verifying Block Construction stage processes the ordered sequence to generate a Merkle root, a block header embedded with signatures, and applies a size/time-based packaging policy. Finally, the Optimized Block Propagation stage distributes blocks via an adaptive Gossip protocol with probability-controlled flooding and fault-tolerant retry mechanisms with blacklisting.

The Data Management layer acts as a secure bridge between the Consistency Layer's ordered blocks and the Hybrid Storage Layer's encrypted persistence, tasked with converting blockchain-verified transactions into executable storage instructions while maintaining cryptographic consistency and data integrity. The Block Parser first receives ordered blocks from the Consistency Layer, and decomposes them into block headers and transaction bodies containing rewritten SQL with ciphertext placeholders, versioned rSets, encrypted wSets, and field-level EM, validating block integrity via chained hashing and digital signatures. The State Validator then performs a two-phase transaction validation, namely read-set validation which uses Merkle proofs to compare the version of rSets with current database state so as to prevent dirty reads, and write-set validation which checks primary key uniqueness, foreign key constraints, and EM completeness to reject invalid transactions. For Storage Preparation, the layer binds the encrypted wSets to corresponding EM fields to generate executable SQL with embedded ciphertexts and JSON metadata, creates lightweight historical records via delta compression, and applies dynamic schema versioning for DDL operations. This module directly produces idempotent SQL transaction blocks. The transaction blocks include business data updates, historical entries, and blockchain metadata. The transaction blocks are streamed to the Storage Layer via Transport Layer Security (TLS) channels in the form of atomic transactions.

The Hybrid Storage layer serves as an encrypted data persistence engine, integrating blockchain records with data storage via a unified SQL execution interface to ensure zero-knowledge security. It executes all storage operations using atomic transaction blocks received via TLS from the Data Management Layer, ensuring cryptographic consistency within a single ACID transaction workflow. Specifically, the SQL Execution Engine processes incoming transaction blocks to atomically execute business data updates, historical records, and blockchain metadata (e.g., block headers and transactions). Security mechanisms include automatic ciphertext zeroization during updates, role-based access control (RBAC) enforcement, and on-write blockchain logging, with execution receipts appended with cryptographic proofs. The Query Processor handles read operations by returning plaintext for non-sensitive fields and ciphertexts with metadata for sensitive fields, optimizing performance via B+ tree and BRIN indexing. The Hybrid Storage layer contains five tables to store data. The Alert_table is used for storing encrypted business data with zero plaintext exposure. The Alert_History is used for storing compressed change logs. The Block_table is used for storing hash-linked block headers. The Transaction_table is used for storing immutable transaction payloads. The Key metadata table is used for storing encryption policy metadata. This design ensures end-to-end encryption, leveraging database-native ACID properties while maintaining auditability and compliance with GDPR standards [15].

3 Design Details

3.1 Data Preprocessing Layer

SQL Analyzer. The SQL analyzer module initiates the sensitive data handling workflow by parsing incoming SQL statements using the ANTLR4 grammar framework [20]. This parsing operation extracts critical structural elements including operation types (INSERT, UPDATE, SELECT, DELETE), target table names, field lists, and value lists. A predefined encryption policy metadata table (*Key_metadata_table*) is then queried to identify sensitive fields requiring cryptographic protection. This policy table maintains mappings between table-column pairs and their corresponding encryption algorithms, expressed as

$$\text{Key\_metadata\_table} : (table\_name, column\_name) \rightarrow (algorithm, key\_id),$$

where $table\_name$ and $column\_name$ identify data locations, $algorithm$ indicates cryptographic schemes (e.g., OPE for range-searchable fields or AES-GCM for full semantic security), and key_id denotes the KMS identifier for key retrieval.

Encryption Engine. The Encryption engine performs cryptographic transformation while restructuring SQL syntax to maintain cryptographic consistency throughout the system. Upon receiving processed SQL metadata, this module executes parallel cryptographic operations through a three-phase workflow. Each sensitive data field undergoes deterministic or randomized encryption based on its pre-assigned cryptographic scheme. Fields requiring range query capabilities employ order-preserving encryption (OPE) follows Boldyreva's scheme [5], expressed as

$$ciphertext = OPE.Enc(K_{ope}, plaintext),$$

where K_{ope} denotes a symmetric key retrieved from the KMS, *plaintext* is the original field value, and *ciphertext* represents the transformed output.

By contrast, sensitive fields requiring full semantic security are encrypted using AES-256-GCM, an authenticated encryption scheme that provides both confidentiality and integrity guarantees [6]. Formally, there is

$$(\text{ciphertext}, \text{IV}, \text{auth\_tag}) = \text{AES-GCM.Enc}(K_{\text{aes}}, \text{plaintext}),$$

where K_{aes} denotes a field-specific key, IV denotes a 12-byte cryptographically random initialization vector(IV), and $auth\_tag$ denotes a 16-byte authentication tag for integrity verification.

Concurrently with encryption, the engine generates field-level EM objects as

$$EM = \{\text{algorithm}, \text{key\_id}, \text{IV}, \text{auth\_tag}\},$$

which are designed to bind cryptographic parameters to each transformed field. Each EM object is structured to contain a unique data reference in the format [table]_[row_key].[column], which maps the metadata to its corresponding table, row, and column, along with the target table name (e.g., "Alert"), column name (e.g., "source_ip"), encryption algorithm identifier (e.g., "AES-GCM" or "OPE"), and the KMS key version identifier for tracking key usage. For randomized encryption schemes like AES-GCM, the EM object includes Base64-encoded IVs and authentication tags (auth_tag) to preserve cryptographic context, while these fields are omitted for deterministic schemes like OPE.

Meanwhile, SQL statements undergo semantic-preserving restructuring. INSERT and UPDATE operations expand column specifications to include "_cipher" and _em suffixes while replacing plaintext values with ciphertext binaries, whereas SELECT statements redirect projection clauses to retrieve ciphertext and metadata columns instead of plaintext, automatically appending necessary metadata. For range queries, the engine preserves predicate structures on OPE-encrypted columns to maintain index compatibility. All transformed SQL incorporates role-based access control predicates to enforce permission constraints at the storage layer, thereby aligning cryptographic enforcement with database permissions in a zero-trust security architecture.

Simulation Execution. The Simulation execution implements conflict detection through Multi-Version Concurrency Control (MVCC) principles [27]. It first converts Data Manipulation Language operations into read-only equivalents using database-specific isolation constructs. For example, this module transforms UPDATE operations into SELECT ... FOR UPDATE statements. Execution against local database replicas produces a read set(rSet). Formally, the rSet is defined as

$$rSet = (table, row\_key, ver)|\forall \text{ rows accessed by the transaction},$$

where *row_key* represents the primary key, and *ver* is a composite version identifier combining block number *BNo* and transaction index *TIdx*. The corresponding wSet captures proposed state modifications. Formally, the wSet is defined as

$$wSet = (op, table, row\_key, new\_val, new\_ver, EM)|\forall write\_operations.$$

In the above equation, the first item *op* denotes the type of the SQL operation, such as INSERT, UPDATE, DELETE. The second item *new_val* denotes ciphertexts, and The item *EM* bound cryptographic metadata. The item *row_key* applies the construct SHA-256$(timestamp\|clientID\|table\|primary_key)$ truncated to 128 bits. The module outputs signed transaction proposals bundling rSet, wSet, and non-sensitive query results for consensus layer submission.

Key Management Service. The Key Management Service is the core security module within the Data Preprocessing layer, enabling secure key derivation and lifecycle management through hardware security modules. Its design adheres to a hierarchical key derivation architecture, ensuring key isolation for sensitive field encryption and forward secrecy. When the Encryption Engine initiates a key request, KMS executes key derivation based on the following input parameters. The first parameter Key identifier denote as *key_id*), indicates the preconfigured encryption policy metadata table, mapping to a master key hierarchy. The second parameter Context parameters denotes as *context*), indicates security context comprising table name, column name, and operation timestamp, binding keys to usage scenarios. The key derivation process employs the HMAC-based Key Derivation Function (HKDF) [14], with pseudocode as follows. As described in Algorithm 1, the function first uses HKDF-Extract and HKDF-Expand comply with RFC 5869 [14]. Then, the function enhances entropy pools via salting and generating deterministic outputs, while the label parameter (e.g., "OPE/AES-key") explicitly distinguishing algorithm types to meet key requirements of different encryption engines (OPE or AES-GCM).

Algorithm 1: HMAC-Based Key Derivation Function

Input: Key identifier *key_id* from $Key\_metadata\_table$; Context parameters *context*

Output: Derived encryption key k

Fetch master key HSM_master from hardware security module;
$seed \leftarrow$ HKDF-Extract(HSM_master, context);
$k \leftarrow$ HKDF-Expand($seed$, "OPE/AES-key", 256);
return k;

3.2 Consistency Layer

The Consistency layer serves as the ordering backbone of SA-aChain, adopting the Execute-Order-Validate (EOV) architecture from aChain [24]. Its core function is to establish a globally agreed-upon sequence of operations through PBFT consensus [23], ensuring deterministic execution across all nodes. This layer operates through Ordering Service Nodes, which perform the following three critical functions.

Transaction Validation and Sanitization. This function processes signed transaction proposal received from the Data Preprocessing layer. Formally, a signed transaction proposal is expressed as

$$m = \langle \mathrm{SQL}_{\mathrm{enc}}, \mathrm{rSet}, \mathrm{wSet}, \mathrm{QRs}, \mathrm{EM}, \mathrm{sig}_{\mathrm{client}} \rangle,$$

where the SQL_{enc} denotes the rewritten SQL statement. The *rSet* and the *wSet* are read and write sets. The *EM* represents the EM. The sig_{client} is the client's ECDSA signature [13]. The proposal is validated via the following logical expression

$$\mathrm{Validate}(m) \equiv \mathrm{VerifySig}_p(m) \wedge \mathrm{SeqUnique}(n) \wedge \mathrm{Digest}(m) = d,$$

SeqUnique(n) indicates sequence number uniqueness. Here, n is a monotonic sequence number generated by the Local Sequencer. Its purpose is to ensure the uniqueness of transaction ordering, preventing duplicates or out-of-order arrangements. This condition verifies the legitimacy of the transaction by checking the uniqueness of the sequence number n. The parameters in the validation expression are sourced as follows. The public key p is from the Certificate Registry for signature verification. Then, the monotonic sequence number n is from the Local Sequencer to ensure ordering uniqueness. Lastly the digest is verifying for data integrity checking as:

$$d = \text{SHA-256}(\mathrm{SQL}_{\mathrm{enc}} \parallel \mathrm{rSet} \parallel \mathrm{wSet}).$$

Self-verifying Block Construction. Given the ordered transaction sequence $T_1, \ldots, T_k$ output by PBFT, the Merkle root is first calculated as [18]

$$\mathrm{tx\_root} = \mathrm{MerkleRoot}\left(h_i = \text{SHA-256}(T_i) \mid h_1, \ldots, h_k\right).$$

In the formula for calculating the Merkle root, h_i represents the SHA-256 hash value of the i-th transaction T_i. The process of computing the transaction Merkle root (tx_root) begins with generating h_i by applying the SHA-256 hash function to each transaction T_i. These hash values $h_1, \ldots, h_k$ then form the basis for constructing the Merkle tree, and the root node of this tree is the tx_root.

The block header is structured as

$$H_i = \langle i, \mathrm{tx\_root}, H_{\text{i-1}}, \mathrm{Sig}_{\mathrm{BFT}} \rangle,$$

where i is the current block height (previous height + 1), *H_i-1* is the preceding block header from the Blockchain State, and Sig_{BFT} is an aggregated signature from at least $2f+1$ nodes to ensure block immutability and consensus validity. Blocks are packaged dynamically based on accumulated transaction size or time intervals to balance storage and propagation efficiency.

Optimized Propagation Mechanism. Key parameters include the neighbor count N_{peers} obtained from the Topology Service and the average latency avg_latency measured by the Network Probe Daemon. The adaptive Gossip protocol adjusts the propagation probability using the piecewise function as follows [8].

Algorithm 2: Latency-Aware Block Propagation Function

Input: Block B_i; Set of neighbor nodes *neighbors*; Average latency latency_{avg}
Output: Propagation status report
// $\phi(N) = \min(5, \lfloor N/2 \rfloor)$ where N is the size of *neighbors*
foreach $p_j \in randomSubset(neighbors, \phi(N))$ **do**
    Send block B_i to peer p_j;
    Start timeout timer $T_{out} \leftarrow 2 \times \text{latency}_{avg}$;
    if *Timer expires* ***and*** *retries* < 3 **then**
        Select backup node p_k from reserve list;
    end
    else
        Add peer p_j to blacklist;
    end
end
return *Propagation status report*

3.3 Data Management Layer

The Data Management layer serves as a secure conduit between the ordered blocks from the Consistency Layer and encrypted persistence in the Storage Layer. Its primary function is to translate blockchain-verified transactions into executable storage operations while enforcing cryptographic consistency and data integrity. The design comprises the following four core modules:

Block Parser. The Block Parser module decomposes incoming blocks into structured components, including block headers. A block header has fields, including block_number, block_hash, parent_hash, consensus_signature. These fields are stored in the Block_Table, and transaction payloads containing rewritten SQL with ciphertext placeholders, versioned rSets, encrypted wSets, and field-level EM. The Block Parser also verifies the integrity of the block. First, the parser computes the hash of the block as

$$block\_hash = SHA-256(block\_header \parallel tx\_root).$$

Then, the parser verifies the digital signature validation (using ECDSA [13]) of the BFT consensus signature, with invalid blocks triggering immediate rejection. If the block fails the verification, it will be rejected immediately.

State Validator. The State Validator module implements a two-phase transaction validation mechanism. Given the rSet, the validator checks whether the current database state version matches the version of rSet using Merkle proofs [18]. Mismatches indicate dirty reads and cause transaction abortion. Given the encrypted wSet, the validator checks if wSet satisfies primary key uniqueness for INSERT operations, foreign key constraints via relational integrity checks, and completeness of EM bindings for all sensitive fields (e.g., absence of EM for source_ip in wSet raises InvalidTransaction).

Storage Preparation. The Storage Preparation module serves as the core component of the Data Management layer, responsible for transforming validated transaction data into executable storage instructions while maintaining EM binding and historical record integrity. The module first binds a triple dataflow processing mechanism, encrypted data binding dynamically associates encrypted fields in the wSet with EM to generate structured objects embeddable in SQL. Then the module constructs lightweight history generation constructs change logs using Delta compression algorithms to store only differential data [22]. After that, the module packages atomic transaction combining business data, historical records, and blockchain metadata into ACID transaction blocks. During data binding, a field-level mapping

$$\Psi_{\text{field}} : \text{new\_val}[\text{column\_cipher}] \mapsto \text{EM}[\text{column}]$$

is constructed to generate structured objects embedding ciphertexts and corresponding metadata. The JSON object embeddable in SQL is generated as

$$\Gamma_{\text{data}} = \bigcup_{col \in \text{sensitive\_fields}} \left\{ \text{col\_cipher} : \text{new\_val}[\text{col\_cipher}], \text{col\_em} : \text{JSON}(\text{EM}[\text{col}]) \right\}.$$

This object serves as input for parameterized SQL statements, ensuring synchronous storage of ciphertexts and their encryption contexts. The historical records are defined as

$$H_\delta = \langle \text{row\_key}, \text{op}, \Delta_{\text{data}}, \Delta_{\text{EM}}, \text{new\_ver} \rangle,$$

where Δ_{data} stores only changed sensitive field ciphertexts. The ciphertexts are full sets for INSERT or differential fields for UPDATE. Δ_{EM} is the corresponding metadata subset, and the version number new_ver inherits from the wSet. The atomic transaction block T_{atomic} consists of three components is defined as

$$T_{\text{atomic}} = \begin{cases} \text{Business Update: } \Phi_{\text{exec}}(\text{table}, \Gamma_{\text{data}}) \\ \text{History Append: } \Phi_{\text{exec}}(\text{Alert\_history}, H_\delta) \\ \text{Metadata Update: } \Phi_{\text{exec}}(\text{Block\_table}, H_i) \end{cases},$$

where Φ_{exec} denotes the SQL execution operator. The T_{atomic} is transmitted to the storage layer via TLS channels, which ensures atomicity between business table updates and historical record writes, version consistency between blockchain metadata and business data, and the inseparability of EM and ciphertexts.

3.4 Hybrid Storage Layer

The Hybrid Storage layer serves as the cryptographically secure persistence engine within the SA-aChain architecture, implementing a unified storage model that integrates blockchain verifiability with relational database management while enforcing zero-knowledge security principles. This layer executes atomic transaction blocks received from the Data Management Layer via TLS-secured channels, maintaining cryptographic consistency through ACID-compliant operations across two core components.

SQL Execution Engine. The SQL Execution Engine processes atomic transaction block T_{atomic} containing three operation types. The first type is business data updating to the encrypted Alert table. The second type is historical records compressed for Alert_history. The third type is immutable blockchain metadata for Block_table and Transaction_table. Each block is processed deterministically through the following workflow.

$$\Gamma_{\text{exec}} = \Phi_{\text{RBAC}} \circ \Phi_{\text{Zeroize}} \circ \Phi_{\text{Integrity}}(T_{\text{atomic}}).$$

The symbol $\circ$ denotes function composition, meaning that functions are applied sequentially from right to left. Specifically, the atomic transaction block T_{atomic} first undergoes processing by $\Phi_{\text{Integrity}}$, which generates cryptographic proofs using Merkle-Patricia commitments. The result of this processing is then passed to Φ_{Zeroize}, which securely erases plaintext buffers via NIST SP 800-88-compliant sanitization. The output from Φ_{Zeroize} is subsequently processed by Φ_{RBAC}, which enforces role-based access control using system-configured permission matrices. The final result of this sequential function application is Γ_{exec}. If the block is processed successfully, then the execution appends verifiable receipts to the blockchain log. Otherwise, automatic state restoration from the latest valid checkpoint will be triggered.

Query Processor. The Query Processor implements dual-mode retrieval for encrypted datasets. For non-sensitive fields, the processor enables sub-millisecond plaintext projection via clustered B+ tree indexing. The processor utilizes clustered B+ tree indexes created on primary keys and frequently filtered columns. The B+ tree has logarithmic complexity, which accelerates point queries and range scans on plaintext data. Index keys are structured as

$$\text{B+ Node} = \langle \text{key}, \text{data\_ptr}, \text{child\_ptr} \rangle,$$

where leaf nodes contain direct pointers to plaintext records in the `Alert_table`. While sensitive fields return ciphertext/EM pairs with OPE-compatible range query support via BRIN indexing, for composite operations, the processor solves the following optimization problem to generate the most efficient execution plan:

$$\min_{P}\{\mathrm{Cost}(P) \mid P \models \mathrm{RBAC} \wedge \mathrm{GDPR}_{25}\}.$$

In this optimization problem, the symbol $\models$ indicates that the execution plan **P** must satisfy two constraints. The first constraint is compliance with Role-Based Access Control policies, which regulate access permissions based on predefined roles. The second constraint is adherence to Article 25 of GDPR, which pertains to requirements for data protection impact assessments [15]. The cost model integrates index selectivity estimates and cryptographic operation weights. All results undergo on-the-fly consistency verification against the blockchain's state root before delivery.

Storage Schema Implementation. SA-aChain utilizes five core relational tables to persist the outputs generated by its SQL Execution Engine and Query Processor, each designed with distinct functionalities and inter-table relationships to ensure data integrity and cryptographic consistency. The Alert Table employs a hybrid plaintext-ciphertext schema to store encrypted business data: non-sensitive fields such as *alert_id*, *timestamp*, *severity*, *status*, and *alarm_type* are stored in plaintext, while sensitive fields like *source_ip* and *content* are encrypted as ciphertexts. Each encrypted column is accompanied by metadata columns that record algorithm specifications, key IDs, IVs, and authentication tags, with *alert_id* serving as the primary key to link with other tables.

The Alert_history Table maintains compressed change logs using delta-encoding for efficient version tracking. Each entry includes *row_key* references to the Alert table, operation types (INSERT/UPDATE/DELETE), version identifiers composed of block height and transaction index, and binary diffs of modified fields along with their EM. BRIN indexes on the version columns facilitate efficient temporal range queries.

The Block_table records immutable blockchain headers with hash-chaining integrity, featuring fields such as *block height*, *creation timestamp*, the Merkle root of transactions, *previous block hash*, and aggregate BFT signatures. The *block height* acts as a foreign key in the Transaction_table, which stores verifiable transaction payloads with cryptographic proofs. These payloads include *transaction IDs*, *block height* references, read/write sets from consensus validation, rewritten SQL operations, field-level EM, and Merkle proofs linking to the Block_table roots, enabling blockchain state reconstruction and audit verification.

The *Key_metadata_table* manages field-level encryption policies as system metadata, with a schema consisting of *table_name*, *column_name*, *algorithm*, and *key_id*. This table governs the encryption behaviors of the Data Preprocessing layer, referenced during both write operations and ciphertext query rewriting.

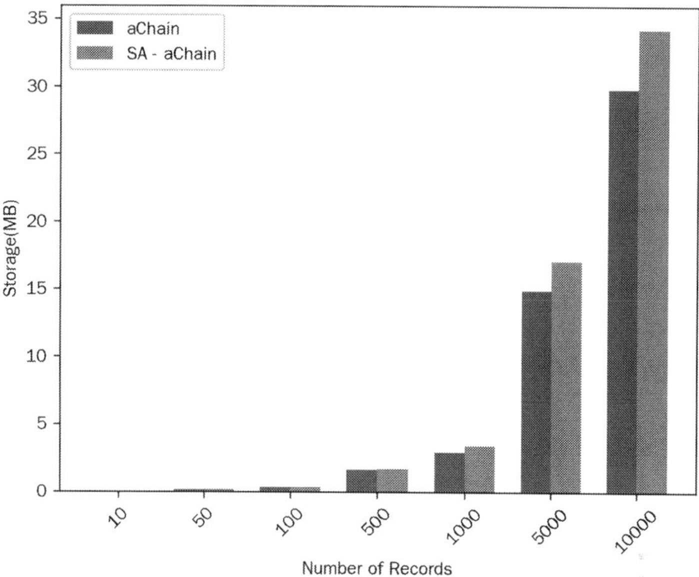

Fig. 2. A comparison between SA-aChain and aChain in terms of storage overhead.

4 Evaluation

To evaluate the performance of SA-aChain, we implement a simple prototype using CouchDB and HyperLedger Fabric [4]. HyperLedger Fabric v2.5.12 is set up with a Raft consensus network, including 2 organizations (1 Peer per organization), and CouchDB 3.3.2 serves as the state database. The related smart contracts are coded in Go. For the experimental data, we employ a self-constructed synthetic security alerts dataset. It includes from 10 to 10,000 records to simulate small-to-medium scale scenarios, with each record containing 2 sensitive fields (e.g., content, src_ip) and 5 non-sensitive fields (e.g., timestamp, severity). All experiments were conducted on a computer equipped with an 11th Gen Intel(R) Core(TM) i7-11850H CPU, 128 GB RAM, and a 1TB NVMe SSD, running the Ubuntu 24.04.2 LTS operating system.

We compare the performance of SA-aChain with that of aChain. First, we conduct simulations to evaluate the storage overhead. Given the number of records, we measure the actual storage size for SA-aChain and aChain at the corresponding record count. The results are shown in Fig. 2. As we can see, both the storage overhead of SA-aChain and the storage overhead of aChain grow linearly with the number of records. The storage overhead of SA-aChain is 5–15% higher than that of aChain. This is mainly because, compared to aChain, SA-aChain's encryption and indexing mechanisms introduce additional storage overhead. The minor storage difference stems from IV and key index storage in sensitive fields, additional key-value pairs and standardized serialization of encrypted data.

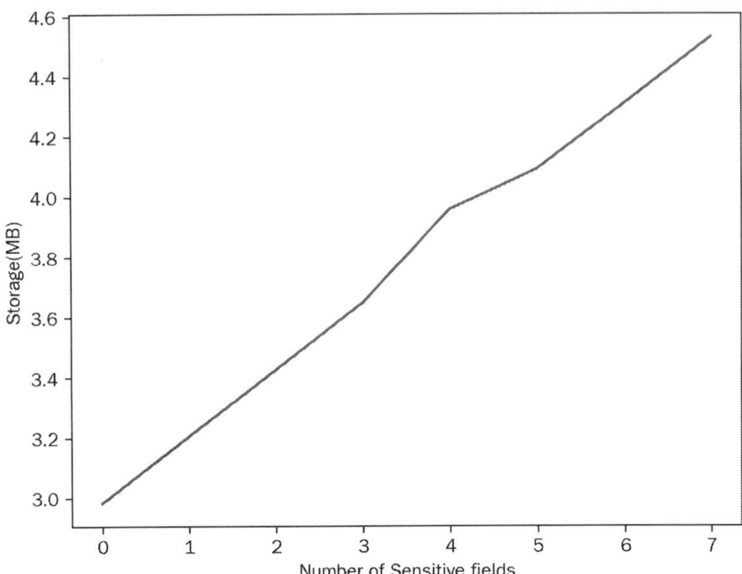

Fig. 3. The storage overhead of SA-aChain under different settings of the number of sensitive fields per record. The total number of transactions is 1000.

To quantify the impact of sensitive field quantity on storage consumption, we conduct tests with fixed transaction volume (1,000 transactions) while progressively increasing sensitive field count from 0 to 7. As demonstrated in Fig. 3, the storage overhead increases non-linearly with sensitive field counts. When all 7 fields are sensitive, storage consumption reaches 4.5MB per 1,000 transactions, reflecting a 52% growth compared to the baseline scenario where all fields are non-sensitive.

We also conduct simulations to evaluate the query performance of SA-aChain. For non-sensitive fields (i.e., plaintext fields), we measure the query latency of both aChain and SA-aChain. For sensitive fields (encrypted fields), we only measure the query latency of SA-aChain, as aChain lacks the capability to query encrypted data. Results are shown in Fig. 4. As we can see, non-sensitive field query latency for both aChain and SA-aChain grows logarithmically with record count, SA-aChain's 3% higher latency is negligible, attributed to lightweight EM processing. For sensitive fields, only SA-aChain supports encrypted queries. The latency grows quasi-linearly (0.324.57 ms) due to hash indexing and per-record decryption. We consider the higher query latency of SA-aChain is acceptable, as aChain cannot handle encrypted data queries at all.

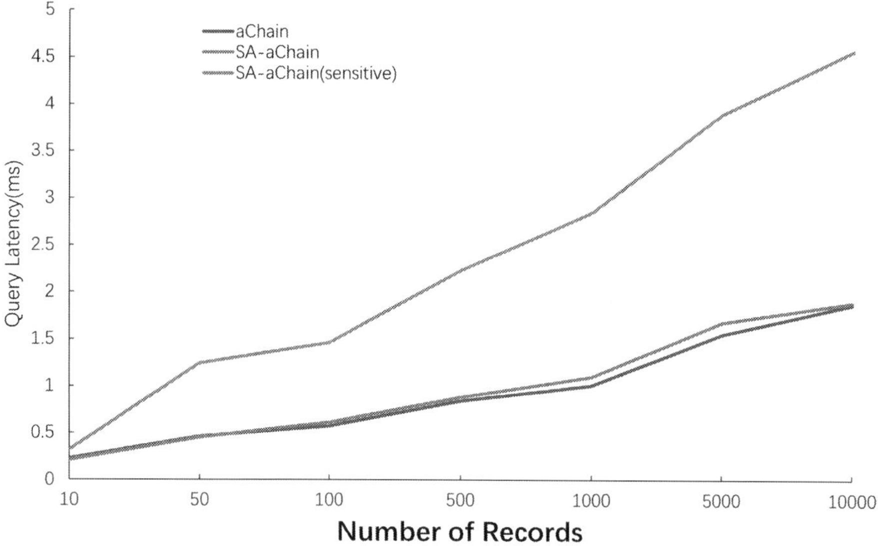

Fig. 4. A comparison between SA-aChain and aChain in terms of query latency. The blue line indicates the result of aChain. The orange line indicates the result of SA-aChain. The gray line indicates the result of SA-aChain for encrypted query. (Color figure online)

5 Conclusion

This paper proposes SA-aChain, a hybrid "blockchain + relational database" architecture designed to tackle the challenges of secure storage and efficient querying of sensitive cybersecurity alert data. Through a four-layer collaborative framework, SA-aChain achieves end-to-end encryption from SQL parsing to storage, safeguarding sensitive fields via AES-GCM and OPE encryption while maintaining query efficiency through a dual-index mechanism. The PBFT consensus layer ensures global transaction ordering and verifiable state transitions, with Merkle proofs preventing dirty reads and delta compression reducing historical storage. The hybrid storage engine integrates encrypted relational data with immutable blockchain metadata, enforcing GDPR compliance through automatic plaintext/ciphertext separation and zero-knowledge security. Simulation results show that SA-aChain introduces a little storage overhead compared to aChain due to EM, yet supports encrypted range queries with acceptable latency while maintaining comparable performance for non-sensitive field queries across varying dataset scales.

While advancing secure SQL operations in blockchain systems, the architecture leaves room for future optimization of encryption algorithms for high-throughput scenarios and exploration of cross-organizational threat intelligence sharing via federated learning, providing a foundational framework for balancing privacy, performance, and compliance in distributed cybersecurity data management. In future work, we will enhance performance by developing a SA-aChain native framework to address generic blockchain performance limitations, validate scalability with 100,000-level datasets via Merkle tree optimization and high-performance hardware, and design dynamic key rotation algorithms to strengthen encryption resilience.

Acknowledgments. This work was supported by National Defense Basic Scientific Research program of China under Grant No. JCKY2023602C026.

References

1. Ali, Khan, A., Ahmed, M., Jeon, G.: Bcals: blockchain-based secure log management system for cloud computing. Trans. Emerg. Telecommun. Technol. **33** (2021). https://doi.org/10.1002/ett.4272
2. Ali, S., Li, Q., Yousafzai, A.: Blockchain and federated learning-based intrusion detection approaches for edge-enabled industrial IoT networks: a survey. Ad Hoc Netw. **152**, 103320 (2024). https://doi.org/10.1016/j.adhoc.2023.103320. https://www.sciencedirect.com/science/article/pii/S1570870523002408
3. Androulaki, E., et al.: Hyperledger fabric: a distributed operating system for permissioned blockchains. In: Proceedings of the Thirteenth EuroSys Conference. EuroSys 2018. ACM (2018). https://doi.org/10.1145/3190508.3190538
4. Bergman, S., Asplund, M., Nadjm-Tehrani, S.: Permissioned blockchains and distributed databases: a performance study. Concurr. Comput. Pract. Exp. **32**(12), e5227 (2020). https://doi.org/10.1002/cpe.5227. https://onlinelibrary.wiley.com/doi/abs/10.1002/cpe.5227, e5227 cpe.5227
5. Boldyreva, A., Chenette, N., Lee, Y., O'Neill, A.: Order-preserving symmetric encryption. In: Joux, A. (ed.) EUROCRYPT 2009. LNCS, vol. 5479, pp. 224–241. Springer, Heidelberg (2009). https://doi.org/10.1007/978-3-642-01001-9_13
6. Dworkin, M.J.: Recommendation for block cipher modes of operation: galoiscounter mode (GCM) and GMAC (2007). https://doi.org/10.6028/NIST.SP.800-38d
7. El-Kosairy, A., Abdelbaki, N., Aslan, H.: A survey on cyber threat intelligence sharing based on blockchain. Adv. Comput. Intell. **3**(3), 10 (2023). https://doi.org/10.1007/s43674-023-00057-z
8. Eugster, P., Guerraoui, R., Kermarrec, A.M., Massoulie, L.: Epidemic information dissemination in distributed systems. Computer **37**(5), 60–67 (2004). https://doi.org/10.1109/MC.2004.1297243
9. Franke, U., Brynielsson, J.: Cyber situational awareness – a systematic review of the literature. Comput. Secur. **46**, 18–31 (2014). https://doi.org/10.1016/j.cose.2014.06.008. https://www.sciencedirect.com/science/article/pii/S0167404814001011
10. Ghafir, I., et al.: Detection of advanced persistent threat using machine-learning correlation analysis. Futur. Gener. Comput. Syst. **89**, 349–359 (2018). https://doi.org/10.1016/j.future.2018.06.055. https://www.sciencedirect.com/science/article/pii/S0167739X18307532
11. Granadillo, G., González-Zarzosa, S., Diaz, R.: Security information and event management (SIEM): analysis, trends, and usage in critical infrastructures. Sensors **21**, 4759 (2021). https://doi.org/10.3390/s21144759

12. Hassija, V., Bansal, G., Chamola, V., Kumar, N., Guizani, M.: Secure lending: blockchain and prospect theory-based decentralized credit scoring model. IEEE Trans. Netw. Sci. Eng. **7**(4), 2566–2575 (2020). https://doi.org/10.1109/TNSE.2020.2982488
13. Johnson, D., Menezes, A., Vanstone, S.: The elliptic curve digital signature algorithm (ECDSA). Int. J. Inf. Secur. **1**(1), 36–63 (2001). https://doi.org/10.1007/s102070100002
14. Krawczyk, H., Eronen, P.: HMAC-based Extract-and-Expand Key Derivation Function (HKDF). RFC 5869 (2010). https://doi.org/10.17487/RFC5869. https://www.rfc-editor.org/info/rfc5869
15. Kuner, C., Bygrave, L.A., Docksey, C., Drechsler, L.: The EU General Data Protection Regulation (GDPR): A Commentary. Oxford University Press (2020). https://doi.org/10.1093/oso/9780198826491.001.0001
16. Liu, Y., Liu, J., Hei, Y., Xia, Yu., Wu, Q.: A secure cross-shard view-change protocol for sharding blockchains. In: Baek, J., Ruj, S. (eds.) ACISP 2021. LNCS, vol. 13083, pp. 372–390. Springer, Cham (2021). https://doi.org/10.1007/978-3-030-90567-5_19
17. McConaghy, T., et al.: Bigchaindb: a scalable blockchain database. Technical report, ascribe GmbH, Berlin, Germany (2016). https://gamma.bigchaindb.com/whitepaper/bigchaindb-whitepaper.pdf, whitepaper
18. Merkle, R.C.: A digital signature based on a conventional encryption function. In: Pomerance, C. (ed.) CRYPTO 1987. LNCS, vol. 293, pp. 369–378. Springer, Heidelberg (1988). https://doi.org/10.1007/3-540-48184-2_32
19. Mridul, M.A., Chang, K., Gupta, A., Seneviratne, O.: Smart contracts, smarter payments: innovating cross border payments and reporting transactions (2024). https://arxiv.org/abs/2407.19283
20. Parr, T., Fisher, K.: Ll(*): the foundation of the ANTLR parser generator. In: Proceedings of the 32nd ACM SIGPLAN Conference on Programming Language Design and Implementation, PLDI 2011, pp. 425–436. Association for Computing Machinery, New York, NY, USA (2011). https://doi.org/10.1145/1993498.1993548
21. PostgreSQL Global Development Group: BRIN indexes (2023). https://www.postgresql.org/docs/current/brin-intro.html. Accessed 01 Oct 2023
22. Suel, T.: Delta Compression Techniques, pp. 1–8. Springer, Cham (2018). https://doi.org/10.1007/978-3-319-63962-8_63
23. Sukhwani, H., Martínez, J.M., Chang, X., Trivedi, K.S., Rindos, A.: Performance modeling of PBFT consensus process for permissioned blockchain network (hyperledger fabric). In: 2017 IEEE 36th Symposium on Reliable Distributed Systems (SRDS), pp. 253–255 (2017). https://doi.org/10.1109/SRDS.2017.36
24. Wang, Y., et al.: aChain: a SQL-empowered analytical blockchain as a database. IEEE Trans. Comput. **72**(11), 3099–3112 (2023). https://doi.org/10.1109/TC.2023.3287036
25. Wei, Q., Li, B., Chang, W., Jia, Z., Shen, Z., Shao, Z.: A survey of blockchain data management systems. ACM Trans. Embed. Comput. Syst. **21**(3) (2022). https://doi.org/10.1145/3502741
26. Wong, E., Ting, H.Y., Atanda, A.: Enhancing supply chain traceability through blockchain and IoT integration: a comprehensive review. Green Intell. Syst. Appl. **4**, 11–28 (2024). https://doi.org/10.53623/gisa.v4i1.355
27. Wu, Y., Arulraj, J., Lin, J., Xian, R., Pavlo, A.: An empirical evaluation of in-memory multi-version concurrency control. Proc. VLDB Endow. **10**(7), 781–792 (2017). https://doi.org/10.14778/3067421.3067427

28. Yin, B., Liu, Y., Xu, B.: VSQ: enabling efficient and verifiable similarity queries in blockchain databases. Expert Syst. Appl. **285**, 127815 (2025). https://doi.org/10.1016/j.eswa.2025.127815. https://www.sciencedirect.com/science/article/pii/S095741742501437X
29. Zhu, C., Li, J., Zhong, Z., Yue, C., Zhang, M.: A survey on the integration of blockchains and databases. Data Sci. Eng. **8**(2), 196–219 (2023). https://doi.org/10.1007/s41019-023-00212-z

OSD: A Graphical Password Scheme Based on Object Shape Drawing on Smartphones

Christina Berry[1] and Wenjuan Li[2(✉)]

[1] Macao Research and Development Centre, Macao SAR, China
[2] Department of Mathematics and Information Technology, The Education University of Hong Kong, Hong Kong SAR, China
lwenjuan@eduhk.hk

Abstract. Smart devices especially smartphones have become type of daily device for people, e.g., acting as a central and multifaceted hub to access social networks and enabling communication through photos and videos. Hence, the information stored on these devices is very private and important. To protect a smartphone from unauthorized access, there is a need to perform user authentication. Traditional authentication methods based on passwords are often short of usability and security; thus, graphical password is considered as an alternative that requires users to create a credential by interacting with images. For graphical passwords, time consumption is usually a limiting factor against a practical deployment. For example, users have to remember and draw something on the image(s). In this work, we develop an efficient graphical password scheme based on object shape drawing–called *OSD scheme*, which only requires the user to draw the shape of selected object. In the user study, we recruit a total of 40 participants and find that most users can perform well on our scheme in terms of both authentication accuracy and time consumption, as compared with Android Unlock Pattern.

Keywords: User Authentication · Shape Drawing · Smartphone Security · Behavioral Authentication · Graphical Password

1 Introduction

IDC report indicated that Worldwide smartphone shipments are forecast to grow 1% year-on-year in 2025 to 1.24 billion units, which represents an improvement from the previous forecast of around 0.6% [1]. At the moment, mobile devices especially smartphones are an important asset of users, used as popular data storage and online banking devices. Cyber-attackers also take such devices as one of the main targets due to many financial profits. Hence, there is an urgent need to protect these devices from unauthorized access and align with regulations (e.g., GDPR [8,19]).

M. Yung et al. (Eds.): AIBlock 2025, LNCS 16314, pp. 143–159, 2026.
https://doi.org/10.1007/978-3-032-16168-0_9

Currently, the practical systems usually take password-based method for user authentication, which requires a user to input correct textual information, e.g., strings. The advantage is the wide adoption by existing users, but such method has know limitations regarding security and usability. One typical instance is that users cannot remember their password for a long time because of the long-term memory limitation [5,36] and multiple password interference [30,37]. Due to this, many users may choose a simple password than a complicated one in their daily lives [6]. Another major concern is threat of cyber-attacks such as recording attacks [39] and charging attacks [34,35]. These attacks can record and leak the passwords, making the password-based method insecure. It is noted that password database is often leaked every year, e.g., the number of compromised records has now hit 16 billion [2].

Aiming to address the limitations, graphical password (GP) is considered as one possible option–in which a user has to create the credential by interacting with one or more images [49]. In practice, Android Unlock Pattern (AUP) is a typical instance that asks users to draw a pattern on a 3×3 grid [20,33]. A number of GP schemes have been developed and discussed in the past decade (see Sect. 2), and many of them showed good authentication performance than traditional password-based methods. However, GP schemes may still have similar issues as password-based method, stated as below.

- **Security aspect.** The same as password-based method, if the GP credential is leaked, an attacker can obtain the access privilege, e.g., recording attacks and touch trail analysis [4]. Some schemes may suffer from 'hot-spot' analysis, so the attacker can perform an effective guess.
- **Usability aspect.** Many GP schemes require users to remember image or object sequence, increasing the memory workload. Some schemes may ask users to perform several steps to create a credential, which greatly increase the time consumption in practical deployment (e.g., *PassPoints* [54]).

To address these challenges, there is a requirement to consider better design of graphical password schemes. The key points are summarized as below.

- **Security aspect.** The scheme should enable dynamic credential creation and verification, which can greatly increase the difficulty for cyber-attackers.
- **Usability aspect.** The scheme should reduce the memory workload on user's side and provide a fast login process.

According to the above design requirements, in this work, we develop an efficient and dynamic graphical password scheme based on object shape drawing (so called *OSD* scheme), which requires a user to draw the shape of an object for authentication. The scheme can offer demanded features: 1) Enhanced security–the shown image is dynamic every time and the object shape is varied, and 2) Enhanced usability–the user only needs to draw the object shape rather than remember any object sequence, making the authentication process straightforward and efficient. The contributions can be summarized as below.

- We design OSD–a graphical password scheme based on object shape drawing, so that a user can draw the shape of selected object for authentication. The scheme is easy to understand and perform that can also provide some benefits. 1) The credential is dynamic as the shown image and the selected object will be varied each time. 2) The process is easy to complete, reducing the time consumption of authentication. 3) It can be integrated with existing solutions including behavioral authentication.
- In the user study, we involve 40 common phone users in order to evaluate the scheme performance regarding the authentication rate and attack success rate under two types of attacks. Based on the authentication performance and users' feedback, it is found that our scheme is secure and usable, as compared with the Android Unlock Pattern.

The paper is organized as follows. Section 2 introduces related work on graphical password and unlock solutions. Section 3 introduces our OSD scheme (e.g., design and steps) in detail. Section 4 presents a user study with collected user feedback and attack tests. We discuss open challenges and future directions with behavioral features in Sect. 5. We conclude our work in Sect. 6.

2 Related Work

This section introduces the background and related work of graphical password and unlock solutions on mobile devices.

2.1 Graphical Password

Broadly, a graphical password-based authentication allows the verification of a user by means of images, patterns or sequences of selections via a visual input-interface. The merit is known as *Picture Superiority Effect* [43], referring that humans are generally better at recognizing and remembering images than textual information. Based on this, many GP schemes are developed in the past decade.

A GP scheme can be classified as Recall-Based Schemes, Recognition-Based Schemes and Cued-Recall Schemes.

- **Recall-Based Schemes.** The user should re-create the credential that they created during the registration phase without any cues. As an example, Jermyn et al. [18] introduced a typical scheme of Draw-A-Secret (DAS), enabling a user to draw something on a grid as the credential.
- **Recognition-Based Schemes.** The user should recognize and select correct images from a set of images. The 'correct images' refer to the ones they pre-selected during registration. PassFaces [3] is one typical example, which requires a user to identify several human faces from a set of images.
- **Cued-Recall Schemes.** Such type can provide a cue to help users recall their secret. The cue is typically one particular image that is able to trigger the memory of users. Wiedenbeck et al. [54] presented an early system called PassPoints, which provides a clue to help users remember the sequence of points on different images.

There many new schemes in each type, for example, Qin et al. [21,22] introduced RoundImage, a GP scheme that requires users to select images in rounds (e.g., three rounds) for authentication. It can resist against some typical threats, such as shoulder-surfing attacks and provide fault tolerance.

At present, hybrid GP schemes are more popular that combines one or more features of Recall-Based Schemes, Recognition-Based Schemes and Cued-Recall Schemes. For example, click-draw based GP scheme [28,29] showed a design layout combining all the features. They particularly transformed the classification as click-based, selection-based and drawing-based schemes, and developed a special action called click-draw, where users can draw something using clicks.

To enlarge the password space, many schemes try to use a world map as the background image. Sun et al. [50] introduced a GP scheme named PassMap in which a password consists of a sequence of two click-points, asking a user to select on a large world map. Thorpe et al. [52] then introduced GeoPass, where a user only needs to select one place as the credential. They also showed that 97% of users were able to remember their places over the span of 8–9 days. For location number, it has been found there is no statistical difference between PassMap and GeoPass [38]. Similarly, RouteMap scheme [32] further extended the idea of using a map, which allows a user to draw a route on a world map as their secret. The user study found that most users could achieve better performance using RouteMap in terms of multiple password memory. Then, CPMap [40] is a click-points map-based GP scheme that allows users to choose one place on a world map at first and then click a point or an object on an image relating to the previously selected location. Some recent similar schemes and research studies can refer to [7,9,11,14,23,41,55,56].

2.2 Mobile Unlock Solutions

To safeguard the security of mobile data, graphical password is an attempt to enhance the existing mobile unlock solutions. On Android devices, the Android Unlock Pattern (AUP) [10,33] is a widely adopted authentication method that allows users to draw a custom pattern on a 3×3 grid. This mechanism is functionally an adaptation of the earlier Pass-Go scheme [51], which also relies on user-defined patterns created over a grid-based image.

There are different approaches designed for mobile devices such as smartphones, e.g., physiological or biometric features. For instance, Face Unlock system [12] employed both frontal and profile facial data to unlock devices during a panoramic shot around the user's head, which leverages integrated camera and motion sensors. Their approach demonstrated a promising authentication success rate of around 90.5%. Izuta et al. [17] presented an unlock system on phones by using sensors like accelerometers and pressure arrays to analyze the motion and pressure distribution of the user's grip. Meng et al. [33] introduced TMGuard by analyzing a user's unique touch movements, such as speed and pressure, in addition to the correctness of AUP. It verifies a user's identity by checking for consistent touch movements over time. Yi et al. [57] introduced WearLock by using acoustic signals for secure smartphone unlocking with a smartwatch. The system generates and receives sound tones between the devices for verification. Wang et al. [53] then proposed an unlock method by using the built-in accelerometer on mobile phones to capture unique heartbeat vibration patterns for user authentication.

SwipeVlock [25,26] is a behavioral mobile unlock mechanism that verifies users based on swiping action. Their results showed that participants could perform well with a success rate of 98% in the best case. Choi et al. [46] introduced VibPath, a simultaneous 2FA scheme that can understand the user's hand neuromuscular system through touch behavior. Their method captures the individual's vibration path responses between the hand and the wrist with the attention-based encoder-decoder network. Hong et al. [13] introduced a mobile unlock solution, called wrist-rolling motion recognition (WRMR) method, which leverages the unique motion patterns that require the sensors embedded in mobile phones. Li and Tan [27] presented DOT-C, a phone unlock scheme based on dot-dot connection, aiming to facilitate the usage based on the grid of Android Unlock Pattern. The obtained results showed the effectiveness of their scheme in practice with 90 users. Fan et al. [15] introduced EmgAuth, a phone unlock system based on electromyography (EMG) via the Siamese network. It could allow users to unlock their devices by leveraging the EMG data collected from Myo armbands. Now it is a very popular direction to design an unlock system by using various sensors and behavioral features.

3 Our Proposed Scheme

As mentioned earlier, we aim to develop an efficient graphical password scheme, which can reduce the memory workload for users. For this purpose, we design OSD–a scheme based on object shape drawing, where a user can draw the shape of selected object for authentication. Figure 1 illustrates the scheme workflow.

Generally, in the first step, the system will randomly present an image and then the user has to choose the object and draw the object shape. The phases of registration and authentication are described as below:

- **OSD registration.** For scheme registration, users have to select an object in a series of images and draw the shape of selected object. In practical deployment, the image numbers and themes can be updated in terms of the requirements. A big image pool may increase the memory burden on users, so a balance should be made.
- **OSD authentication.** For scheme authentication, users have to select the correct object from the presented image and draw the object shape. Please note that the shown image may vary each time. Any failure will result in an unsuccessful login trial.

Scheme Implementation. Figure 2 presents an example implementation of our OSD scheme. To balance the security and usability, we set six images in the image pool. To start, the system will present an image randomly. Then the user has to choose the pre-selected object and draw the object shape.

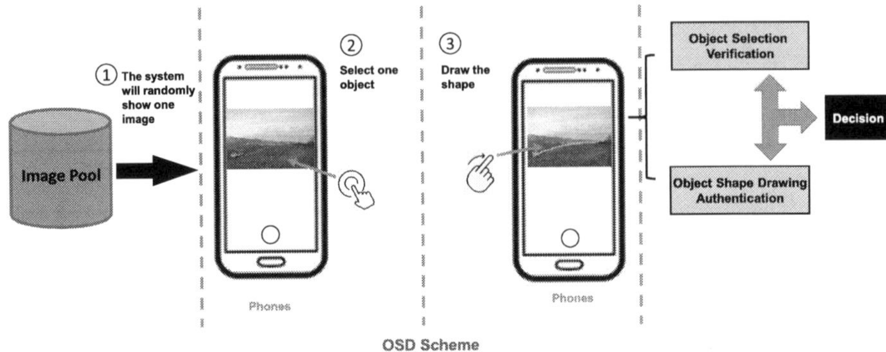

Fig. 1. Workflow of OSD scheme: (1) Step1: the system will randomly present an image (from an image pool); (2) Step2: the user has to select the object; and (3) the user has to draw the object shape.

Please note that how to draw the object shape depends on users' preference, i.e., the user can draw a full shape or partial shape of the object. As shown in Fig. 3, some examples (Fig. 3(a)–(c)) are provided of drawing different shapes of objects. It is seen that different objects can be selected with varied shape drawing. In the end, the system will check whether both the object selection and the shape drawing are correct.

To improve the usability of the scheme, we set the touch error-tolerance to a 21×21 pixel box around the selected location, based on evaluation results from the previous work [25,38].

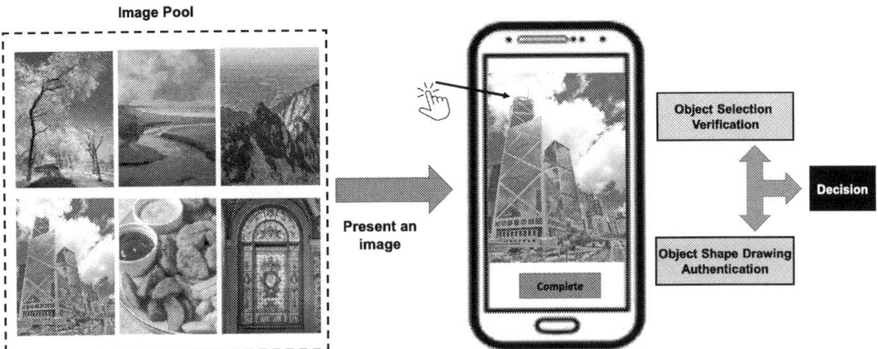

Fig. 2. A case implementation of our OSD scheme. 1) An image pool with six images and an image is randomly shown; 2) User selects the pre-selected object and draws the object shape; 3) The system verifies object selection and shape drawing.

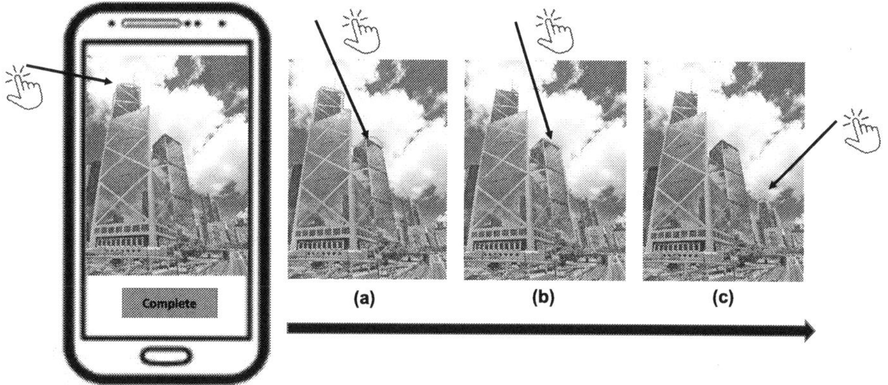

Fig. 3. An example of different drawing shapes. a) The shape drawing covers three buildings (the left side on the image), b) the shape drawing covers one building (the middle on the image), and 3) the shape drawing covers three buildings (the right side on the image).

Practical Deployment and Scheme Advantages. To deploy the scheme in practice, there is a need to consider adjusting the settings: 1) image number: generally, a higher number indicates a higher security, i.e., an attacker has to spend more time exploring the correct object selected for each image; 2) image theme: a diverse theme can help enhance the security level, especially an image contains multiple objects that can be selected.

With these settings, our proposed OSD scheme can provide many desirable benefits as follows:

- *Time efficiency.* Our OSD scheme only requires a user to draw the object shape, which is straightforward and easy-to-understand for general phone users. Hence, the authentication time can be reasonable in comparison with most existing schemes.
- *Enhanced usability.* Our scheme does not require the user to remember numerous images or the image sequence, so the memory burden is widely acceptable on user's side. In modern applications, most users would prefer a fast, lightweight and convenient authentication process.
- *Enhanced security.* Each time, the presented image may be different, increasing the cracking difficulty for attackers. Even for the same image, attackers have to guess the correct object and draw the shape (either partial or full shape), in which the scheme can greatly reduce the possibility of a fast cracking. A high security level can be achieved by enlarging the image pool.
- *High extensibility.* The scheme can also consider involving behavioral features (like touch dynamics [45]) during the authentication, e.g., adding another round of verifying the touch behavior when drawing the shape. Hence, our scheme opens much extensibility for future design.

4 User Study

In this section, we aim to discuss the evaluation results on the scheme performance. In particular, we organize a user study with 40 regular phone users (e.g., 23 of them are using an Android phone, 10 of them are using iPhone and the rest are using both types of phones). The background of participants is summarized in Table 1.

For the participants, we have 20 males and 20 females who aged from 20 to 60, including university students (bachelor, master and Ph.D.), university staff or faculty, and company employees. Each participant would get a $20 gift voucher after completing the tasks.

Table 1. Background on participants in the user study.

Information	Male	Female	Occupation	Male	Female
Age < 25	10	8	University Students	13	10
Age 25–40	5	6	University Faculty&Staff	4	6
Age 40–60	5	6	Company Employees	3	4

Comparison Scheme. To compare the scheme performance, we choose the popular *Android Unlock Pattern (AUP)* [10,20] in our study. The selection is based on two main points: 1) Android Unlock Pattern has been widely adopted by phone users, so it can provide a good performance baseline; 2) Users can perform an efficient login trial by inputting the unlock pattern quickly, making it an ideal scheme in the comparison, as the time efficiency is one main goal of our proposed scheme.

There are some common rules for generating a valid Android Unlock Pattern.

- *Connect at least 4 points and 9 points at most:* A valid pattern must involve a minimum of four available dots on the grid.
- *Each point can only be used once:* A valid pattern cannot revisit a dot that has already been connected as part of the pattern.
- *No jumping over unvisited dots:* If a line between two dots you are connecting passes through the center of another dot, then the middle dot must be part of the generated pattern, unless it has already been used.

Authentication Metrics. To evaluate the scheme performance, we adopt two main metrics: 1) *authentication rate* indicates the percentage of successful trials from legitimate users divided by the total trials, and 2) *attack success rate* indicates the percentage of successful attack trials from illegal users divided by the total trials.

To measure the performance under adversarial scenarios, we consider two types of guessing attacks as follows.

Table 2. Authentication rate and average completion time for the step of confirmation, login and retention in the study.

AUP Scheme	Confirmation	Login	Retention
Authentication Rate	188/200 (94%)	192/200 (96%)	181/200 (90.5%)
Avg. Completion Time (seconds)	9.4	9.1	9.7
Standard Deviation (seconds)	4.1	4.3	3.5
OSD Scheme	Confirmation	Login	Retention
Authentication Rate	186/200 (93%)	187/200 (93.5%)	180/200 (90.0%)
Avg. Completion Time (seconds)	17.6	8.3	9.2
Standard Deviation (seconds)	2.2	2.8	3.1

- Guessing attack on object selection (GAOS): attackers can guess the selected object on an image.
- Guessing attack on object drawing (GAOD): attackers can guess the object drawing on the target object. This is a stronger attack as the attackers can know the target object.

Study Steps. In this user study, we recruited 40 participants (see Table 1). First, we explained our objectives to all participants and explained what kind of data would be collected. A consensus form was collected from each participant. Also, each participant could have three trials to get familiar with the OSD scheme as well as Android Unlock Pattern. During the study, participants would obtain an Android phone (Samsung Galaxy Note) and performed the study in our lab area. All participants would create a credential for both AUP and OSD, but the creation sequence is random (that is, the creation could start from either OSD or AUP). The study steps are summarized as follows.

- **Step 1. Creation phase:** participants need to register their credentials according to either OSD or AUP steps.
- **Step 2. Confirmation phase:** participants have to confirm the created credential by inputting it for 5 times. Participants can change their credentials if they want to create a new one or are simply failed.
- **Step 3. Distributed memory:** participants are given one paper-based finding tasks to distract them for 20 min.
- **Step 4. Login phase:** participants should input the credential to unlock the device for 5 trials.
- **Step 5. Feedback1:** participants are provided with a set of questions (*feedback from*) regarding the scheme usage.
- **Step 6. Retention phase:** after five days, participants are invited to unlock the phone for 5 times.
- **Step 7. Feedback2:** participants have to fill up another *feedback from* regarding the scheme usage.

Study Results. Table 2 presents the authentication rate and average completion time (plus standard deviation) for both schemes regarding confirmation, login and retention. We adopted Chi-square tests to decide whether the results are statistically significant between two rates. It is a statistical test that analyzes differences between observed frequencies and expected frequencies.

- *Confirmation phase.* In this phase, it is seen that participants could perform similarly for both schemes, e.g., an authentication rate of 94% and 93% for AUP and OSD. There was no statistical difference between these two schemes. For the time consumption, in this phase, our OSD scheme is more time consuming as a user has to confirm all the object drawing for six images. Also, it observed that our scheme of OSD could provide a lower SD.
- *Login phase.* It is found that the authentication rate is a bit higher for AUP (96%) than OSD (93.5%). The main errors caused for OSD are: 1) users perform a drawing out of the error tolerance, and 2) users forget the drawn shape. For AUP, the main error is the wrong pattern input. However, we found there was no statistical difference between these two schemes. For the time consumption, it is worth noting that our OSD could achieve lower rate (8.3 s) compared with a rate of 9.1 s for AUP. In our formal interview, it is found users can quickly complete the shape drawing. It is the same that our scheme of OSD could reach a lower SD.
- *Retention phase.* It is seen that participants performed very similarly during the retention phase, where the rate is 90% and 90.5% for OSD and AUP, respectively. Hence, there was no statistical difference between these two schemes. For time consumption, our scheme only required 9.2 s, while AUP scheme required 9.7 s. It is noticed that in this phase, users may need more time to recall their credential, as the average time consumption was higher than the previous two phases. Again for SD, our scheme could reach a lower rate than AUP.

Overall, the results indicate that our scheme of OSD could have a similar usability level as AUP, which can have a great potential in practical usage. We observe that 1) the authentication rate is similar between these two schemes and there is no statistical difference; and 2) participants should need more time in confirmation phase but require less time in login phase.

User Feedback. As stated in the study steps, two feedback forms were provided to receive the feedback from all participants regarding the scheme usage (e.g., security, usability). Ten-point Likert scales are used for each question: 1-score indicates strong disagreement and 10-score indicates strong agreement. The major questions and scores are shown in Table 3.

- *Feedback in login phase.* Based on the first two questions, we found most participants could create and confirm the OSD credential easily (with a score of 8.1 and 8.4 respectively). The following two questions check whether the time consumption is acceptable for confirmation and login; it is found some participants believed the confirmation phase is a bit time consuming, but

Table 3. Major questions and average scores from the participants.

Questions (Login Phase)	Average Scores
1. I could easily create a credential under OSD	8.1
2. I could easily confirm a credential under OSD	8.4
3. The time consumption for confirmation is acceptable	6.1
4. The time consumption for login is acceptable	8.8
5. I could easily make a login attempt	8.9
6. I think Android Unlock Pattern is more usable than OSD	5.2
7. I think Android Unlock Pattern is more secure than OSD	3.8
Questions (Retention Phase)	Average Scores
1. I could easily recall my credential under OSD	8.3
2. I can remember AUP better than OSD	4.8
3. I can remember my selected object on the image under OSD	8.1
4. I can remember my drawn shape on the image under OSD	7.8
5. The time consumption for login is acceptable	8.8
6. I think Android Unlock Pattern is more secure than OSD	3.5
7. I think 8-digit PIN code is more secure than OSD	4.7

most of them believed that the login phase is very efficient. This is verified by the fifth question, where most participants stated that they can easily make a login attempt. For the last two questions, we aim to check users' attitude towards the comparison between OSD and AUP. It is found that many participants considered OSD has a similar usability level as AUP, but most of them believed that OSD is more secure than AUP.

– *Feedback in retention phase.* The question list is a bit different from the form used in login phase. The first question indicated that most participants could remember the OSD credential well. The second question indicated that participants could remember both schemes (AUP and OSD) at the similar level. The following two questions present that most participants could remember their created object and drawn shape. Then most participants were satisfied with the login process. Regarding security, participants believed that OSD could be much more secure than AUP, and even better than the security of a 8-digit PIN (some of them may consider they are similar).

In terms of the user feedback, we found that most participants were positive on security and usability of OSD scheme. They believed that as compared with AUP, the proposed OSD scheme could reach a similar usability level, while providing much better security enhancement, e.g., they considered OSD could reach a similar or better security than a 8-digit PIN. The main issue of OSD is: participants have to spend much more time during creation and confirmation phase, as they have to perform object shape drawing for each image.

Table 4. Attack success rates under Guessing attack on object selection (GAOS) and Guessing attack on object drawing (GAOD).

Attack Type	Attack success rate
GAOS	33.1% (119/360)
GAOD	9.17% (33/360)

Attack Impact. To test the scheme security, we explore two types of attacks: GAOS and GAOS. We randomly selected 20 out of 40 participants, called *attack group*, and the rest participants called *user group*. Table 4 summarizes the attack success rate.

- **GAOS impact.** For such type of attack, we randomly selected 6 images from user group and asked the attack group to guess the selected object on each image. Each attack group member can guess 3 times on each image. Table 4 shows that attackers could have a success rate of 33.1% by selecting the correct object.
- **GAOS impact.** For this type of attack, we randomly selected 6 images with target object from user group and asked the attack group to guess the shape drawing. Each attack group member can guess 3 times on each object. Table 4 shows the attack success rate is 9.17%.

As compared with AUP, it is found that our scheme can greatly leverage the security level. First, attackers could have 33.1% possibility to identify the correct object on an image (it depends on the image theme, as some themes may have few objects). Then with the target object, attackers could have only around 9% success rate to guess the correct shape drawing. If the attacker has to guess the object, then the final guess success rate should be lower than 9%. Overall, our scheme can greatly increase the cracking difficulty level for attackers.

5 Discussion

In this section, we discuss the open challenges and the potential improvement with behavioral features.

5.1 Open Challenges

- *Object selection.* As our scheme requires a user to select an object from an image, there could be an issue of 'hot-spot' that most participants would like to choose. If attackers can explore this issue, they can perform a dictionary attack. This issue can be one of our future work.
- *Image pool.* In this work, we have 6 images in the pool, but a balance should be made between time consumption and security. The future work can explore the scheme performance with different image numbers.

- *Participant size.* Our participant number can be further improved, which can provide more credential samples. This can help understand how a user may create a credential under OSD scheme.
- *Advanced attacks.* In this work, we considered two types of attacks, but some forms of advanced attacks can be made, e.g., shoulder-surfing attacks. For example, an attacker can video-record the whole process. This can be one of our future work.

5.2 Behavioral Features

As our OSD scheme involves a shape drawing, it is intuitive to involve behavioral features to further enhance the security. That is, our scheme can examine the behavioral features when users perform a shape drawing, which can greatly reduce the cracking possibility of cyber-attackers. In the literature, there are many prior studies explored the use of behavioral features, e.g., touch features, on smart devices, such as [16,24,28,31,44,47,48]. The idea can be further extended with multi-touch features given specific scenarios (e.g., designing an intrusion detection system [42]).

6 Conclusion

It has become an important task to protect smartphones (e.g., stored data) from unauthorized access. In this work, we develop a graphical password scheme based on object shape drawing, shortly OSD scheme, in which a user can draw the shape of selected object for authentication. The scheme can provide many benefits–1) Enhanced security: the appeared image is dynamic each time and the object shape is varied; and 2) Enhanced usability: the user only needs to draw the object shape rather than remember any object or image sequence. In the user study, we involved 40 participants to examine the scheme performance in both security and usability aspect. It is found that most participants believed that our scheme can reach a similar usability level (e.g., an authentication rate above 90%) while providing much better security compared with Android Unlock Pattern. We further examined the scheme security under two types of attacks, and it verified that our scheme could provide much higher security level than Android Unlock Pattern (e.g., an attack success rate of 9.17%).

Acknowledgments. We would like to thank the participants for their hard work in the user study.

References

1. Worldwide Smartphone Market Forecast to Grow 1% in 2025, Driven by Accelerated 3.9% iOS Growth, according to IDC. https://my.idc.com/getdoc.jsp?containerId=prUS53767725

2. 16 Billion Apple, Facebook, Google and Other Passwords Leaked. https://www.forbes.com/sites/daveywinder/2025/06/20/16-billion-apple-facebook-google-passwords-leaked---change-yours-now/. Accessed 23 June 2025
3. Passfaces. http://www.realuser.com/
4. Aviv, A.J., Gibson, K., Mossop, E., Blaze, M., Smith, J.M.: Smudge attacks on smartphone touch screens. In: Proceedings of the 4th USENIX Conference on Offensive Technologies, pp. 1–7. USENIX Association (2010)
5. Andriotis, P., Kirby, M., Takasu, A.: Bu-Dash: A Universal and Dynamic Graphical Password Scheme. In: HCI (32), pp. 209–227 (2022)
6. Bonneau, J.: The science of guessing: analyzing an anonymized corpus of 70 million passwords. In: Proceedings of the 2012 IEEE Symposium on Security and Privacy, pp. 538–552 (2012)
7. Binbeshr, F., Khaw, C.S., Por, L.Y., Imam, M., Al-Saggaf, A.A., Abudaqa, A.A.: A systematic review of graphical password methods resistant to shoulder-surfing attacks. Int. J. Inf. Sec. **24**(1), 46 (2025)
8. Meng, W., Chiu, W.Y.: DataVaults: a secure, distributed and privacy preserving personal data management platform. In: The 43rd IEEE International Conference on Distributed Computing Systems (ICDCS 2023), pp. 997–1000 (2023)
9. Fu, H.C., Li, W., Wang, Y.: PassFile: graphical password authentication based on file browsing records. In: ML4CS 2023, pp. 28–43 (2023)
10. De Luca, A., Hang, A., Brudy, F., Lindner, C., Hussmann, H.: Touch me once and i know it's you!: implicit authentication based on touch screen patterns. In: Proceedings of CHI, pp. 987–996. ACM (2012)
11. Feng, T., et al.: Continuous mobile authentication using touchscreen gestures. In: Proceedings of the 2012 IEEE Conference on Technologies for Homeland Security (HST), pp. 451–456. IEEE, USA (2012)
12. Findling, R.D., Mayrhofer, R.: Towards face unlock: on the difficulty of reliably detecting faces on mobile phones. In: MoMM 2012, pp. 275–280 (2012)
13. Hong, Z., He, Y., Cao, L., Liu, L.: A wrist-rolling motion recognition method for mobile phone unlocking. IEEE Internet Things J. **12**(8), 10388–10403 (2025)
14. Frank, M., Biedert, R., Ma, E., Martinovic, I., Song, D.: Touchalytics: on the applicability of touchscreen input as a behavioral biometric for continuous authentication. IEEE Trans. Inf. Forensics Secur. **8**(1), 136–148 (2013)
15. Fan, B., Su, X., Niu, J., Hui, P.: EmgAuth: unlocking smartphones with EMG signals. IEEE Trans. Mob. Comput. **22**(9), 5248–5261 (2023)
16. Gomez-Barrero, M., Galbally, J.: Reversing the irreversible: a survey on inverse biometrics. Comput. Secur. **90**, 101700 (2020)
17. Izuta, R., Murao, K., Terada, T., Iso, T., Inamura, H., Tsukamoto, M.: Screen unlocking method using behavioral characteristics when taking mobile phone from pocket. In: MoMM 2016, pp. 110–114 (2016)
18. Jermyn, I., Mayer, A., Monrose, F., Reiter, M.K., Rubin, A.D.: The design and analysis of graphical passwords. In: Proceedings of the 8th Conference on USENIX Security Symposium, pp. 1–14. USENIX Association, Berkeley (1999)
19. Larrucea, X., Moffie, M., Asaf, S., Santamaria, I.: Towards a GDPR compliant way to secure European cross border Healthcare Industry 4.0. Comput. Stand. Interfaces **69**, 103408 (2020)
20. Li, W., Gleerup, T., Tan, J., Wang, Y.: A security enhanced android unlock scheme based on pinch-to-zoom for smart devices. IEEE Trans. Consum. Electron. **70**(1), 3985–3993 (2024)
21. Qin, X., Li, W.: A graphical password scheme based on rounded image selection. In: SciSec 2023, pp. 97–114 (2023)

22. Qin, X., Li, W., Rosenberg, P.: RoundImage: towards secure graphical password authentication via rounded image selection in IoT. IEEE Internet Things J. **12**(2), 20473–20483 (2025)
23. Li, Y., et al.: A closer look tells more: a facial distortion based liveness detection for face authentication. In: AsiaCCS 2019, pp. 241–246 (2019)
24. Li, Y., Cheng, Y., Meng, W., Li, Y., Deng, R.H.: Designing leakage-resilient password entry on head-mounted smart wearable glass devices. IEEE Trans. Inf. Forensics Secur. **16**, 307–321 (2021)
25. Li, W., Tan, J., Meng, W., Wang, Yu., Li, J.: SwipeVLock: a supervised unlocking mechanism based on swipe behavior on smartphones. In: Chen, X., Huang, X., Zhang, J. (eds.) ML4CS 2019. LNCS, vol. 11806, pp. 140–153. Springer, Cham (2019). https://doi.org/10.1007/978-3-030-30619-9_11
26. Li, W., Tan, J., Meng, W., Wang, Y.: A swipe-based unlocking mechanism with supervised learning on smartphones: design and evaluation. J. Netw. Comput. Appl. **165**, 102687 (2020)
27. Li, W., Tan, S.: DOT-C: a smartphone unlock scheme based on dot-dot connection in IoT-enabled smart cities. Int. J. Inf. Sec. **24**(3), 153 (2025)
28. Meng, Y.: Designing click-draw based graphical password scheme for better authentication. In: Proceedings of the 7th IEEE International Conference on Networking, Architecture, and Storage (NAS), pp. 39–48 (2012)
29. Meng, Y., Li, W., Kwok, L.-F.: Enhancing click-draw based graphical passwords using multi-touch on mobile phones. In: Proceedings of the 28th IFIP TC 11 International Information Security and Privacy Conference (IFIP SEC), IFIP Advances in Information and Communication Technology 405, pp. 55–68 (2013)
30. Meng, W., Li, W., Jiang, L., Meng, L.: On multiple password interference of touch screen patterns and text passwords. In: ACM Conference on Human Factors in Computing Systems (CHI 2016), pp. 4818–4822 (2016)
31. Meng, W., Wong, D.S., Furnell, S., Zhou, J.: Surveying the development of biometric user authentication on mobile phones. IEEE Commun. Surv. Tutor. **17**(3), 1268–1293 (2015)
32. Meng, W.: RouteMap: a route and map based graphical password scheme for better multiple password memory. In: Proceedings of the 9th International Conference on Network and System Security (NSS), pp. 147–161 (2015)
33. Meng, W., Li, W., Wong, D.S., Zhou, J.: TMGuard: a touch movement-based security mechanism for screen unlock patterns on smartphones. In: Proceedings of the 14th International Conference on Applied Cryptography and Network Security (ACNS), pp. 629–647 (2016)
34. Meng, W., Lee, W.H., Liu, Z., Su, C., Li, Y.: Evaluating the impact of juice filming charging attack in practical environments. In: Proceedings of ICISC, pp. 327–338 (2017)
35. Meng, W., Fei, F., Li, W., Au, M.H.: Harvesting smartphone privacy through enhanced juice filming charging attacks. In: Proceedings of ISC, pp. 291–308 (2017)
36. Meng, W., Li, W., Kwok, L.-F., Choo, K.-K.R.: Towards enhancing click-draw based graphical passwords using multi-touch behaviours on smartphones. Comput. Secur. **65**, 213–229 (2017)
37. Meng, W., Li, W., Lee, W., Jiang, L., Zhou, J.: A pilot study of multiple password interference between text and map-based passwords. In: Proceedings of the 15th International Conference on Applied Cryptography and Network Security (ACNS), pp. 145–162 (2017)

38. Meng, W., Lee, W.H., Au, M.H., Liu, Z.: Exploring effect of location number on map-based graphical password authentication. In: Pieprzyk, J., Suriadi, S. (eds.) ACISP 2017. LNCS, vol. 10343, pp. 301–313. Springer, Cham (2017). https://doi.org/10.1007/978-3-319-59870-3_17
39. Nyang, D., et al.: Two-thumbs-up: physical protection for PIN entry secure against recording attacks. Comput. Secur. **78**, 1–15 (2018)
40. Meng, W., Fei, F., Jiang, L., Liu, Z., Su, C., Han, J.: CPMap: design of click-points map-based graphical password authentication. In: SEC 2018, pp. 18–32 (2018)
41. Meng, W., Zhu, L., Li, W., Han, J., Li, Y.: Enhancing the security of FinTech applications with map-based graphical password authentication. Future Gener. Comput. Syst. **101**, 1018–1027 (2019)
42. Meng, W.: Intrusion detection in the era of IoT: building trust via traffic filtering and sampling. IEEE Comput. **51**(7), 36–43 (2018)
43. Shepard, R.N.: Recognition memory for words, sentences, and pictures. J. Verbal Learn. Verbal Behav. **6**(1), 156–163 (1967)
44. Smith-Creasey, M., Rajarajan, M.: A continuous user authentication scheme for mobile devices. In: Proceedings of the 14th Annual Conference on Privacy, Security and Trust (PST), pp. 104–113 (2016)
45. Casanova, A., Cascone, L., Castiglione, A., Meng, W., Pero, C.: User recognition based on periocular biometrics and touch dynamics. Pattern Recogn. Lett. **148**, 114–120 (2021)
46. Choi, S., Yim, J., Kim, S.J., Jin, Y., Wu, D., Jin, Z.: VibPath: two-factor authentication with your hand's vibration response to unlock your phone. Proc. ACM Interact. Mob. Wearable Ubiquitous Technol. **7**(3), 91:1–91:26 (2023)
47. Shahzad, M., Liu, A.X., Samuel, A.: Behavior based human authentication on touch screen devices using gestures and signatures. IEEE Trans. Mob. Comput. **16**(10), 2726–2741 (2017)
48. Sharma, V., Enbody, R.: User authentication and identification from user interface interactions on touch-enabled devices. In: Proceedings of the 10th ACM Conference on Security and Privacy in Wireless and Mobile Networks (WiSec), pp. 1–11 (2017)
49. Suo, X., Zhu, Y., Owen, G.S.: Graphical passwords: a survey. In: Proceedings of the 21st Annual Computer Security Applications Conference (ACSAC), pp. 463–472. IEEE Computer Society, USA (2005)
50. Sun, H., Chen, Y., Fang, C., Chang, S.: PassMap: a map based graphical-password authentication system. In: Proceedings of AsiaCCS, pp. 99–100 (2012)
51. Tao, H., Adams, C.: Pass-Go: a proposal to improve the usability of graphical passwords. Int. J. Netw. Secur. **2**(7), 273–292 (2008)
52. Thorpe, J., MacRae, B., Salehi-Abari, A.: Usability and security evaluation of GeoPass: a geographic location-password scheme. In: Proceedings of the 9th Symposium on Usable Privacy and Security (SOUPS), pp. 1–14 (2013)
53. Wang, L., et al.: Unlock with your heart: heartbeat-based authentication on commercial mobile phones. Proc. ACM Interact. Mob. Wearable Ubiquitous Technol. **2**(3), 140:1–140:22 (2018)
54. Wiedenbeck, S., Waters, J., Birget, J.-C., Brodskiy, A., Memon, N.: Passpoints: design and longitudinal evaluation of a graphical password system. Int. J. Hum. Comput. Stud. **63**(1–2), 102–127 (2005)
55. Ray, P., Giri, D., Meng, W., Hore, S.: GPOD: an efficient and secure graphical password authentication system by fast object detection. Multim. Tools Appl. **83**(19), 56569–56618 (2024)

56. Meng, W., Li, W., Calugar, A.N.: BANN-TMGuard: towards touch movement-based screen unlock patterns via blockchain-enabled artificial neural networks on IoT devices. IEEE Internet Things J. **12**(2), 1856–1866 (2025)
57. Yi, S., Qin, Z., Carter, N., Li, Q.: WearLock: unlocking your phone via acoustics using smartwatch. In: ICDCS 2017, pp. 469–479 (2017)
58. Zheng, N., Bai, K., Huang, H., Wang, H.: You are how you touch: user verification on smartphones via tapping behaviors. In: Proceedings of the 2014 International Conference on Network Protocols (ICNP), pp. 221–232 (2014)

Author Index

M. Yung et al. (Eds.): AIBlock 2025, LNCS 16314, p. 161, 2026.
https://doi.org/10.1007/978-3-032-16168-0

Zeitfracht Medien GmbH
Ferdinand-Jühlke-Straße 7
99095 Erfurt, Deutschland
produktsicherheit@kolibri360.de